# Benaras

RITU JHINGON

Celebrating
30 Years of Publishing
in India

First published in India by HarperCollins Publishers 2023
4th Floor, Tower A, Building No. 10, DLF Cyber City,
DLF Phase II, Gurugram, Haryana – 122002
www.harpercollins.co.in

2 4 6 8 10 9 7 5 3 1



P-ISBN: 978-93-5699-404-1



Typeset in Miller Banner and Abigail
Design by Haitenlo Semy

Printed and bound at
Thomson Press (India) Ltd

# CONTENTS

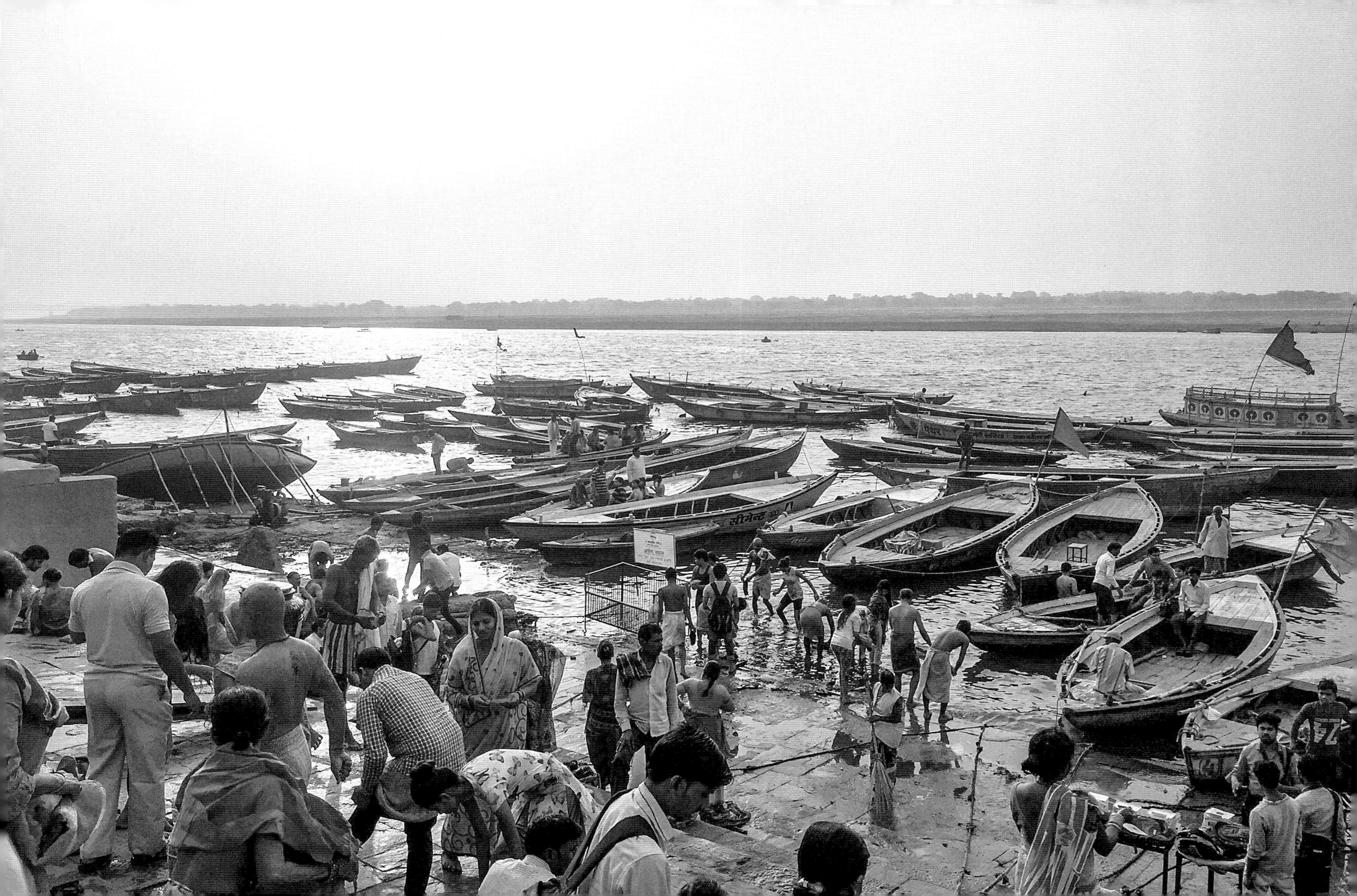

# PREFACE

It is dawn ... the sun is threatening to break through the grey and orange sky ... there is fine mist everywhere. I sit in a small boat bobbing in the river. The cold water of the Ganga pulses and dances through my fingers as the flowers in leaf bowls swirl away from me in gentle rhythmic waves. Around me, pilgrims dip into the water. The sounds of chants swell and ebb with the temple bells. And while the city and the river are about to wake—this mist-filled dawn feels like a precious secret where the day and its promises haven't yet revealed themselves. Just being present in this moment feels both like a prayer and a benediction.

The ghats are an impressionist painting: the thin glassy river shimmering in the foreground; women bathing in colourful saris; thin muscular yogis perfecting their yoga asanas; sadhus deep in meditation, or chanting the mahamrityunjaya jaap—the death-conquering mantra; pot-bellied businessmen dipping into the waters; a group of elderly pilgrims gingerly making their way down the slick narrow steps; convoys of boats taking people on their final journeys; the crowds of mourners and always, always, the pyres. The pyres burn all day, and some all night—the sweet stench of sandalwood and ghee, and grey smoke smudging the sky. Not a moment goes by when death is not alive and vibrant and even celebrated in Benaras, not a minute when it isn't blazing and crackling in the air—a constant reminder of where we all are inexorably marching towards.

A narrow alley, just wide enough for two people to walk side by side, winds its way past tiny shops towards the banks of the Ganga. I see everyone jostling endlessly through the crowds: men, women, sadhus, bullocks, shopkeepers selling everything from mineral water bottles to mouth-puckeringly delicious chaat to the most luxurious and glittering fabrics. Beggars beg, pilgrims throng, kids duck in and out of legs and doors—there is life being lived and salvation being chased by the many residents and visitors, all of whom seem to be right here in front of me in this narrow alley. This is what chaos and confusion and messy pulsating life looks like. Also, luminous grace.

Benaras is amongst the oldest continuously inhabited cities in the world, evidence of human settlement goes back 2,500 years[1]. But the legends and myths about the city go way back to tens of thousands of years. They are all incredible, contradictory, impossible to prove and deeply embedded in the collective consciousness of most Indians. Over centuries, millions and millions of people have been drawn to Benaras due to devotion, tradition, the search for salvation, wanderlust, the love of beauty and truth and experiences.

[1] Varanasi, Wikipedia, https://en.wikipedia.org/wiki/Varanasi

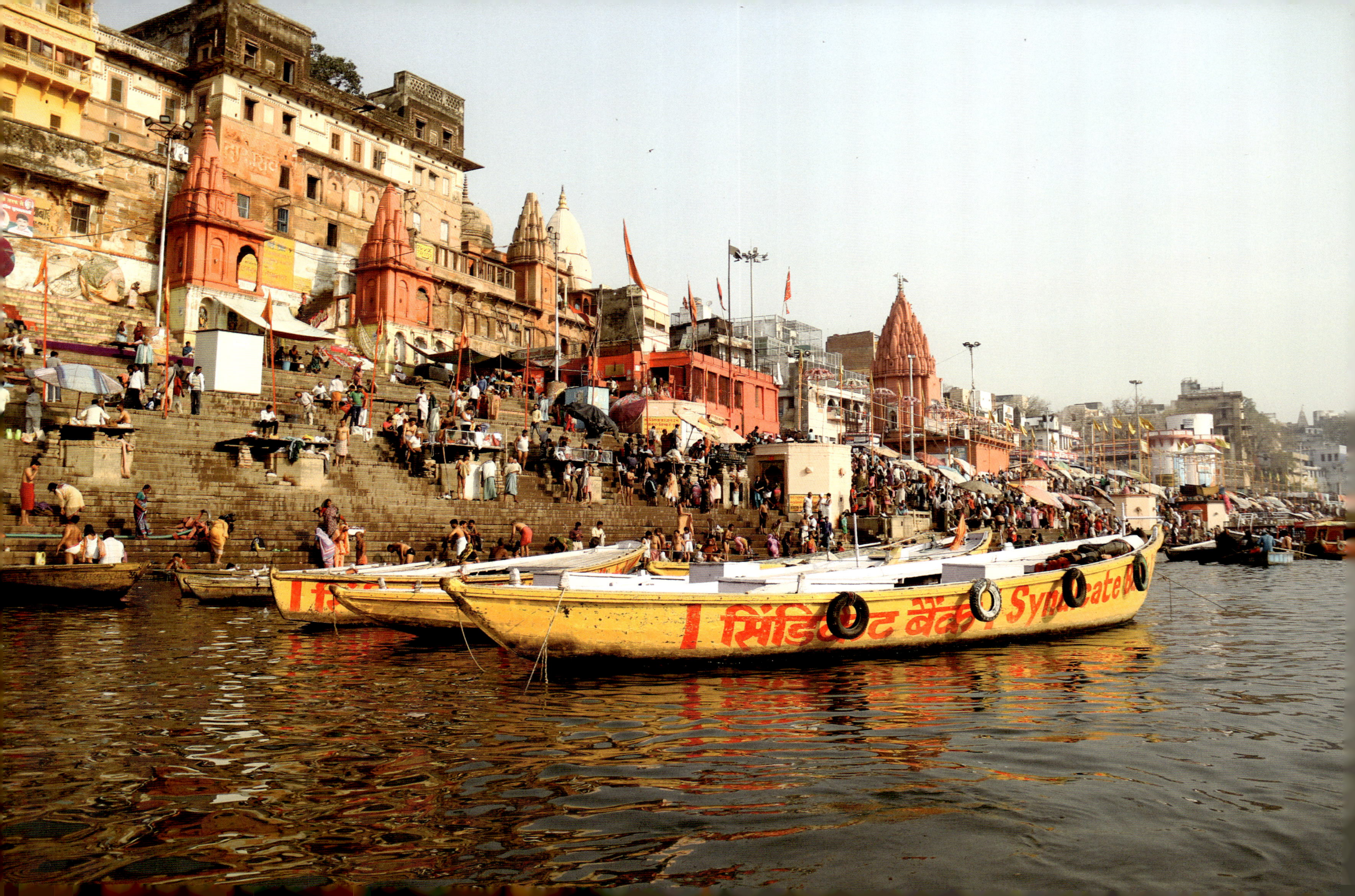

And somewhere in those millions is me—for whom the mystical pull of Benaras has been a very personal revelation and journey. As someone who would never identify as being religious or ritualistic, it's natural that it's the river that drew me in first, the call of the water that proved irresistible for the one-time national swimmer who still lives on in me. But over the years, the experience that is Benaras has settled itself into my being. A force—pure and ancient—that has its roots somewhere in this milieu, replenishes and revitalizes me every time I visit. Coming back here feels like coming home, the idea of Benaras is just the tonic for my weary soul.

The spiritual guru, Sadhguru, says that if you learn how to sit correctly, then you can download the entire cosmos[2]. Sitting in one of the many temples on the riverbank, or on the ghats, or even bobbing in a boat in the river, I begin to understand what this might mean. For when I close my eyes, I can feel the earth move on its axis. I become the pulse of its movement, its heartbeat. Vast. Free. Joyous. A speck in the air enjoying my fleeting moments of ecstasy.

There is a famous adage: *Kankar mein Shankar*. Or even *kann kann mein Shankar*. It is believed that every pebble has the essence of Shiva in this city. After so many years and so many visits, to me this feels like a truth I experience at a primal level. Because it's not just the gifts this city gives me, it's what it absolves me of that is life-affirming and liberating. Some mystical force in the city allows me to lay down the weariness of everyday life, to unclench the petty concerns that dominate my mind, and helps shine a gentle light on the ephemerality of the materialistic, temporal world I inhabit. This is where I can shrug off the burden of mortal existence weighing heavily on my shoulders. And for a few moments and days feel light and enlightened.

To sum up, I am smitten. This book and all the images in it are my love song to Benaras. The energy, the fervour, the life force, the exquisite beauty, the pulsating life, the ever-present death—everything that makes this magnificient city so magical. From the magnificent Ganga Arti at the banks that is surreal to watch to the bells resounding in harmony in the surrounding temples, the aromas of delicious food wafting through the air, the weavers working skillfully at their craft, the youthful laughter, the ambling cows, the mysterious aghoris, the yogis, the sadhus—Benaras is all this and so much more.

Essentially, Benaras is a wise teacher and guide, teaching mere mortals like me the ultimate truth—to be aware of our mortality. Every minute spent in Benaras underlines for me that my time here on earth is limited, and how I use it, is up to me. I can spend it enamoured by myself, my beauty, my body, my youth, my wealth and power or I can focus on something less ephemeral, more timeless. Sitting on its ghats and in its temples and even in passing through its bazaars, I have realized that I am not my thoughts or hopes or regrets or aspirations. I am not even the garments I have draped my body with or the talents or achievements of my life of which I am justifiably proud. But eventually none of that will endure, it will all be stripped down to ash and bone and borne away by the gushing water or be strewn in the wind.

And to me, that is the essence of Benaras. The vitality of life contrasted with the certainty of death. And the omnipresent hand of the Divine orchestrating the two. Benaras gives me the faith that the founder of creation is also its benefactor. And that all of us creatures have the potential to be carried to the other side towards the ultimate non-existence. Tathastu!

[2] 'Kashi Conundrum - Prasoon Joshi with Sadhguru', Youtube video, 22 May 2018, https://youtu.be/0ks6kmCVERg

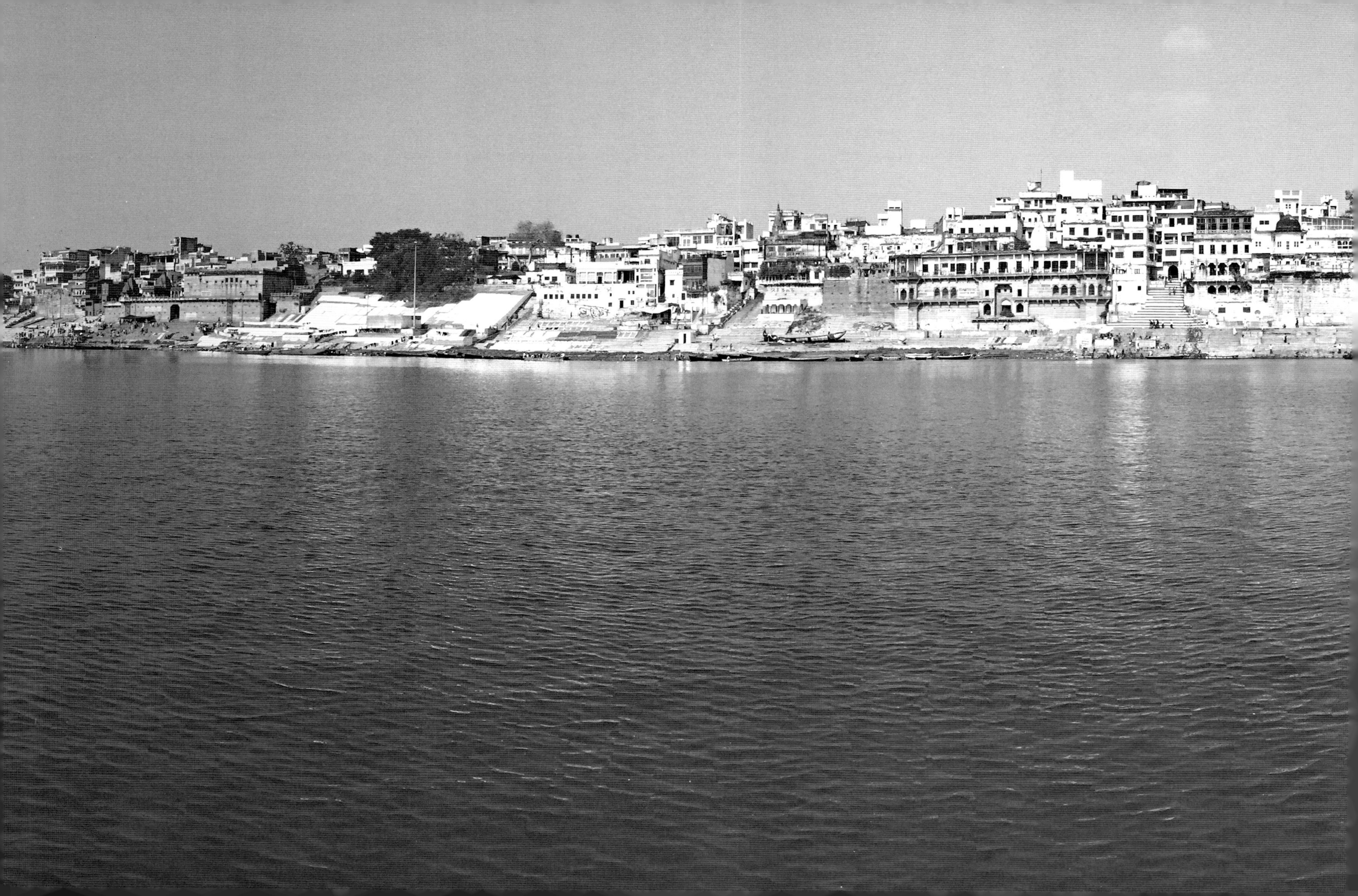

# Ghats

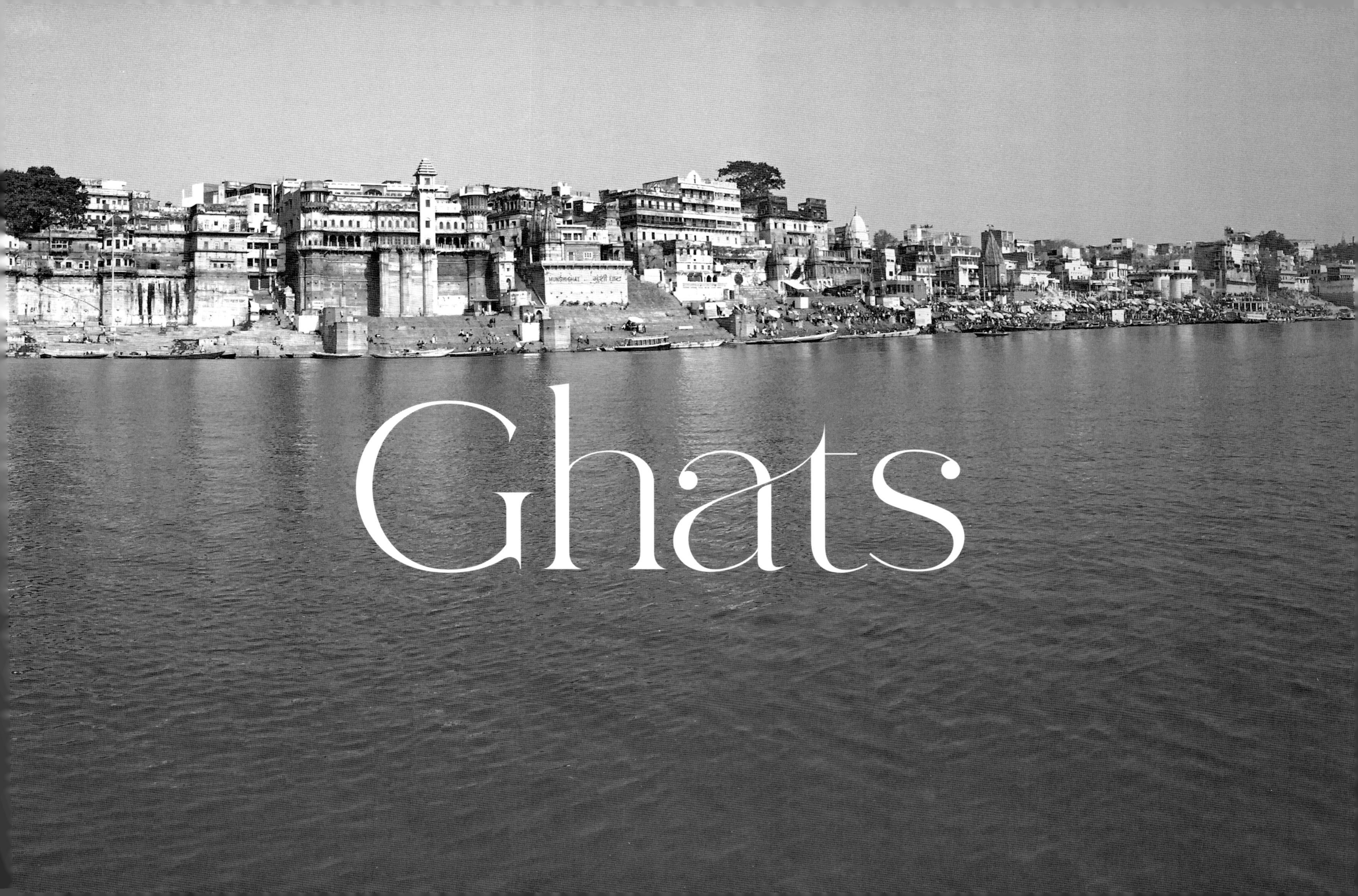

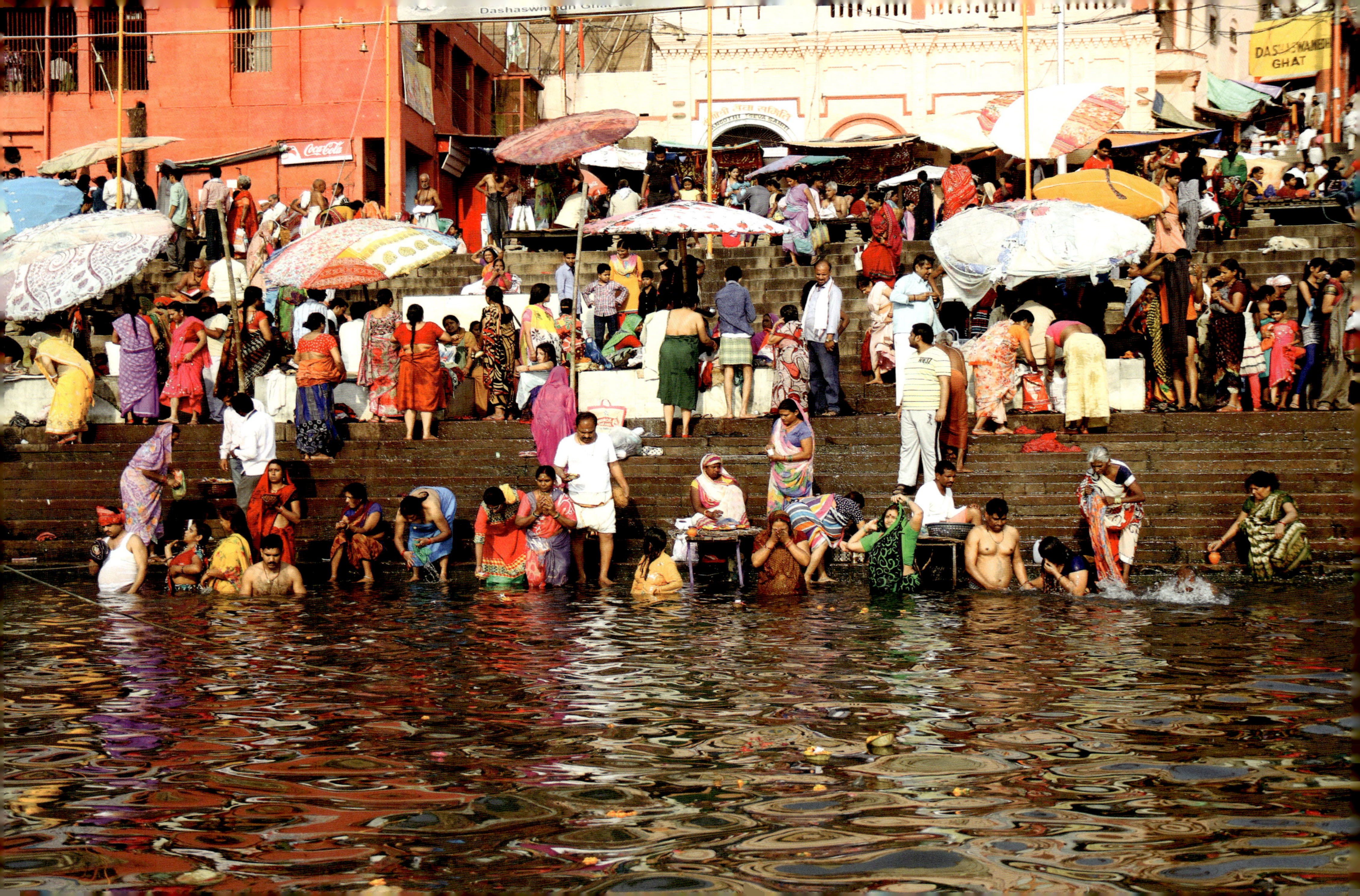
Coca-Cola
GHAT

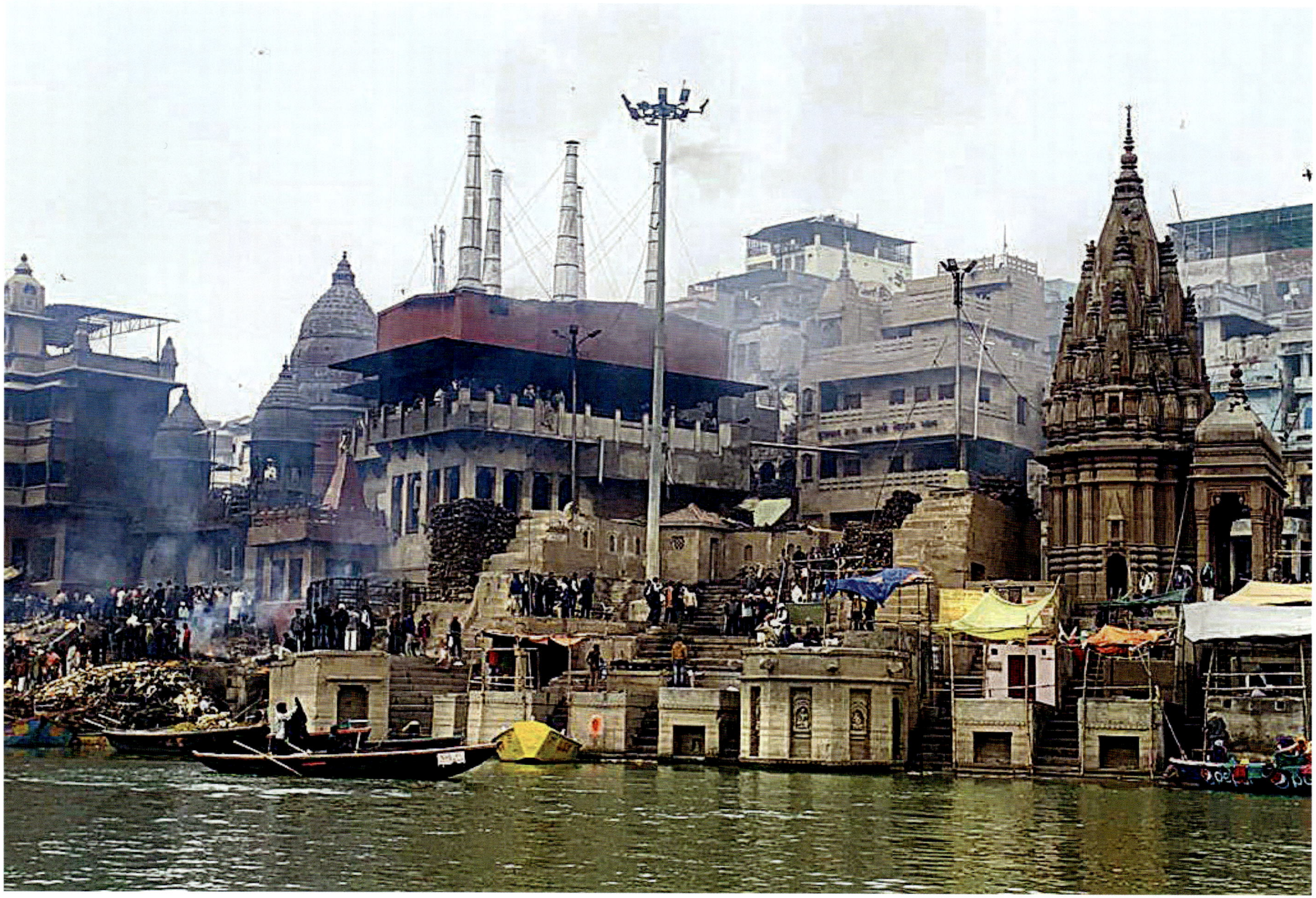

Panchabhuta—the five mahabhutas or great elements—in a single frame depicting a full cycle of life.

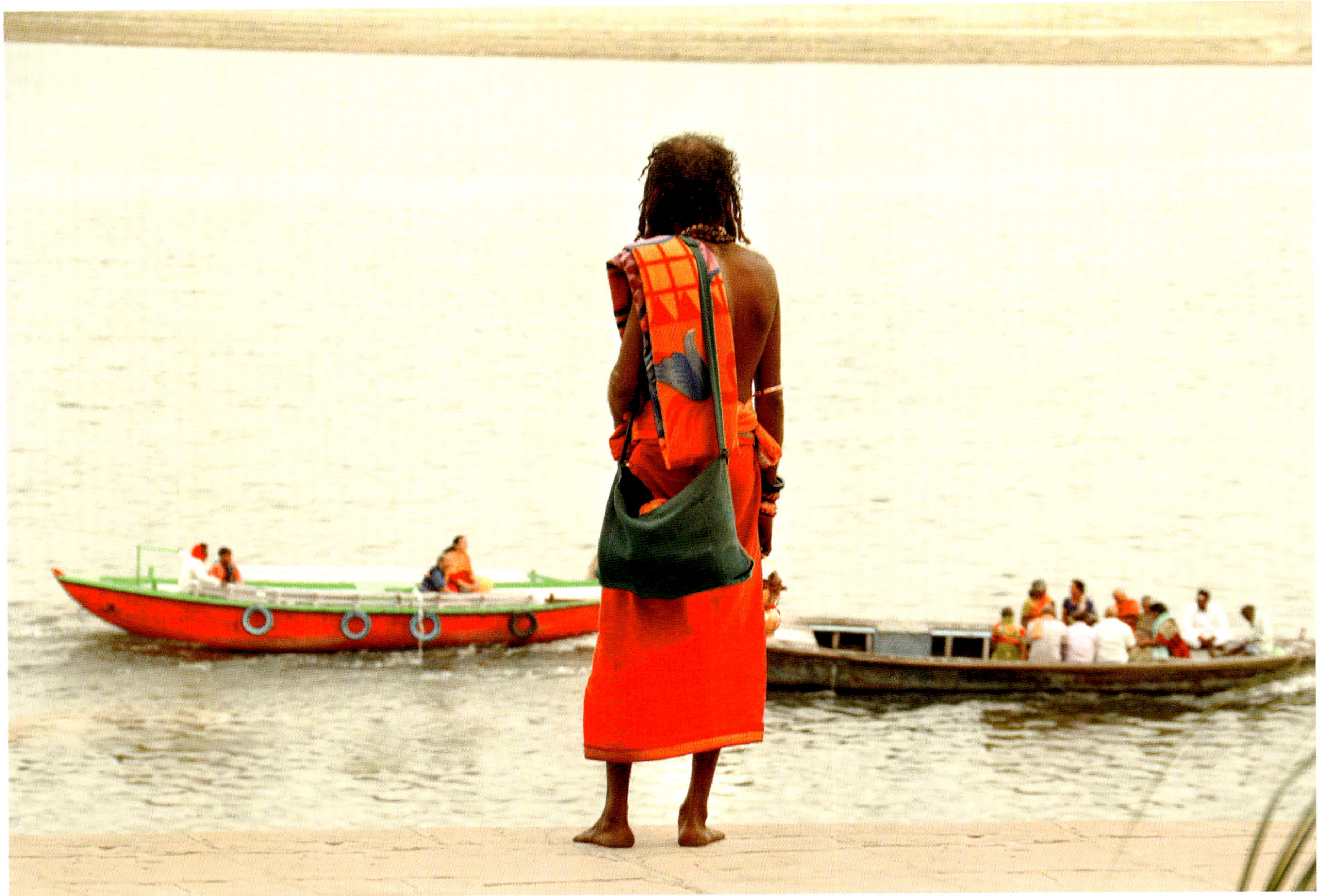

*'Do not be led by others, awaken your own mind, amass your own experience and decide your own path.'*—Rig Veda

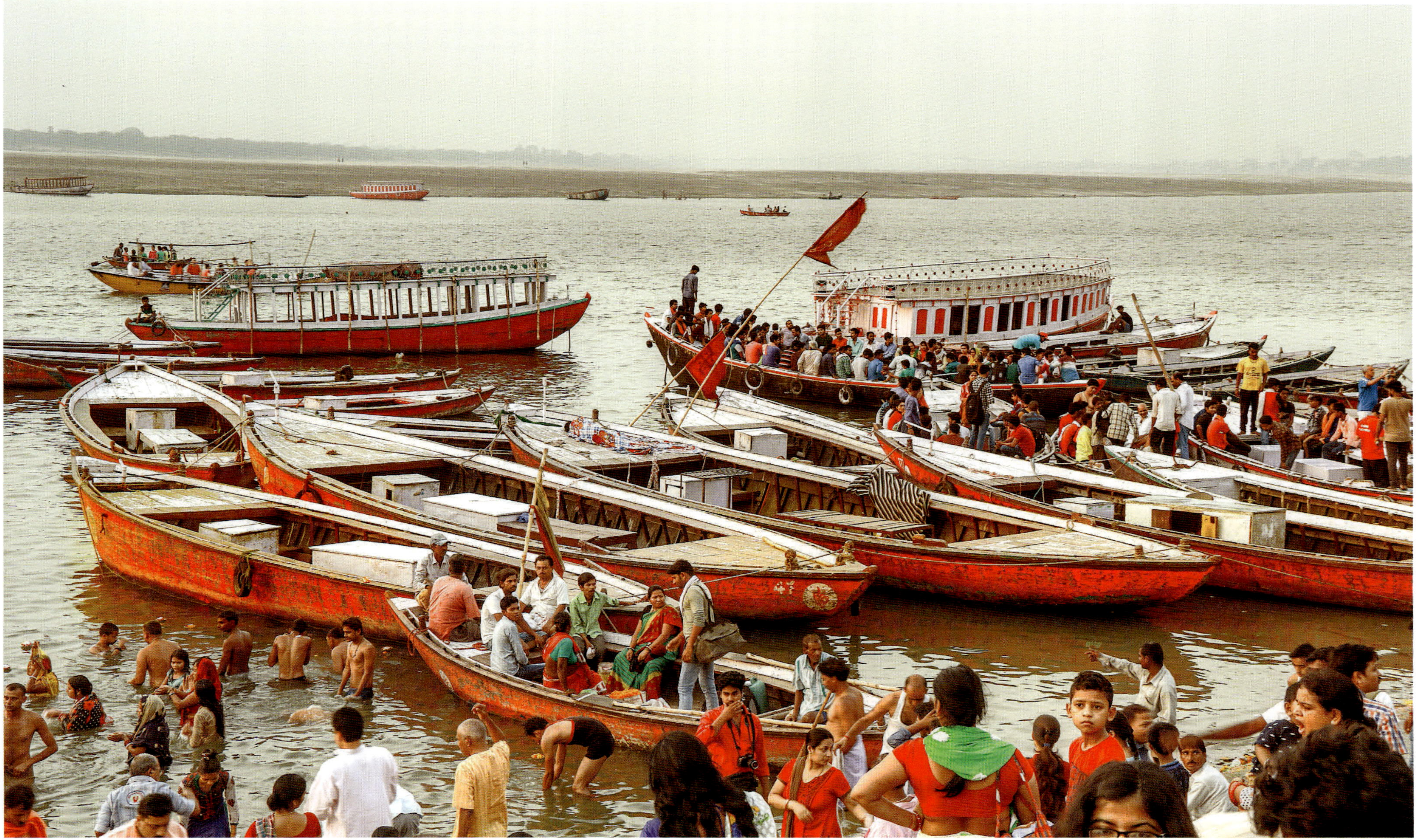

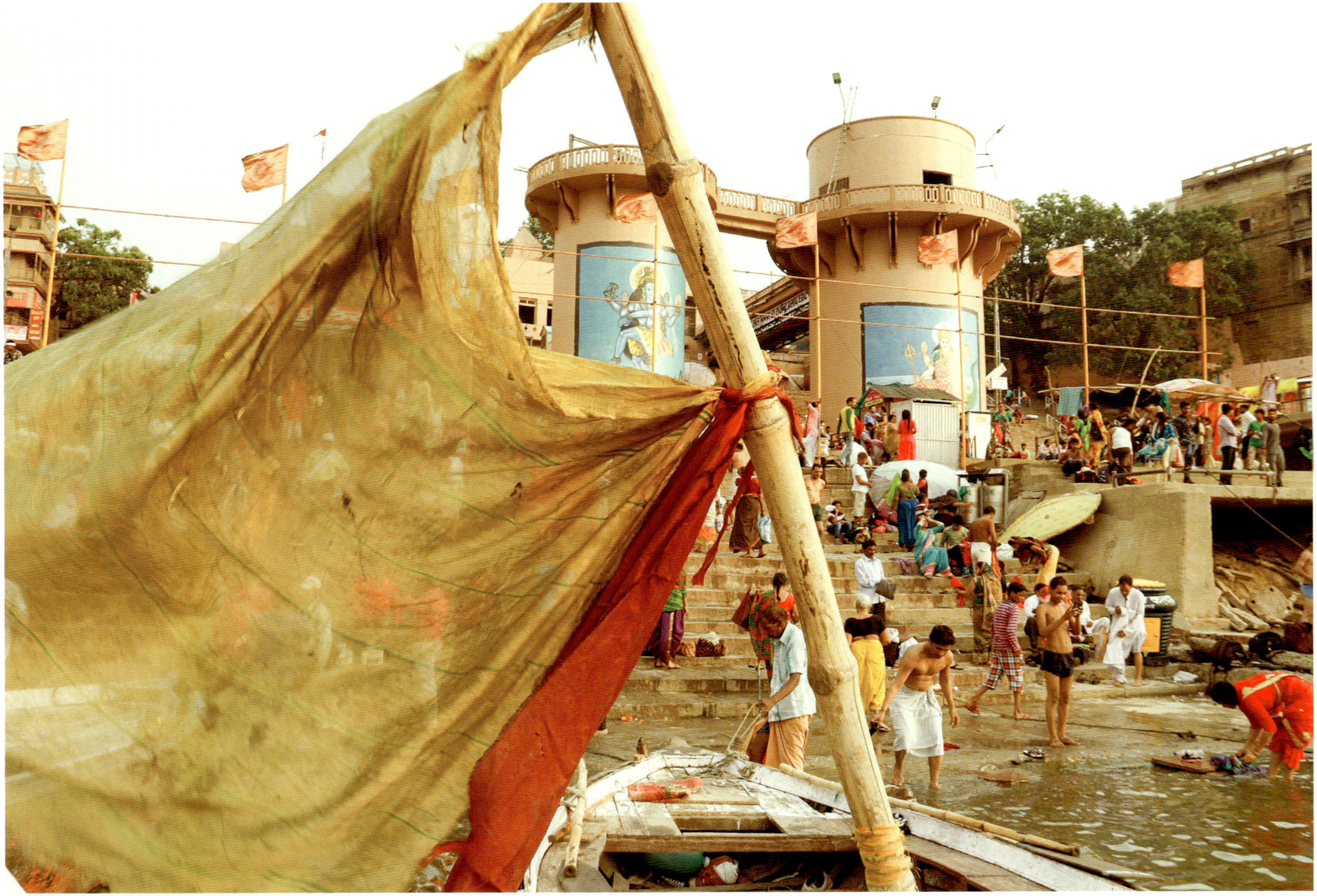

The mere hope of receiving the benevolence of shade from the scorching sun from a torn mast of a boat can create joy in the heart.

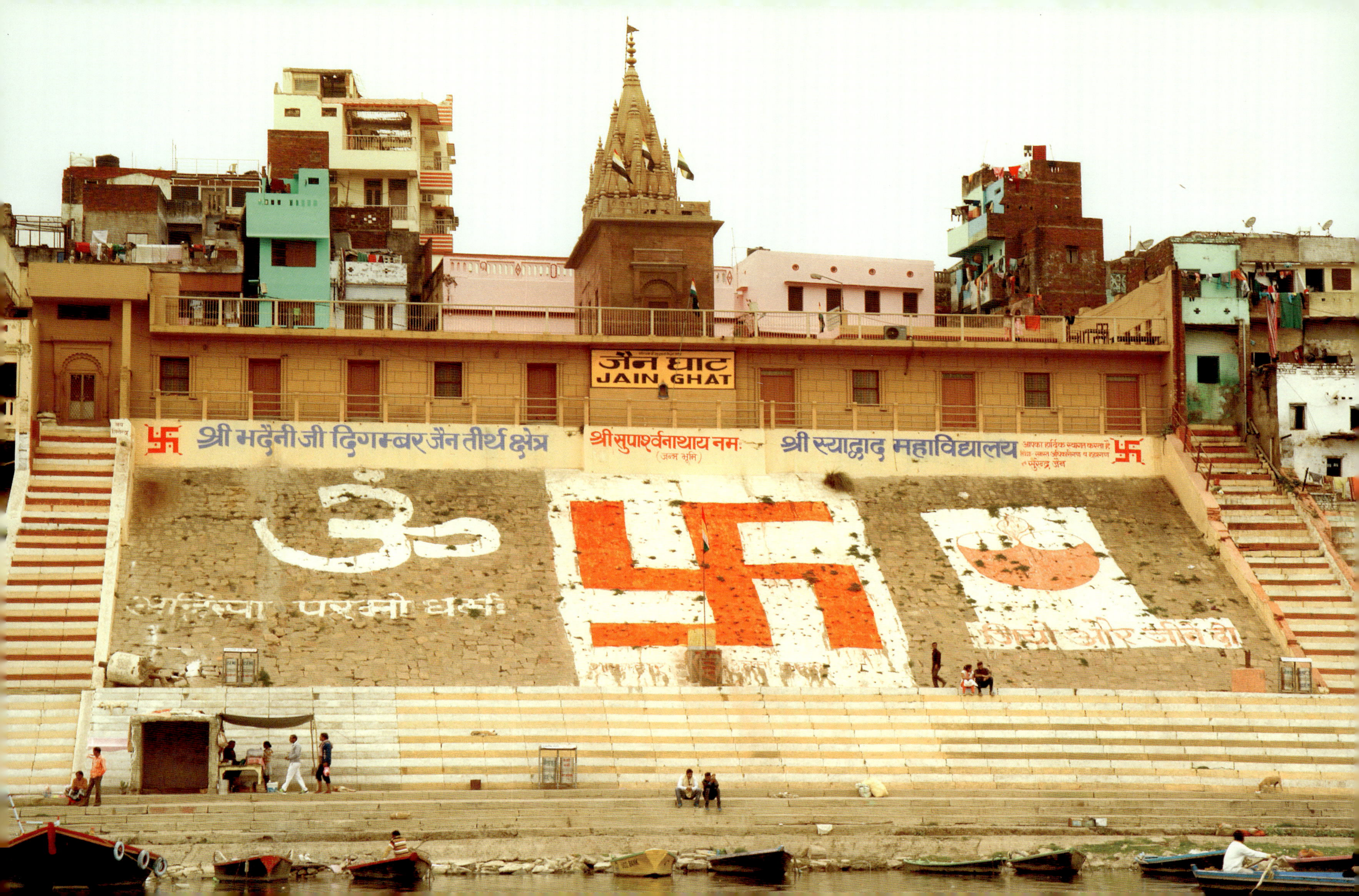
जैन घाट
JAIN GHAT
श्री भदैनी जी दिगम्बर जैन तीर्थ क्षेत्र
श्री सुपार्श्वनाथाय नमः
श्री स्याद्वाद महाविद्यालय

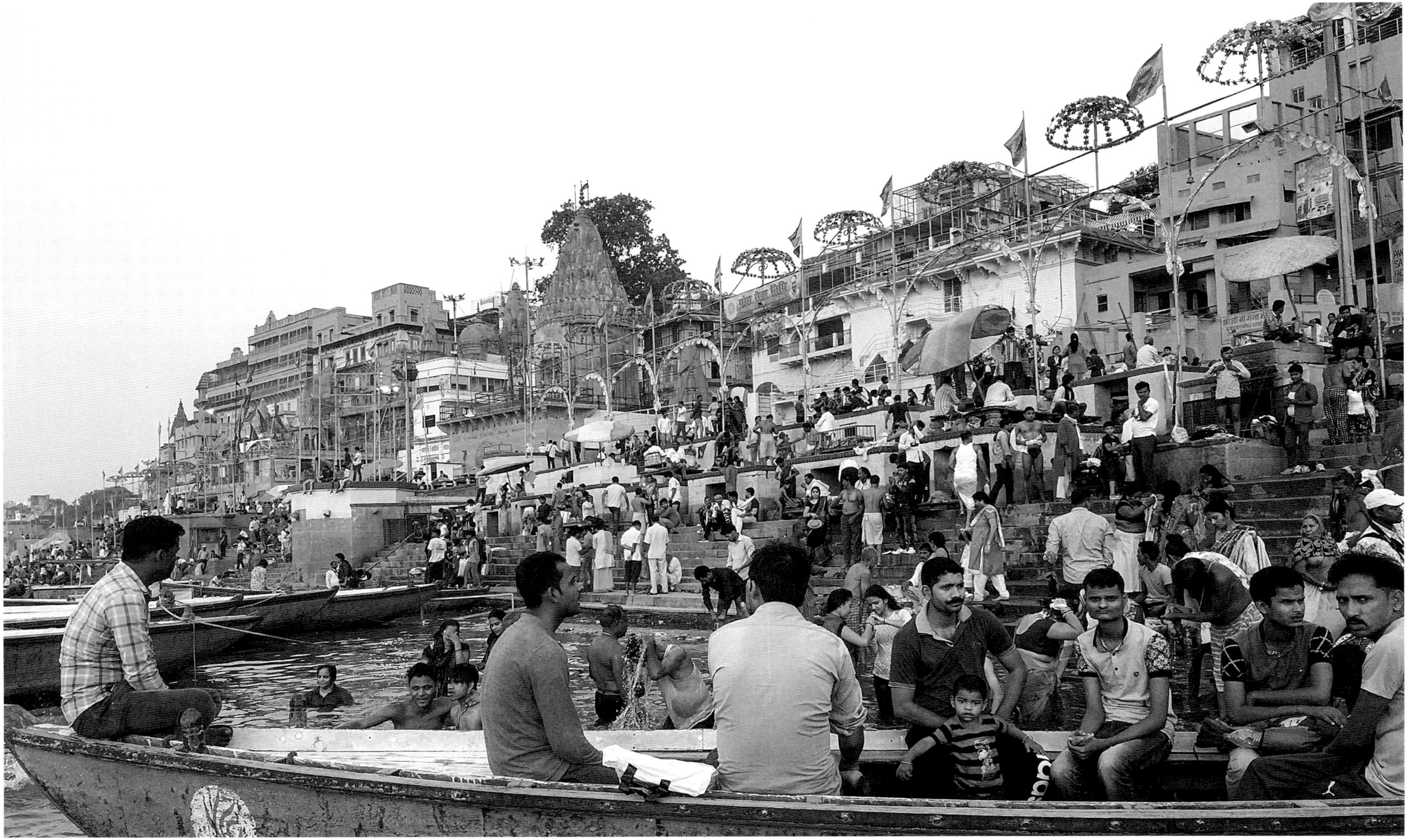

The sadhu energetically shaking his damru seems to be saying that all roads lead to Benaras.

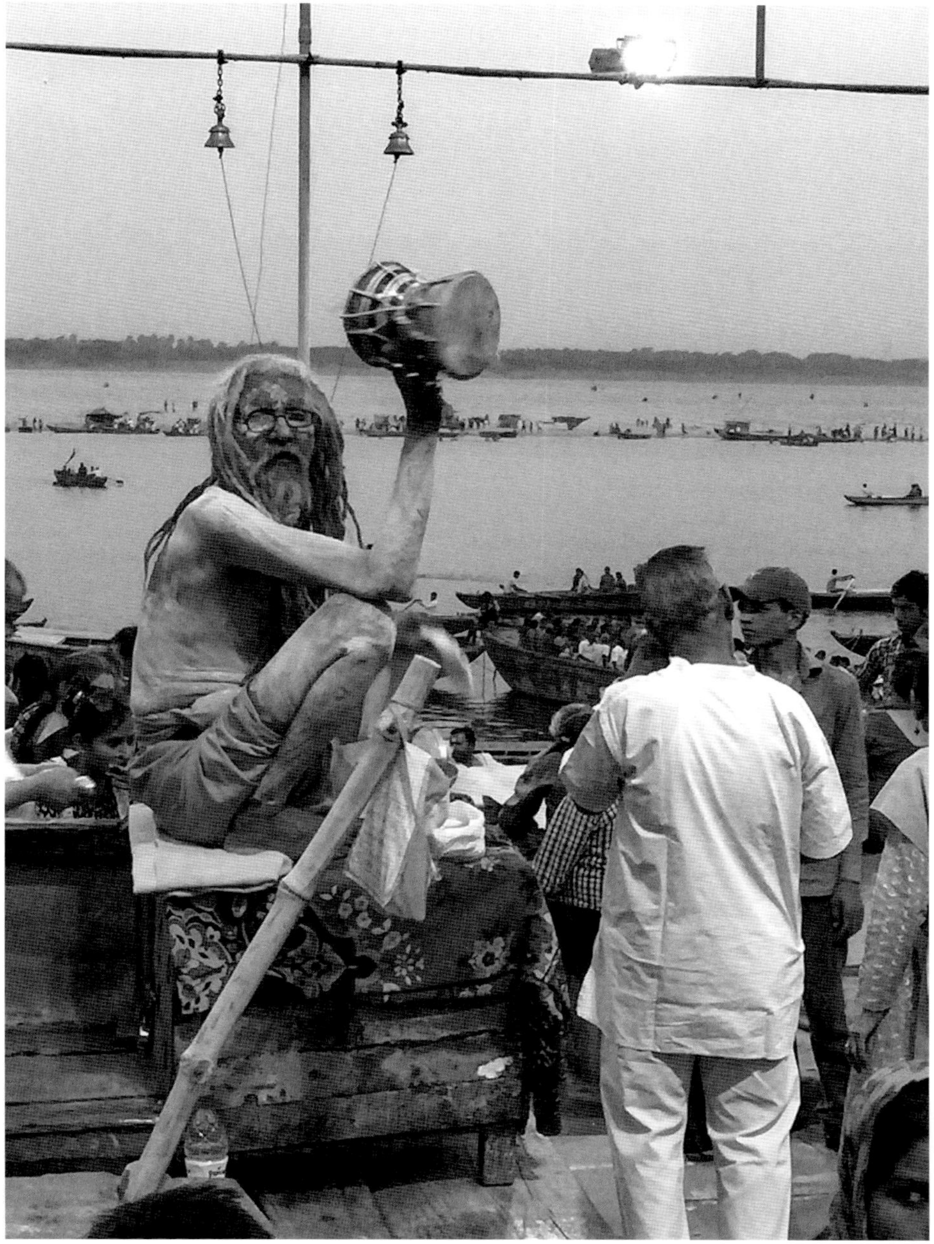

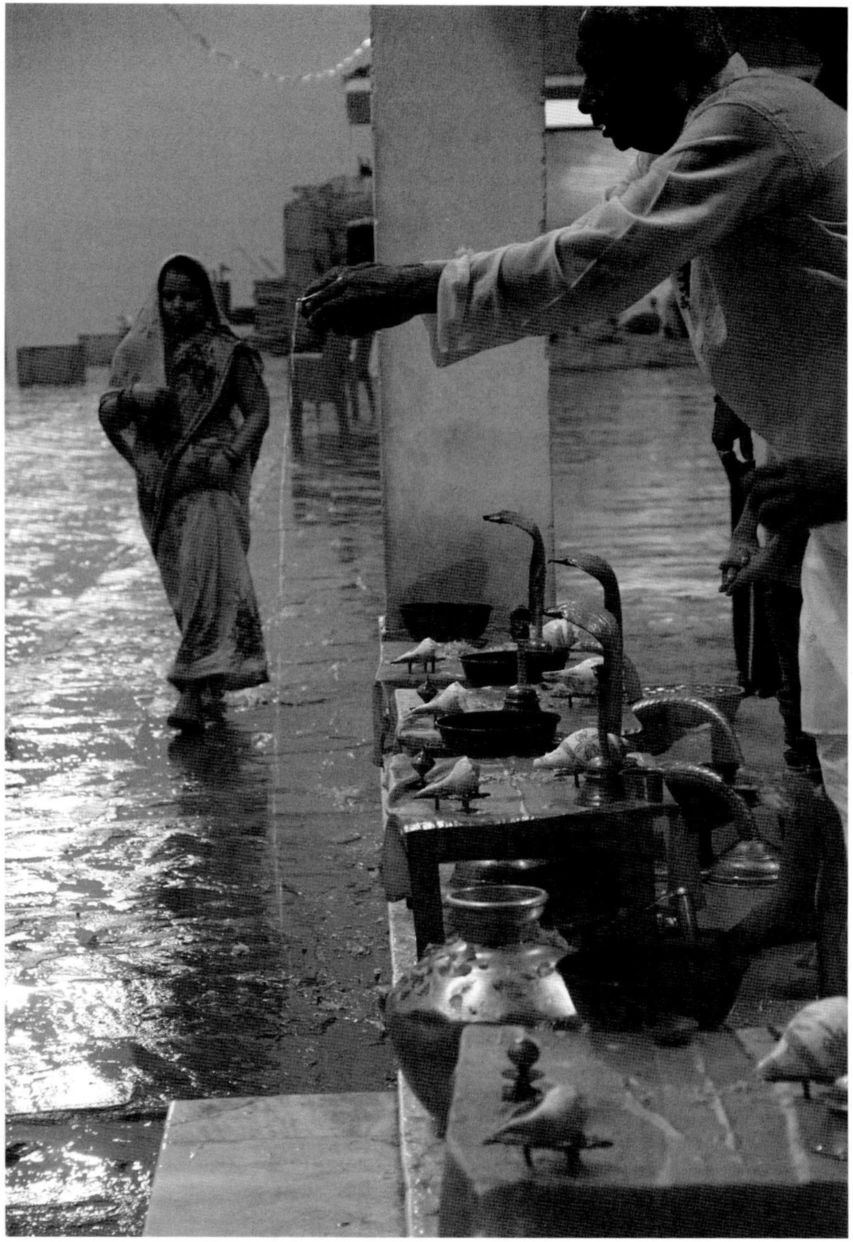

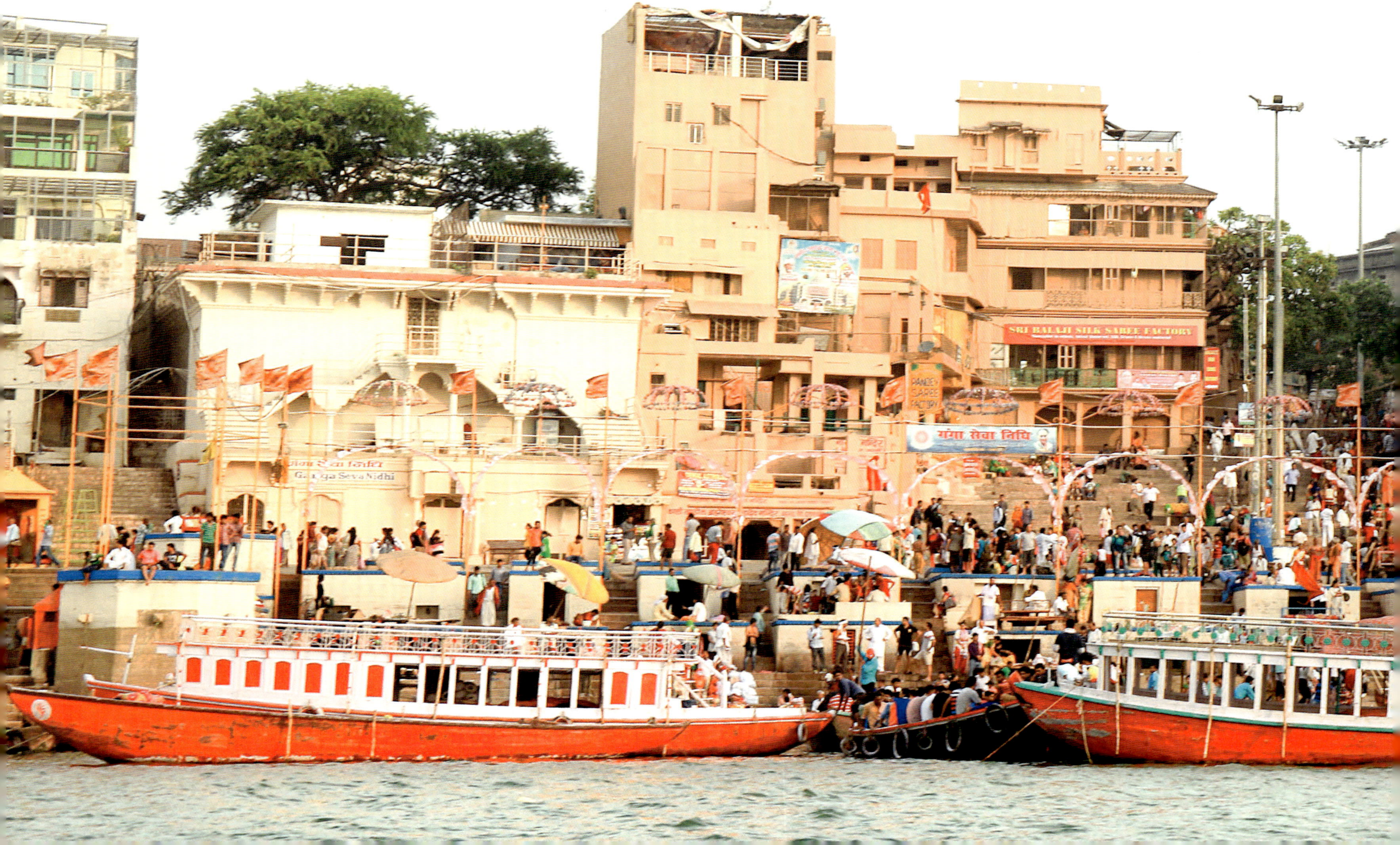
SRI BALAJI SILK SAREE FACTORY
गंगा सेवा निधि
Ganga Seva Nidhi

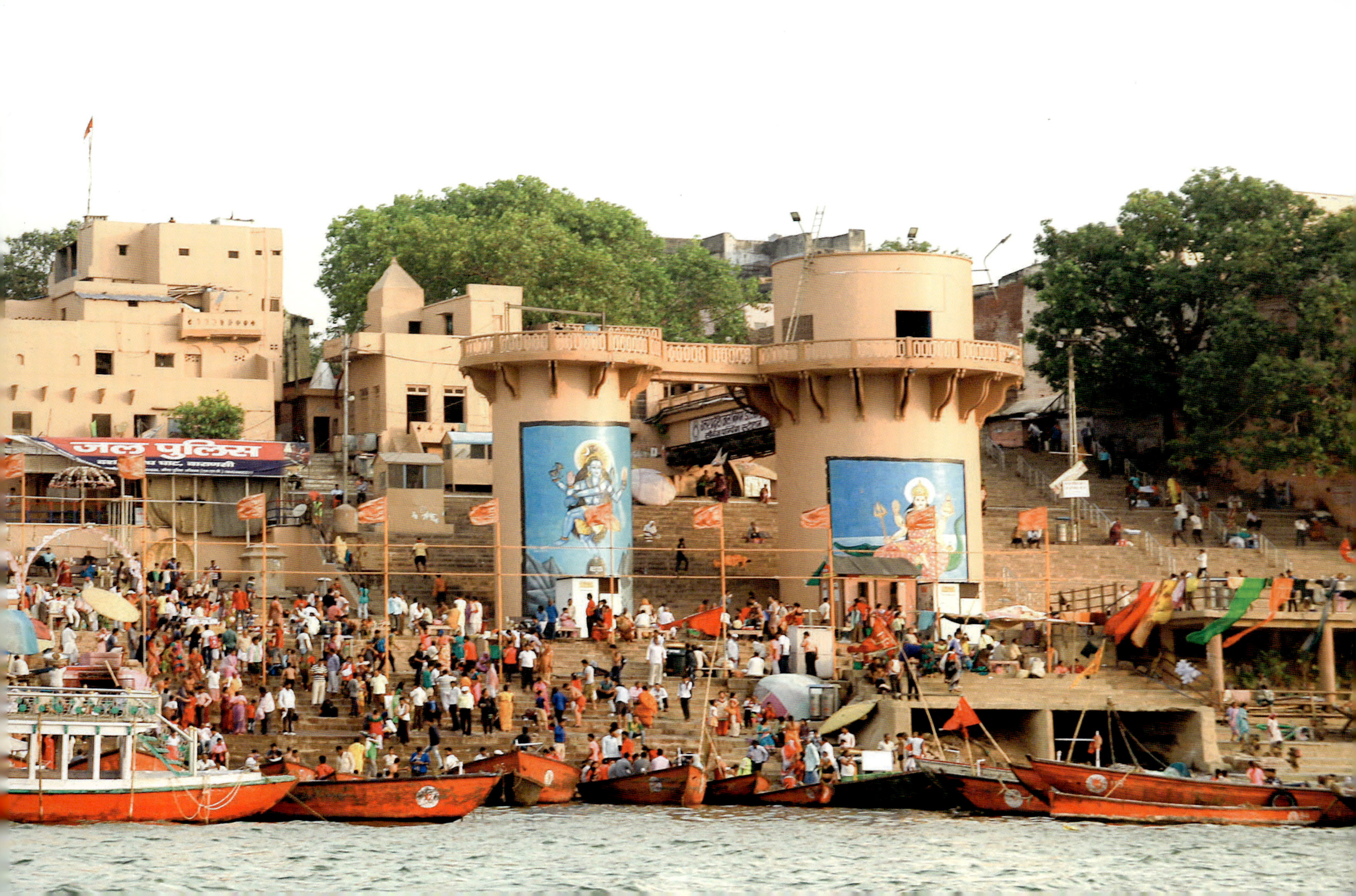
जल पुलिस

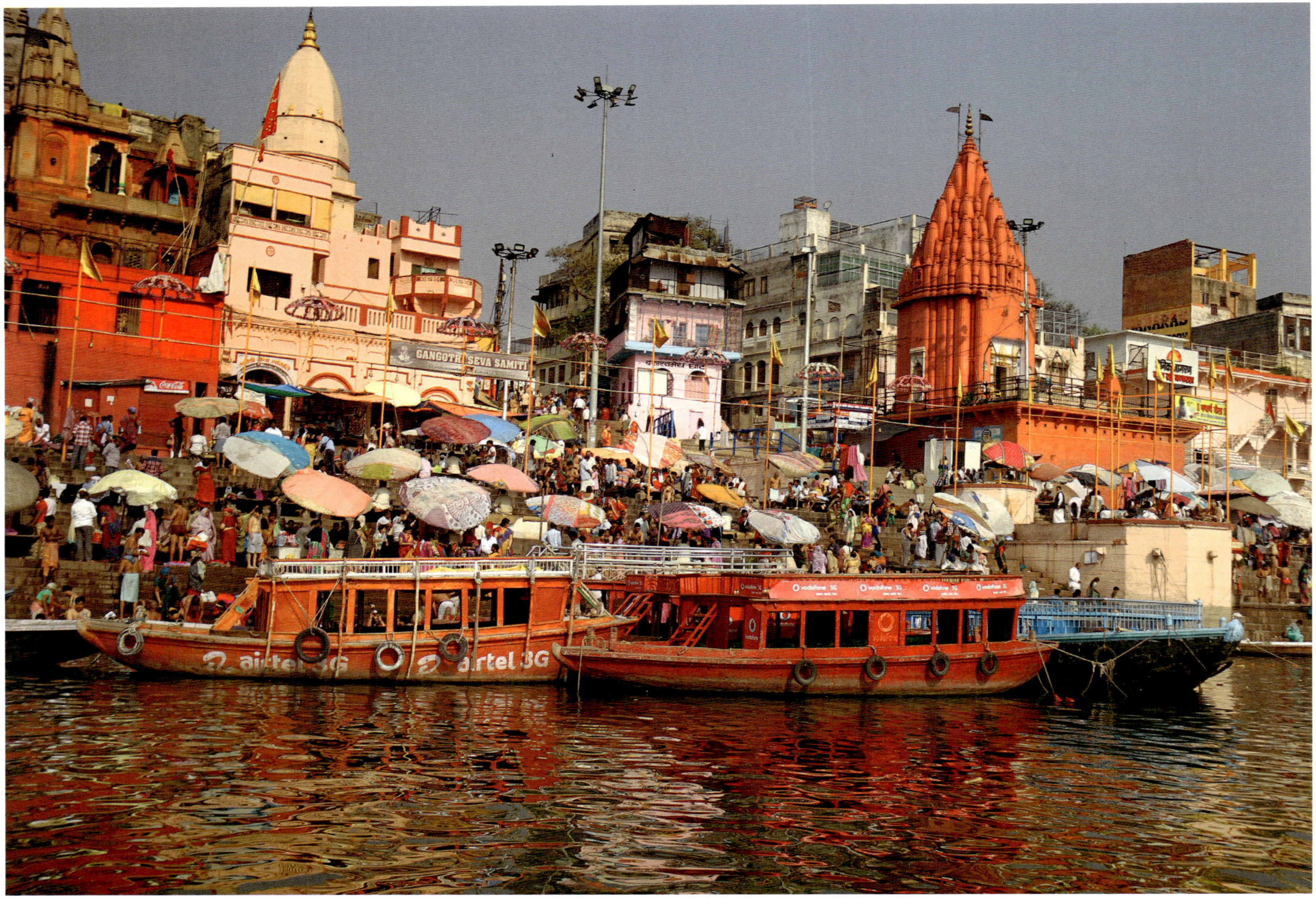


A sea of humanity beyond race, caste, creed, gender, economic barriers and personal inhibitions.

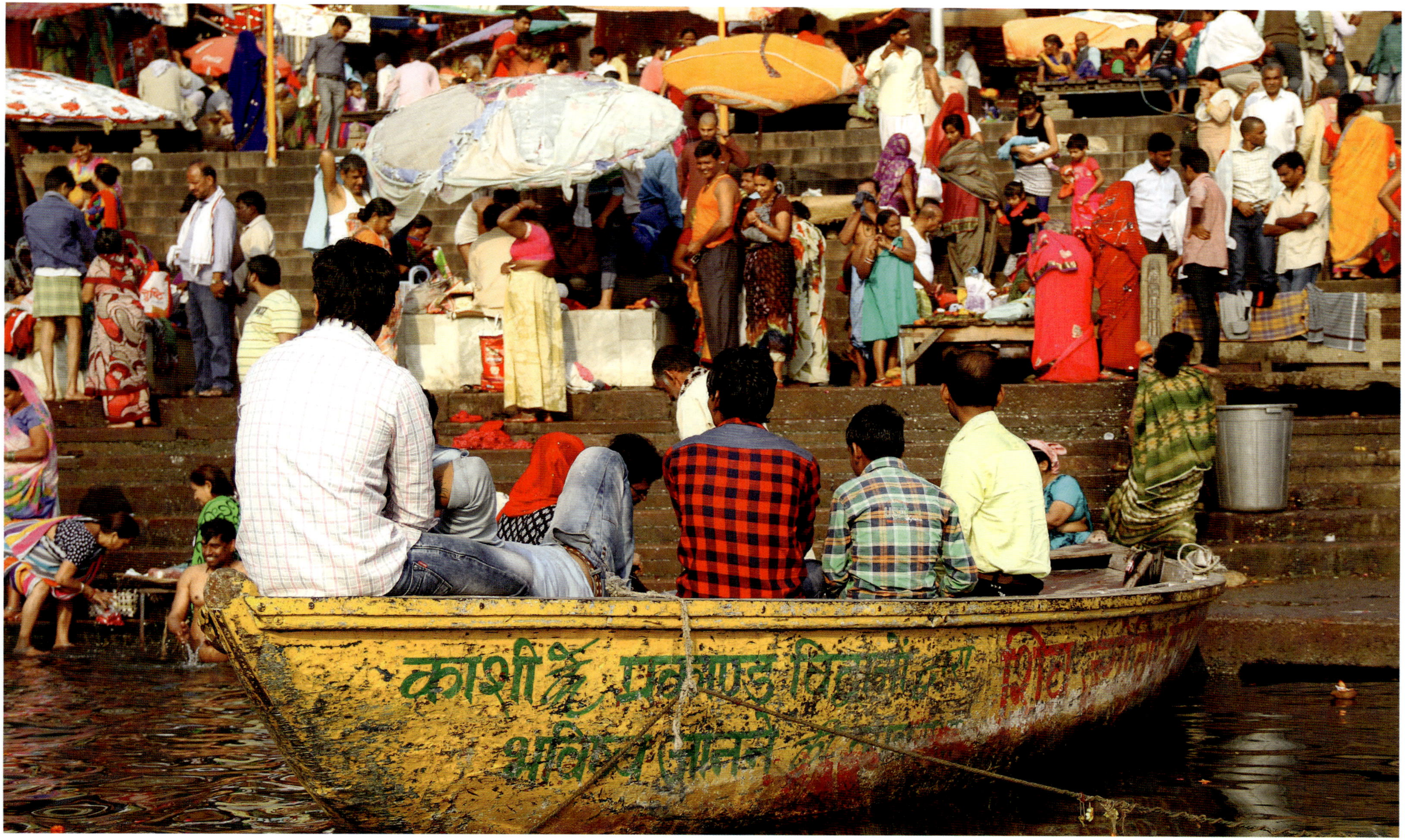
काशी के प्रकाण्ड विद्वानों
भविष्य जानने

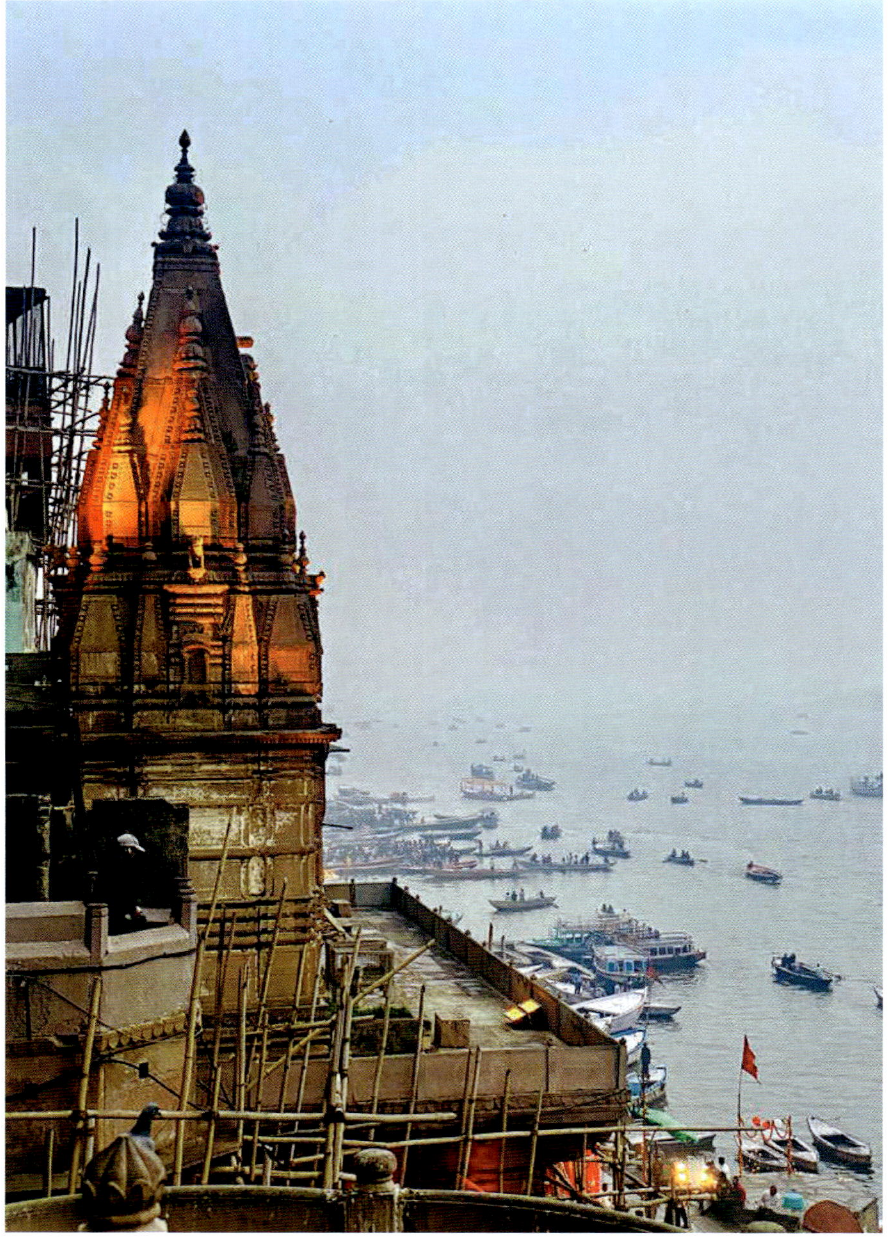

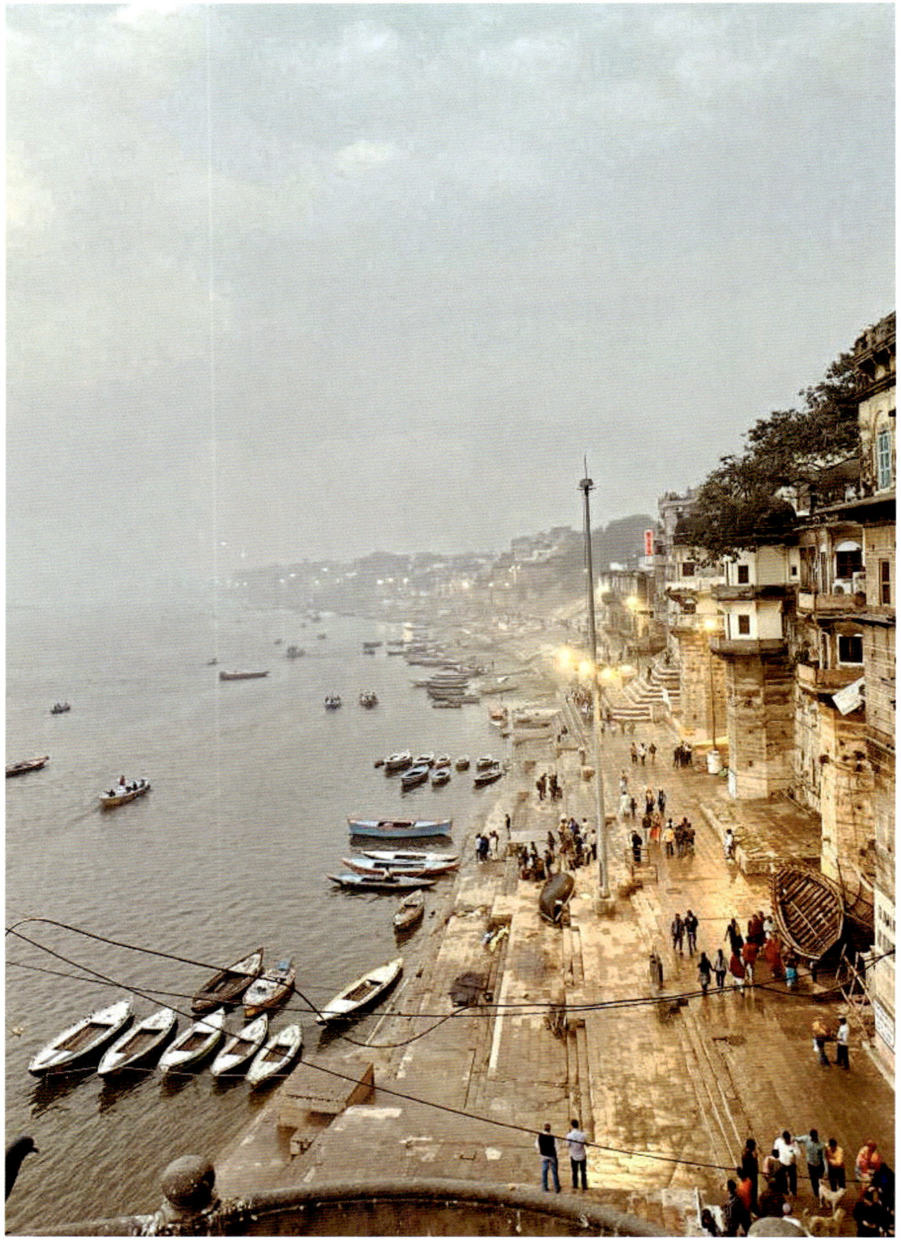

Paap Naashini:
*O mother, the one*
*who has bathed*
*in your holy water,*
*will attain moksha.*

In the quest to purify and redeem our tainted souls, we offer earnest prayers to Maa Ganga.

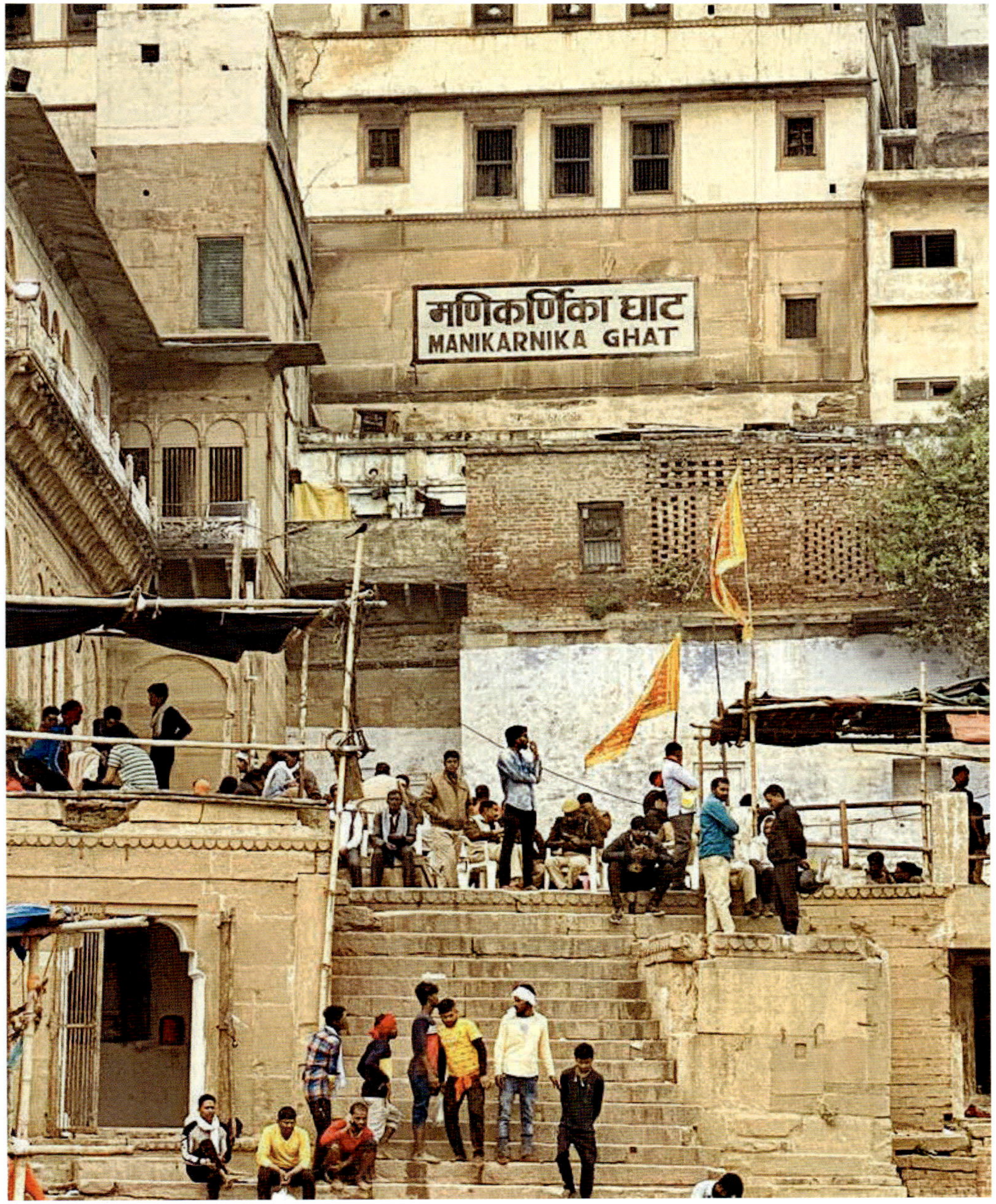
मणिकर्णिका घाट
MANIKARNIKA GHAT

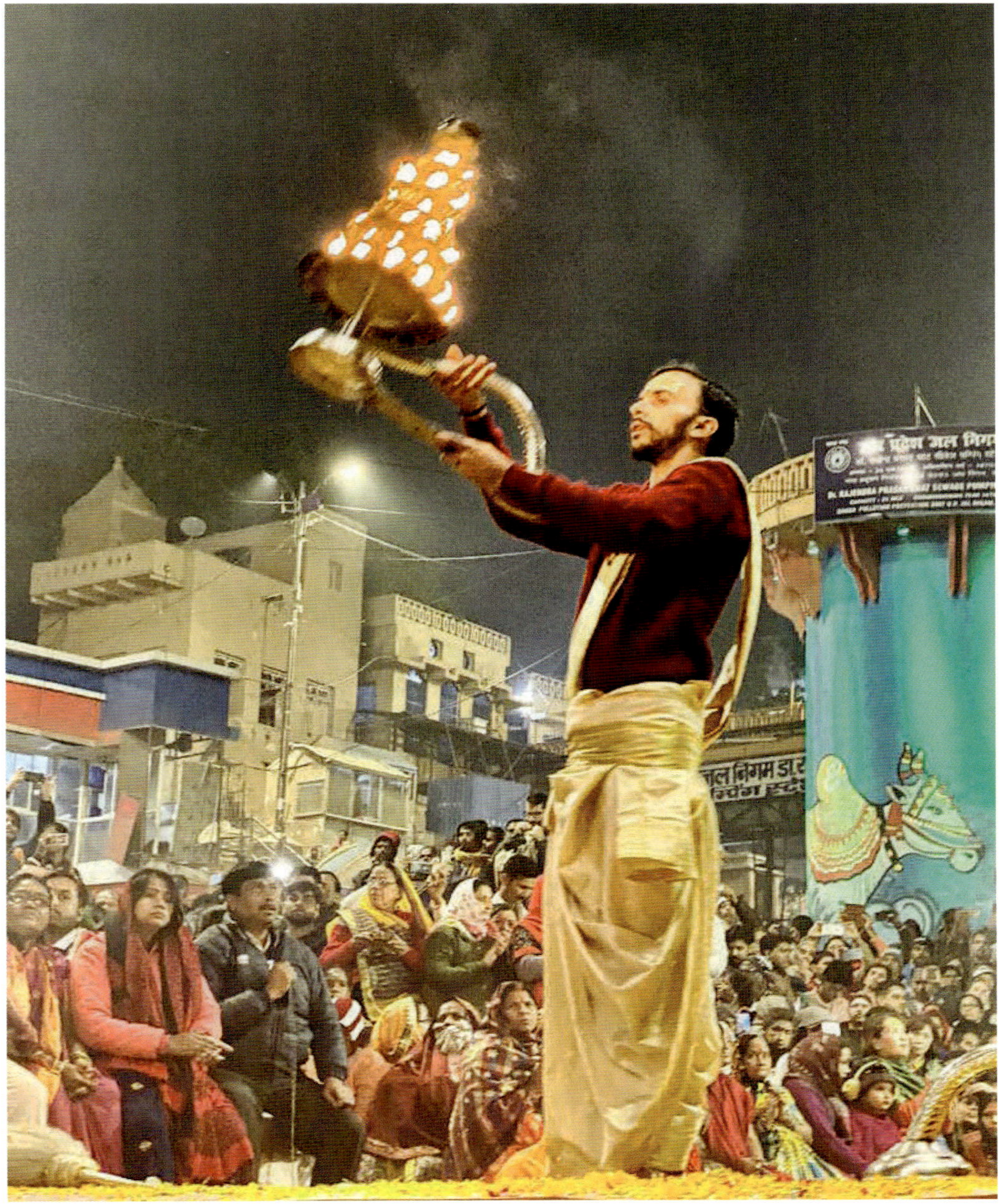

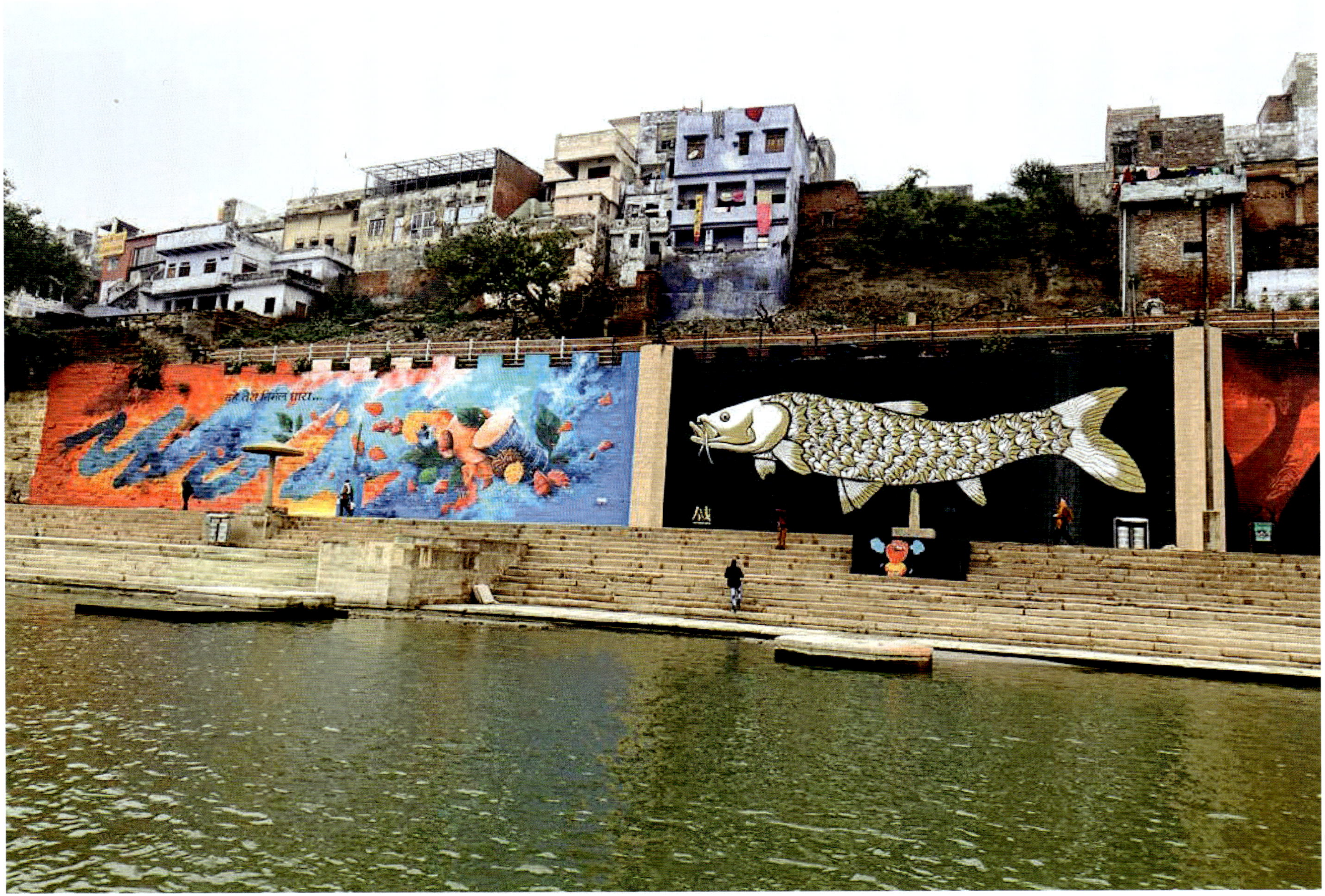

Creator and Destroyer: Rudrasarovar or Dasashvamedh Ghat in the heart of the city that Brahma created and is dwelled upon by the supreme destructor Shiva.

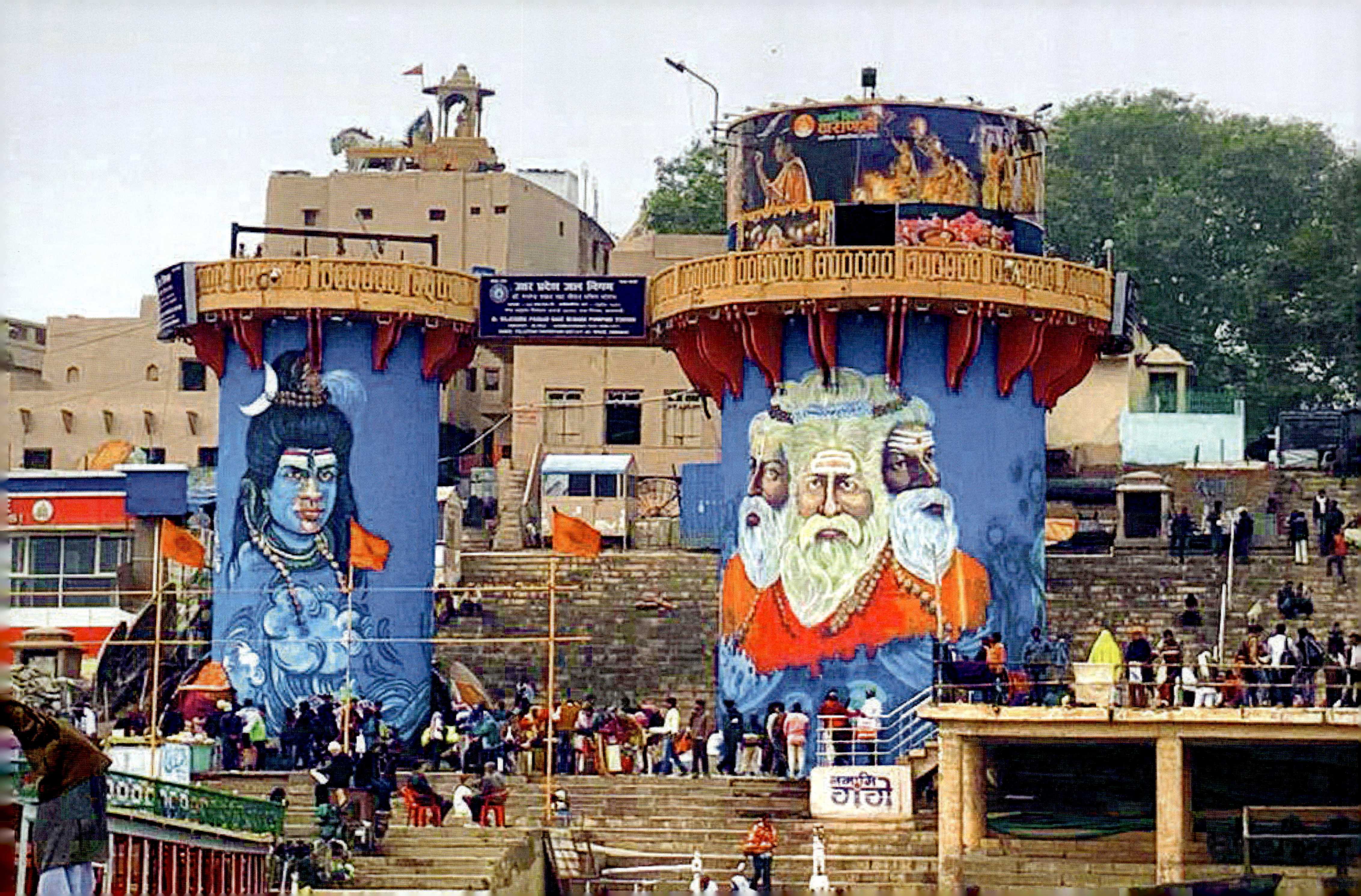
उत्तर प्रदेश जल निगम
नमामि गंगे

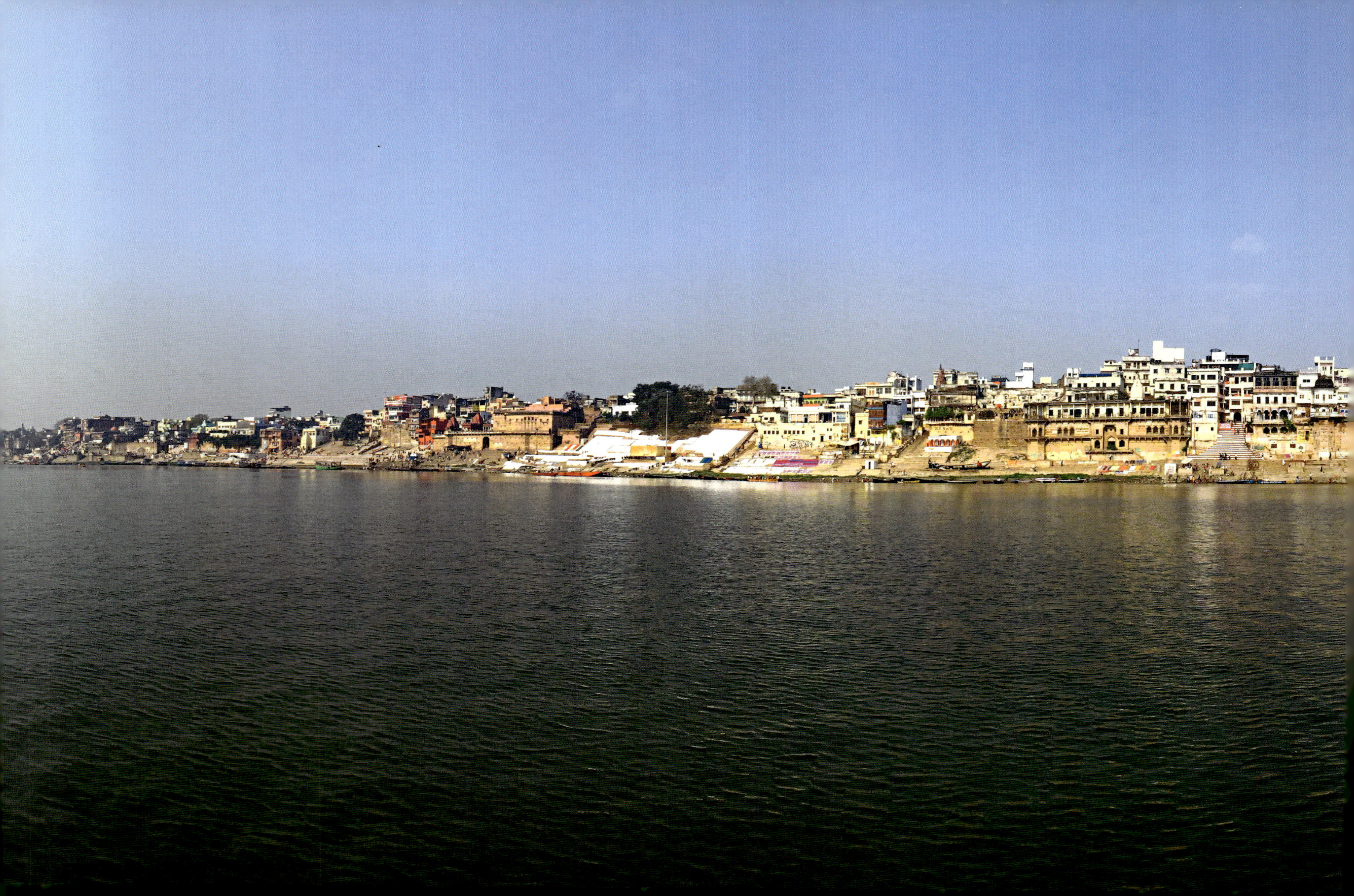

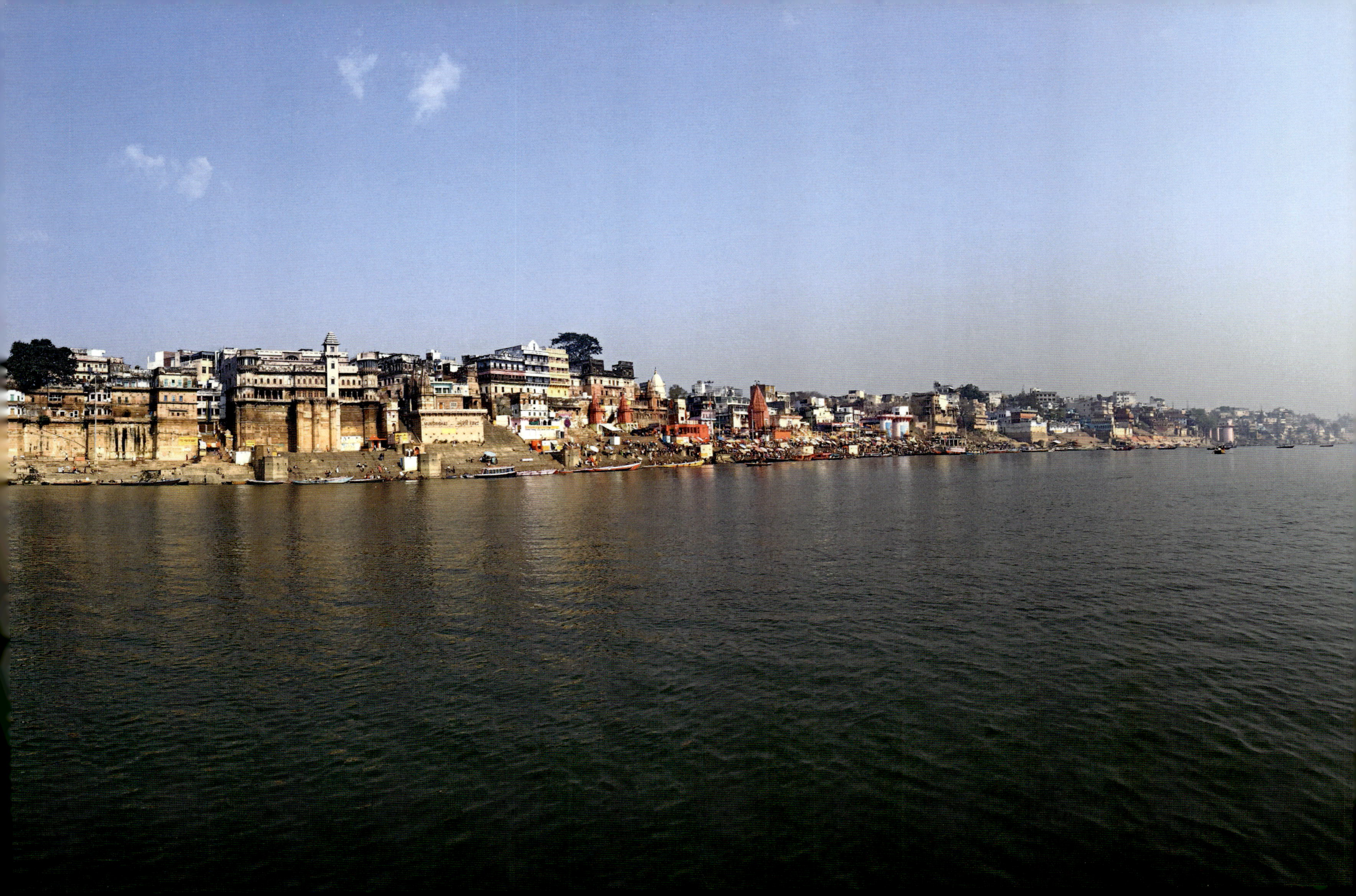

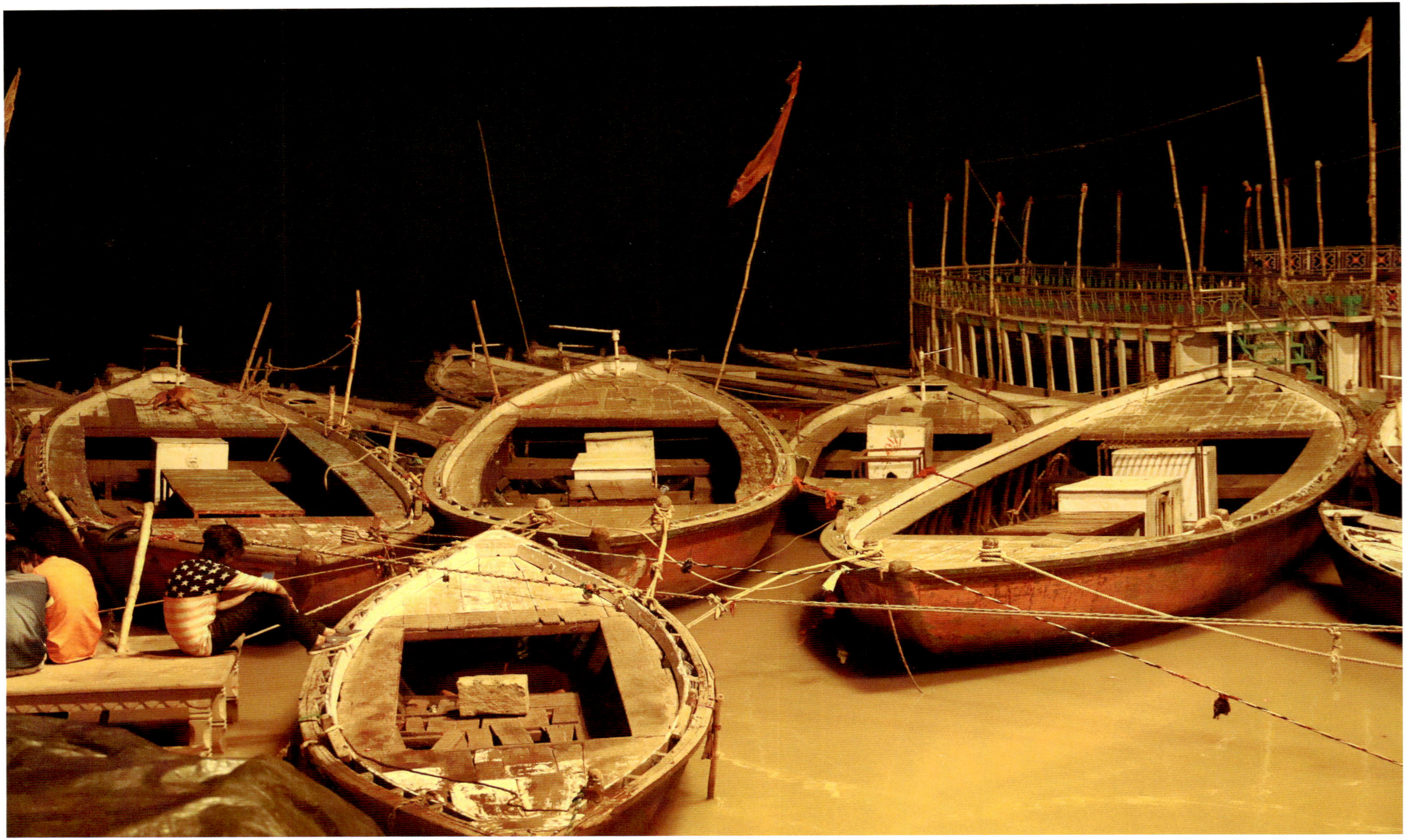

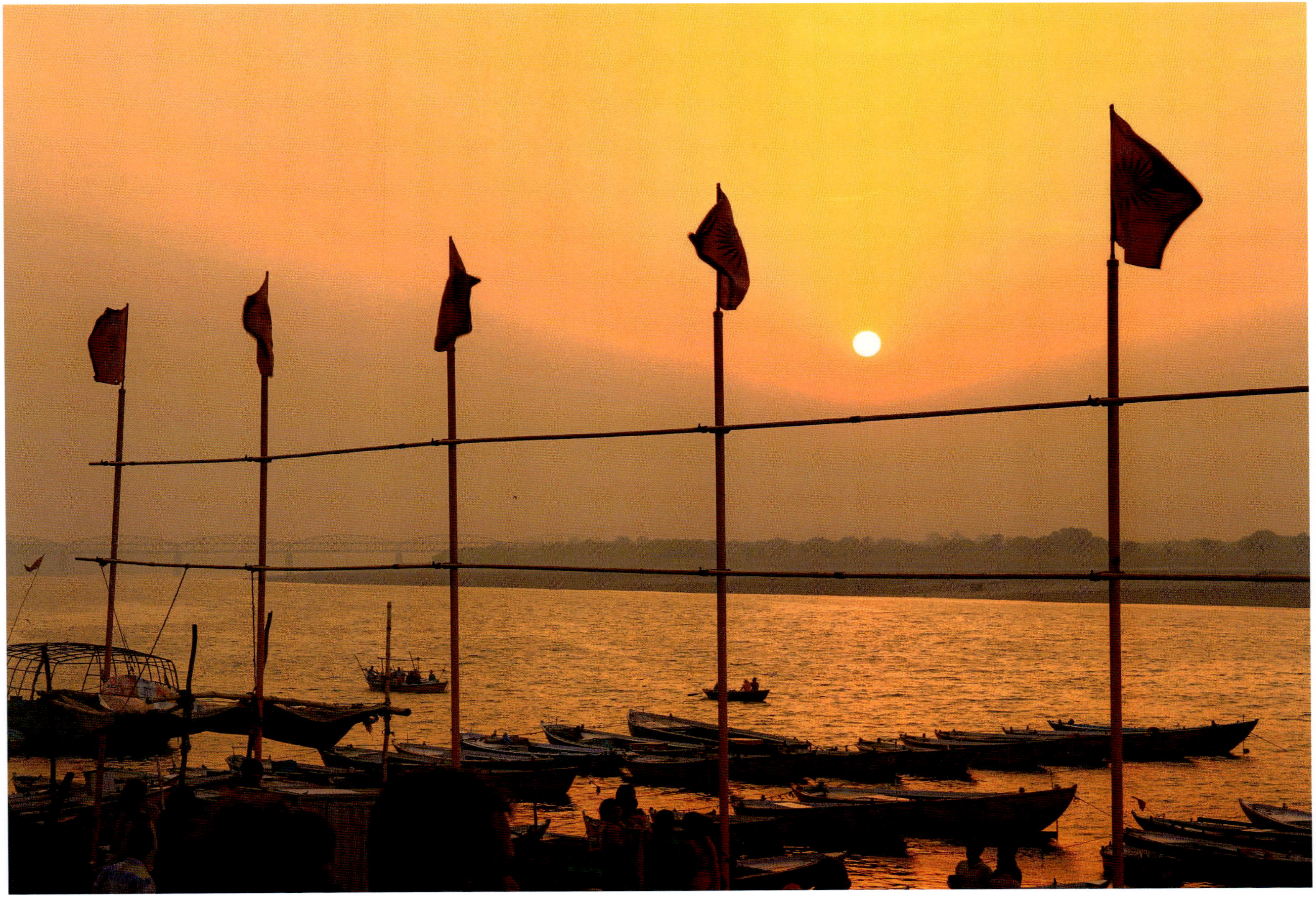

Dwaita: Dualities everywhere in the form of darkness and light, despair and hope, night and day depict the true colours of the soul, and their endless cyclic repetition.

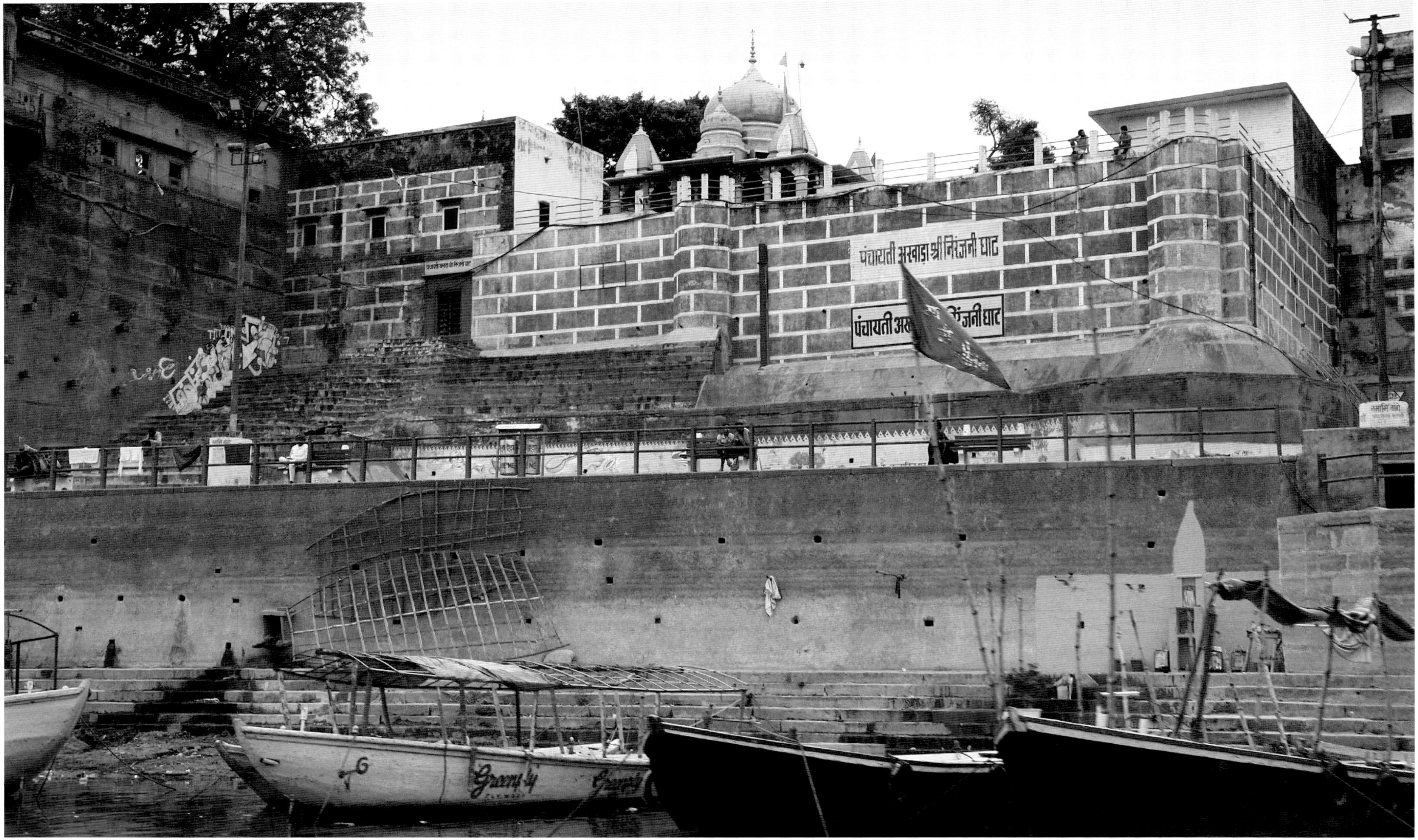
पंचायती अखाड़ा श्री निरंजनी घाट

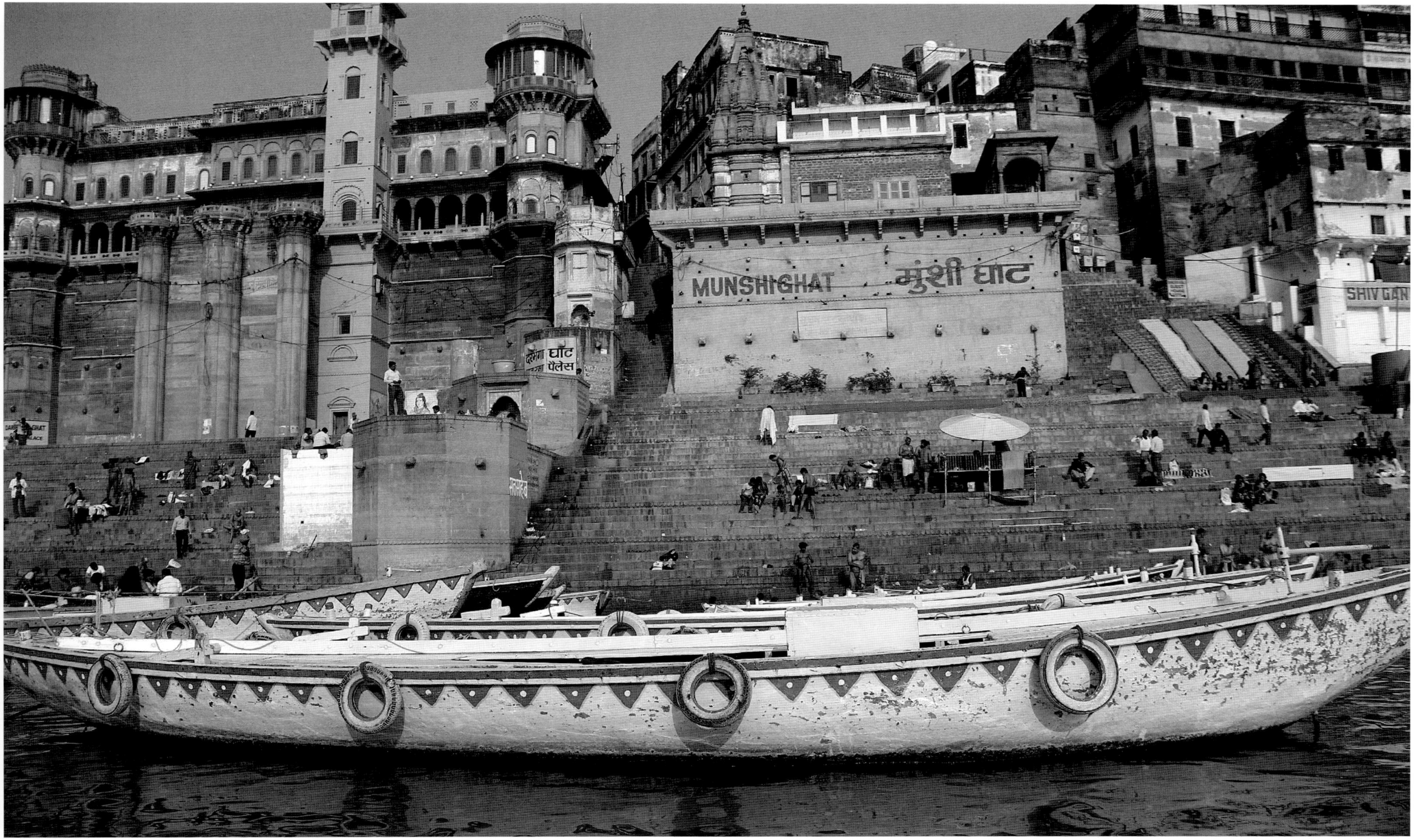
MUNSHIGHAT
मुंशी घाट

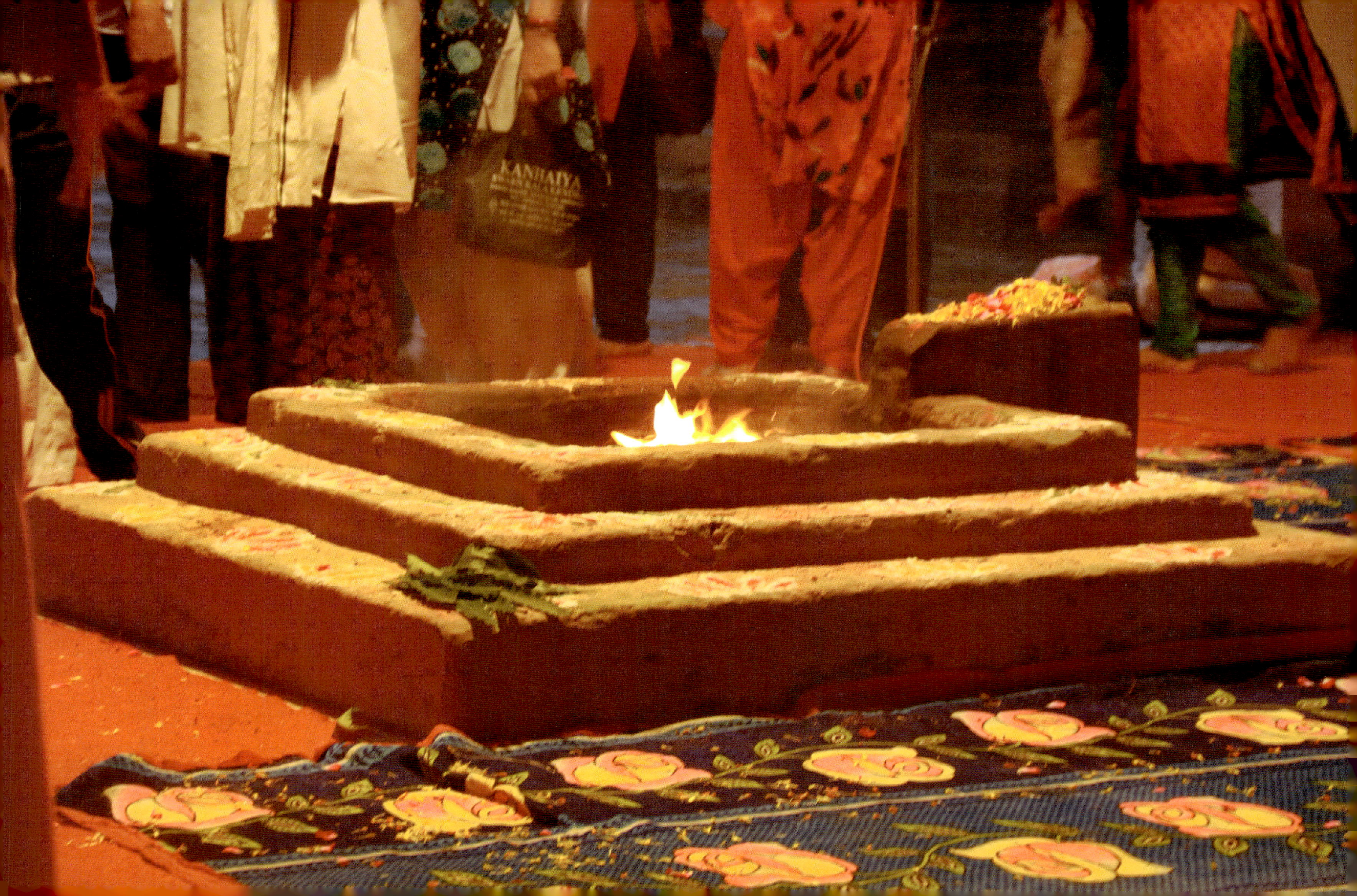
KANHAIYA

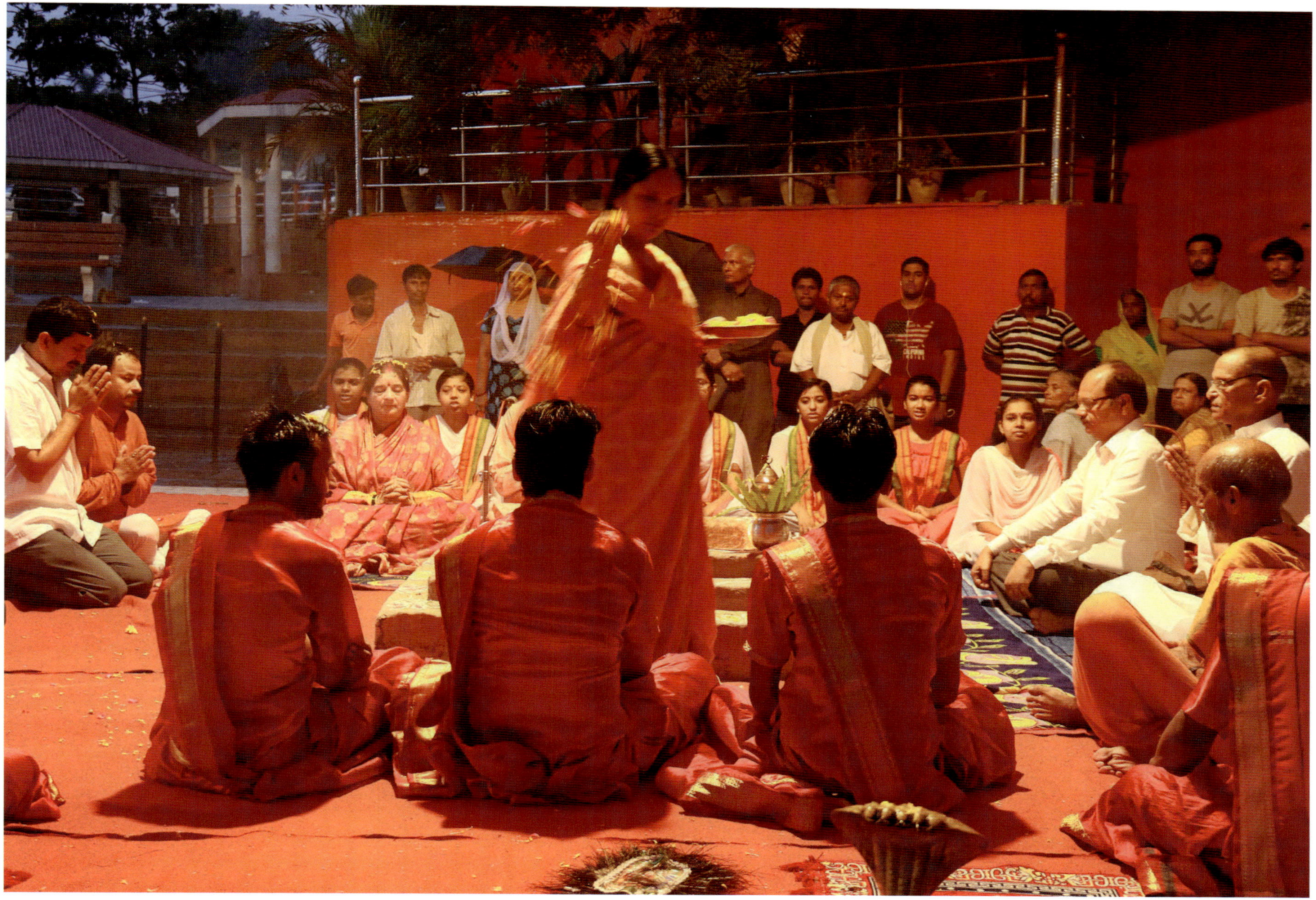

Hawan: The pious mantras resound in the air as sacred offerings are made to the holy fire, dispelling all negativity—a deeply soul-stirring experience.

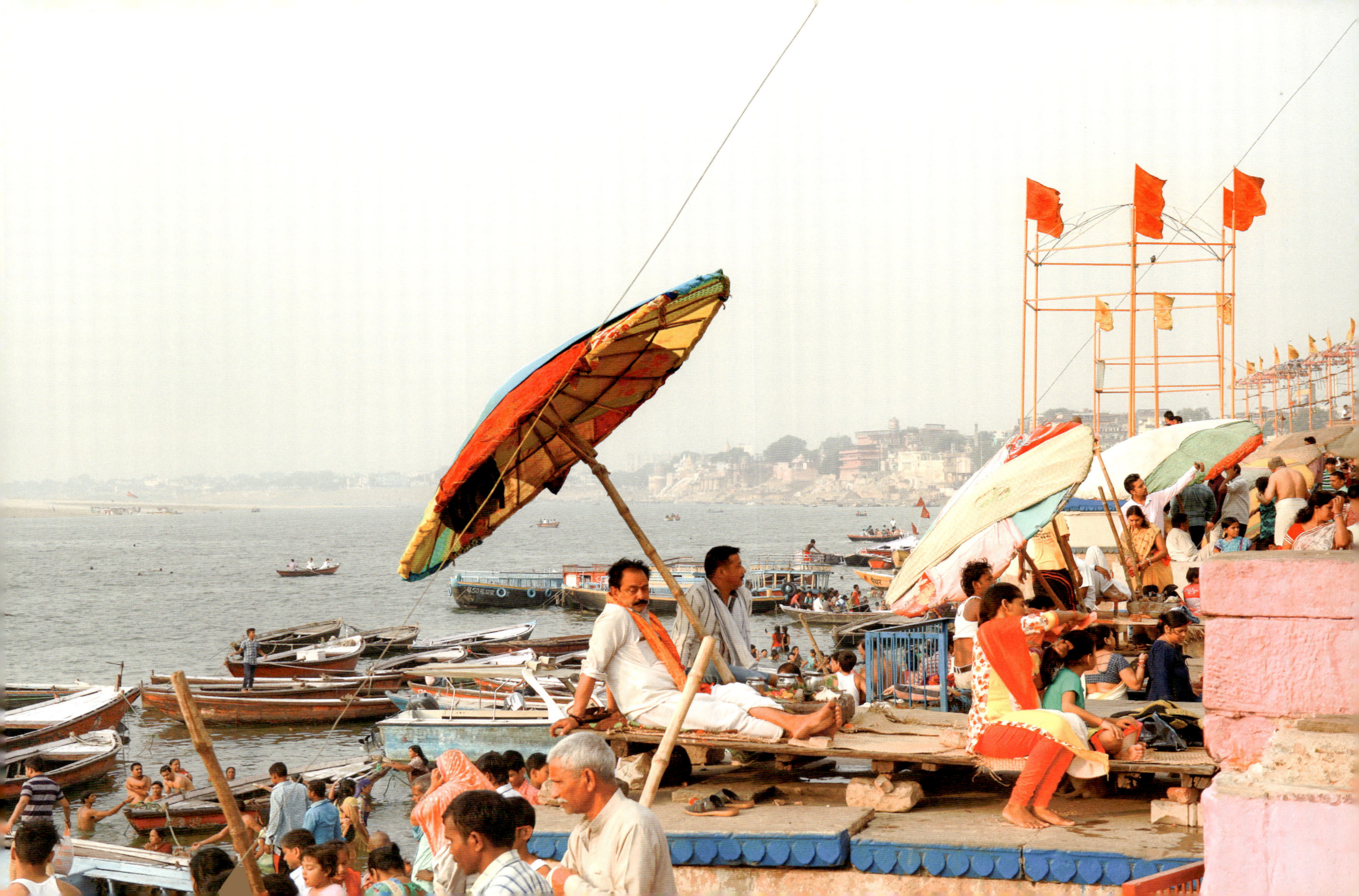

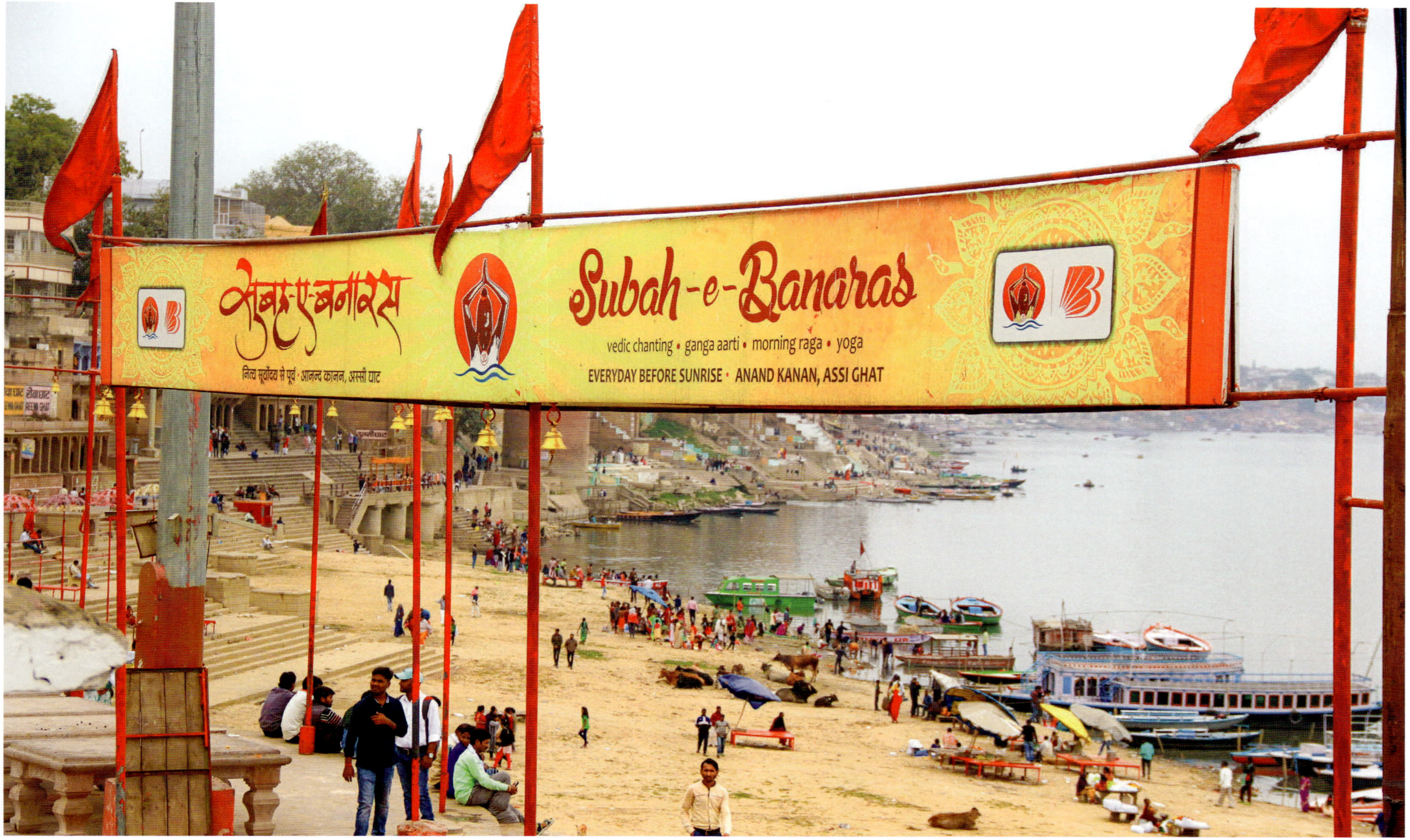
सुबह-ए-बनारस
नित्य सूर्योदय से पूर्व · आनन्द कानन, अस्सी घाट
Subah-e-Banaras
vedic chanting • ganga aarti • morning raga • yoga
EVERYDAY BEFORE SUNRISE • ANAND KANAN, ASSI GHAT

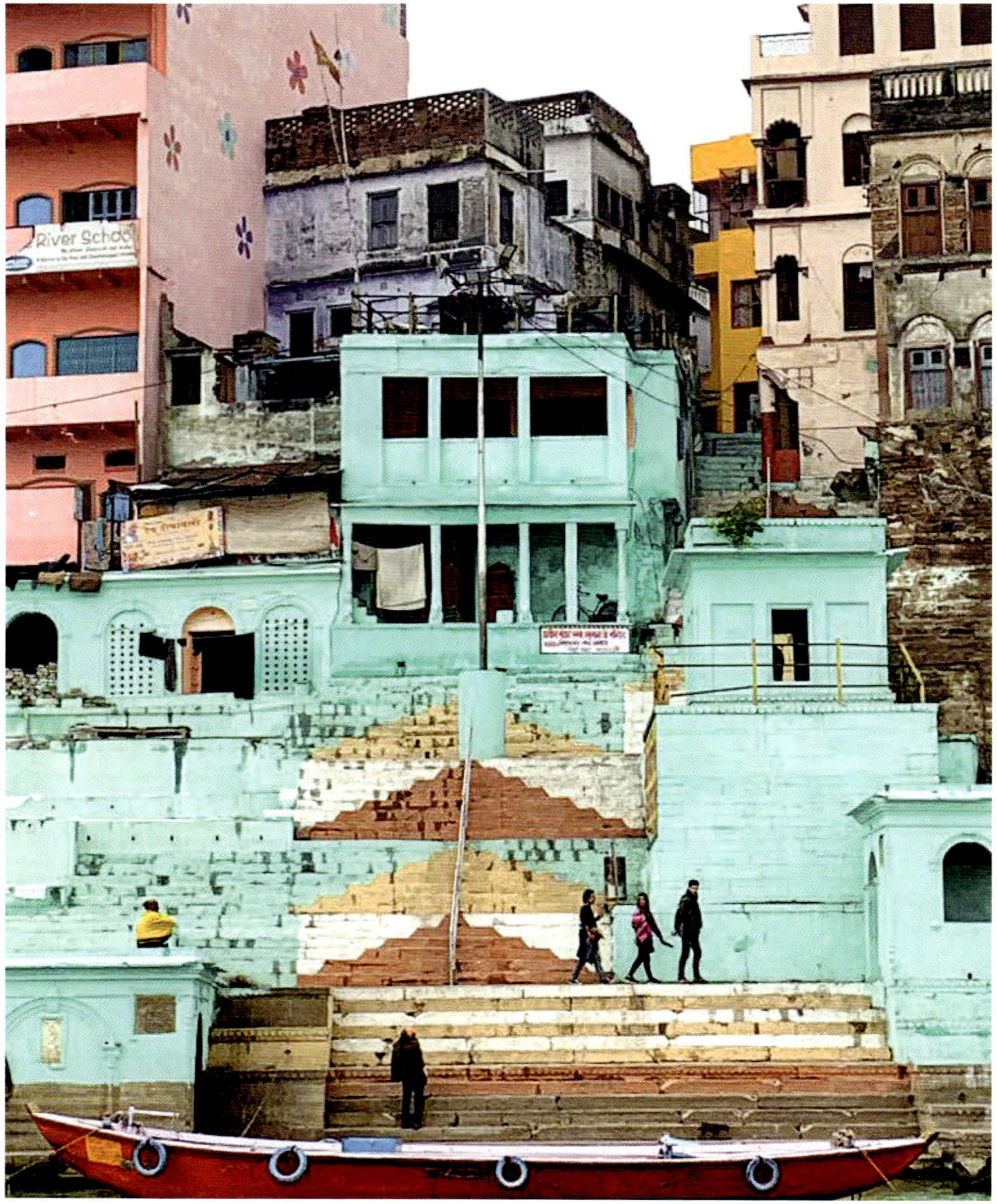

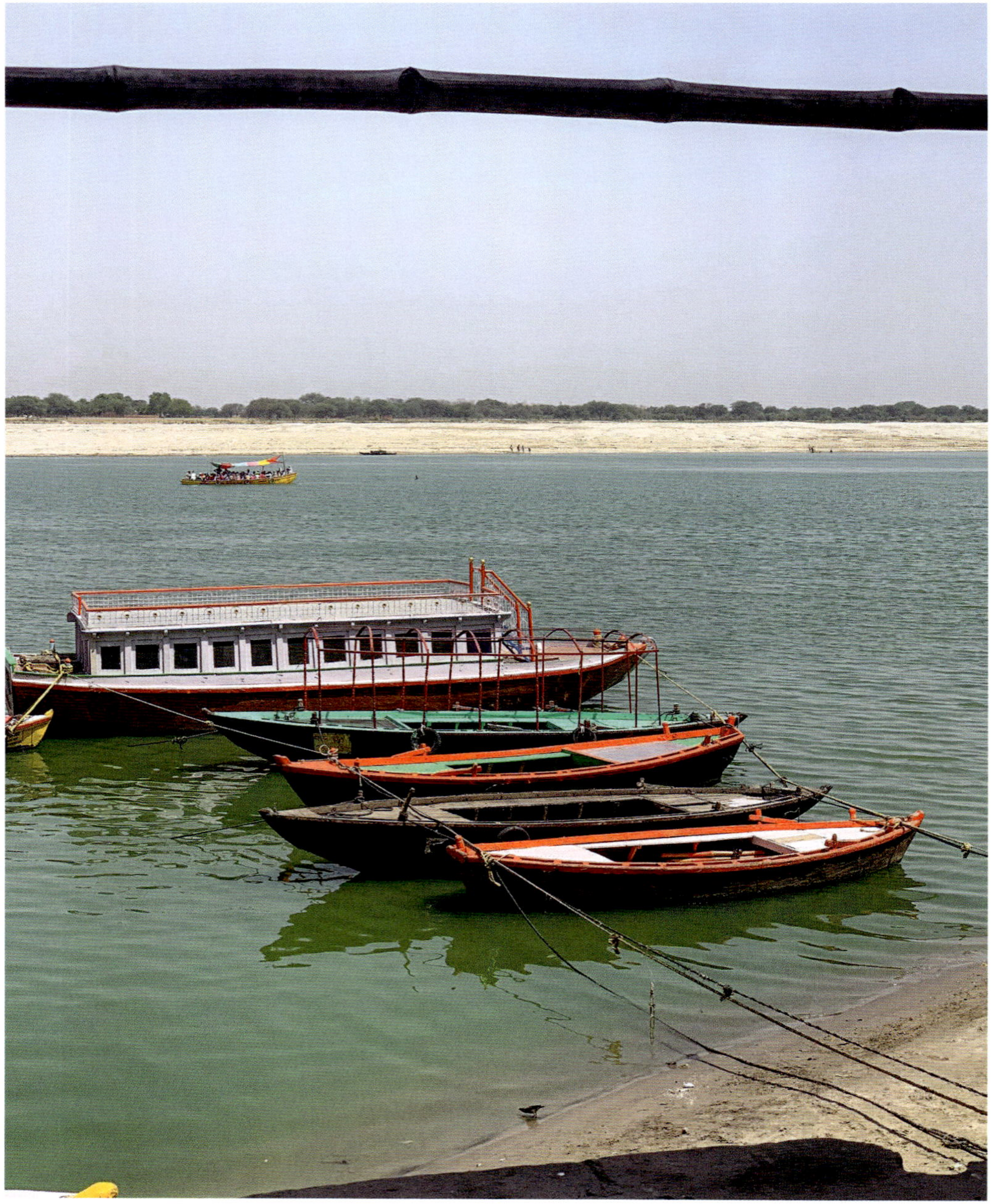

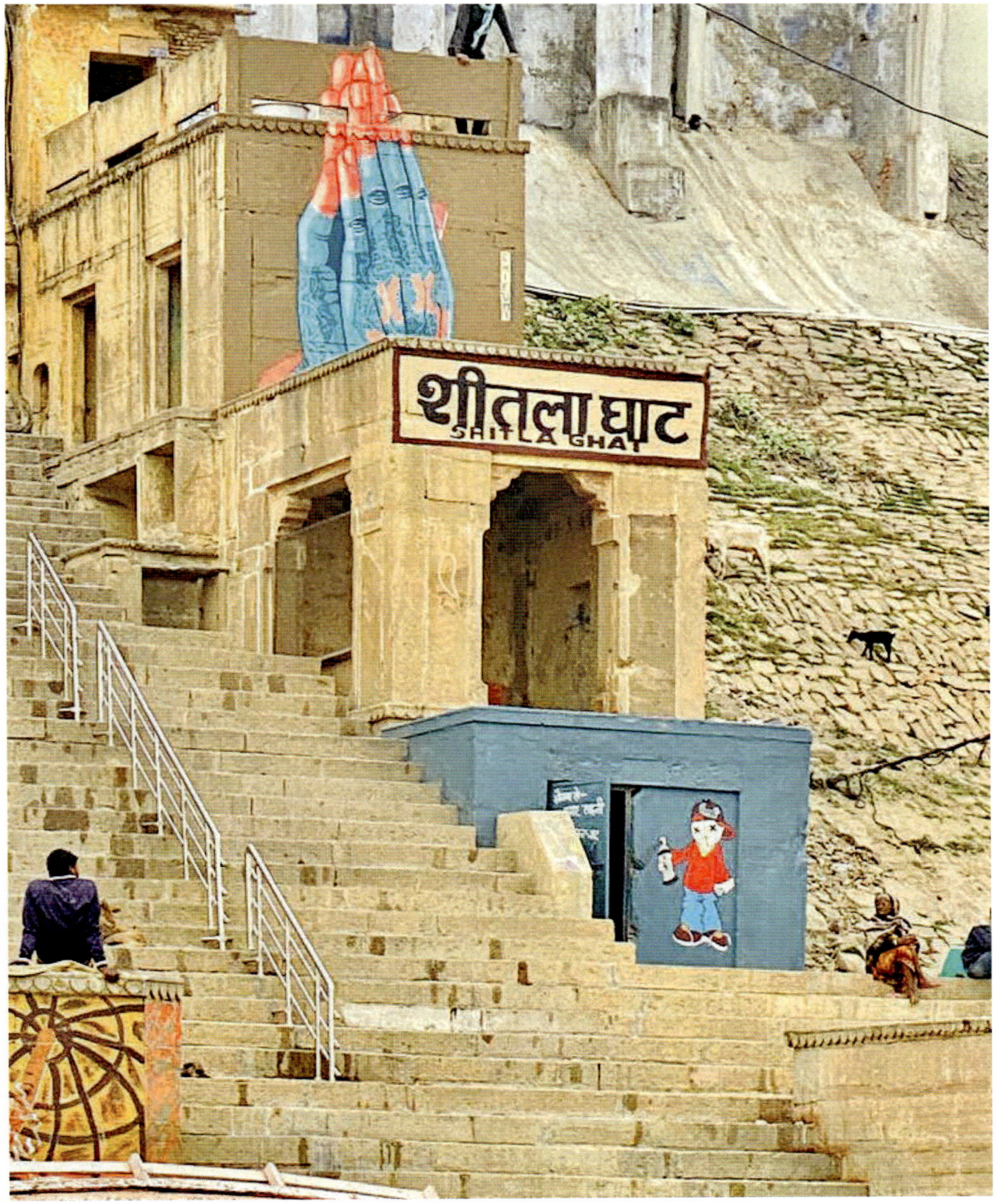
शीतला घाट
SHITLA GHAT

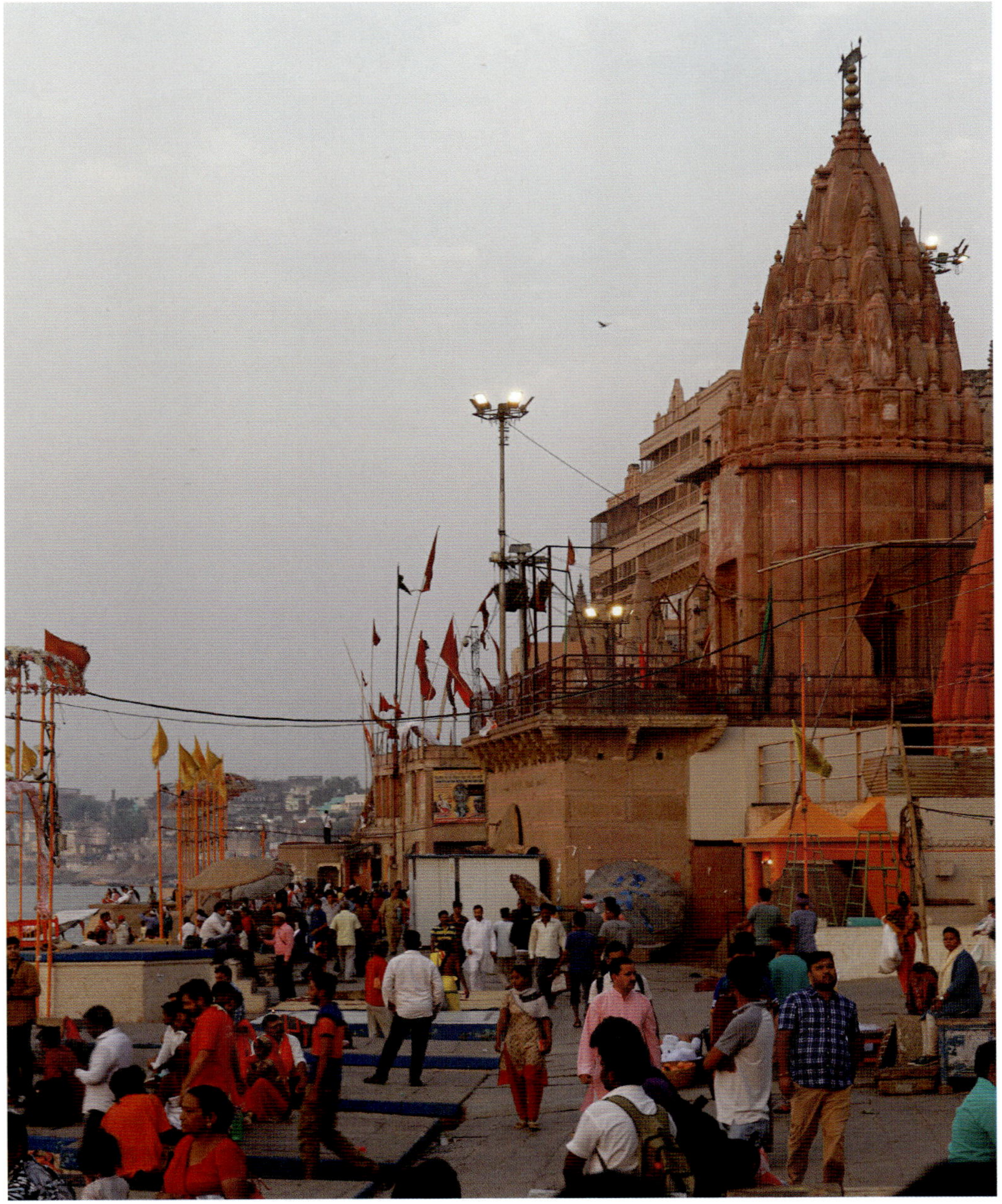

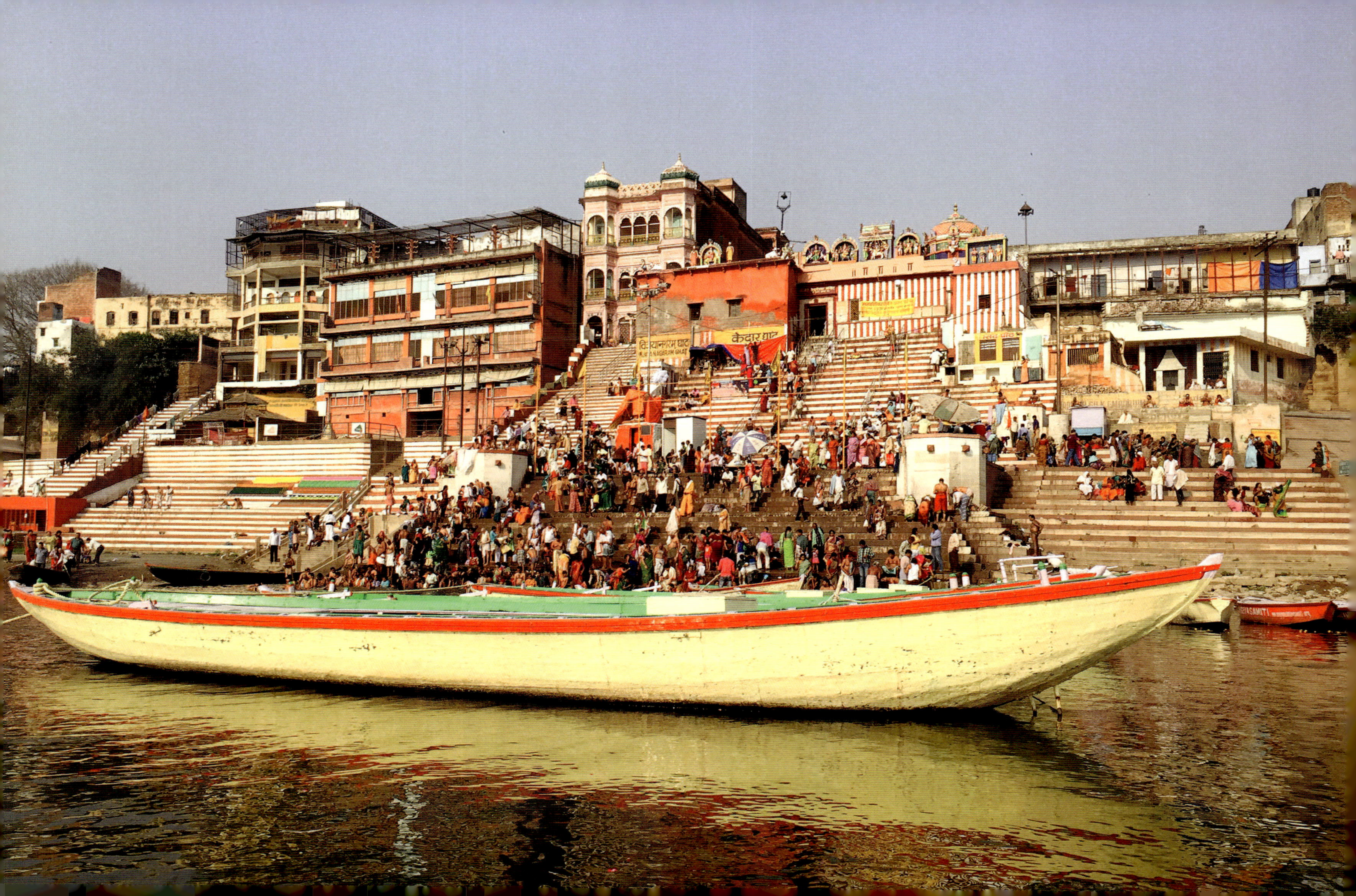
केदार घाट

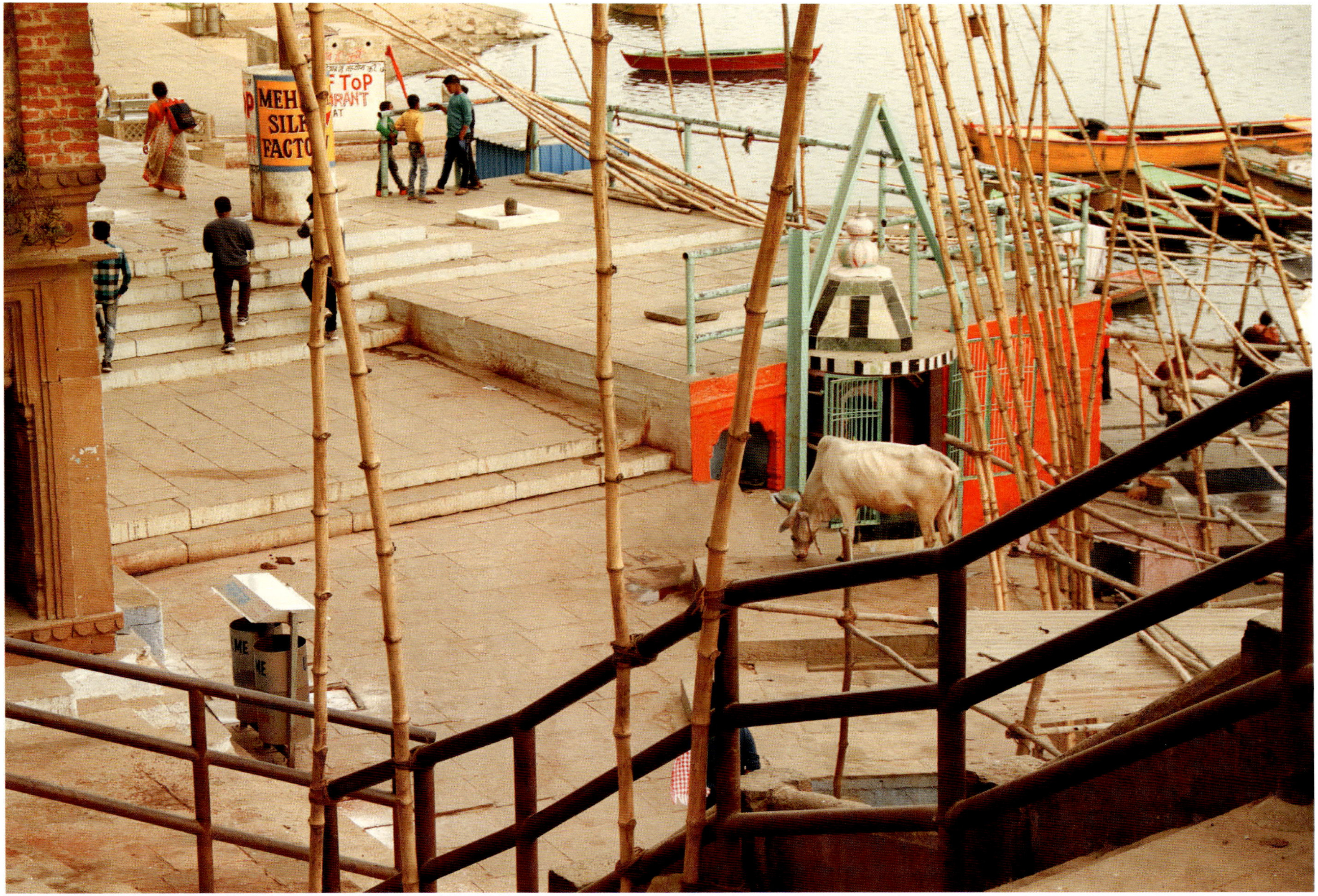

Punarnava (to be reborn): Between the two abysses of Before and After, there is this enduring flash of consciousness where one experiences the whole gamut of mortal emotions and happenings.

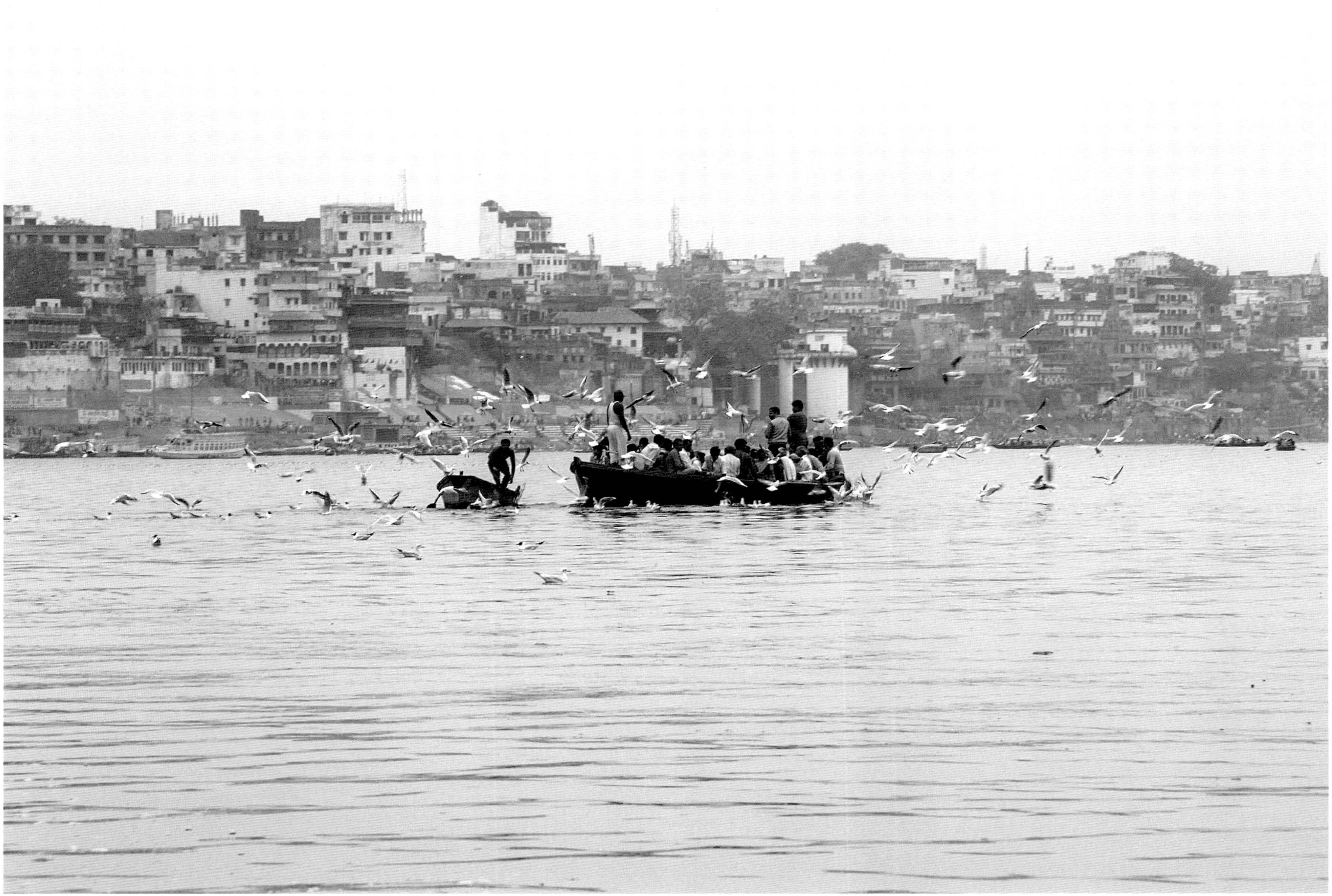

Moksha:
In the stillness
of the morning,
the birds, flying
in the direction of
their choice, mock
the travellers below
and remind them
that the supreme
goal of life is to
be free.

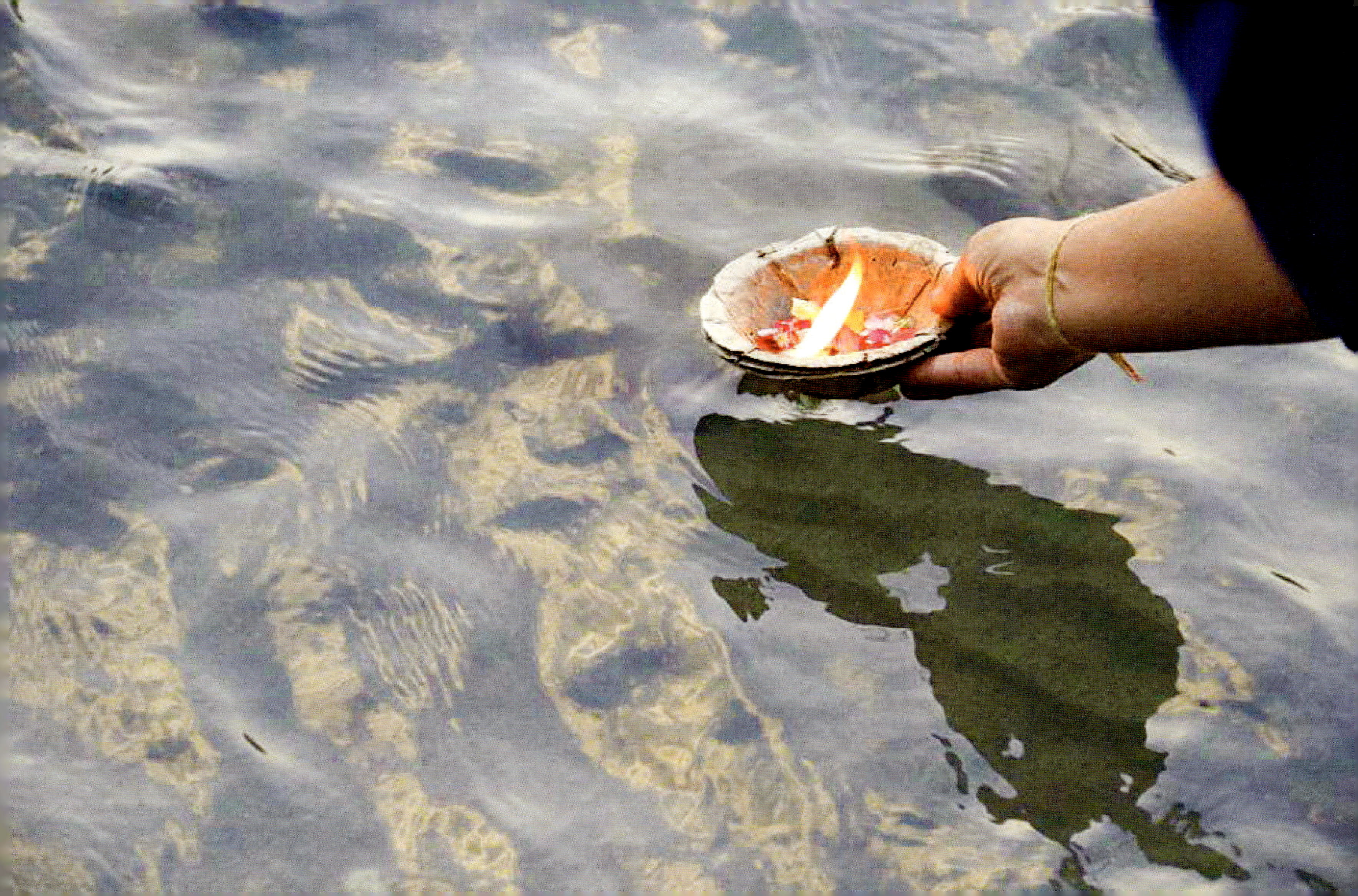

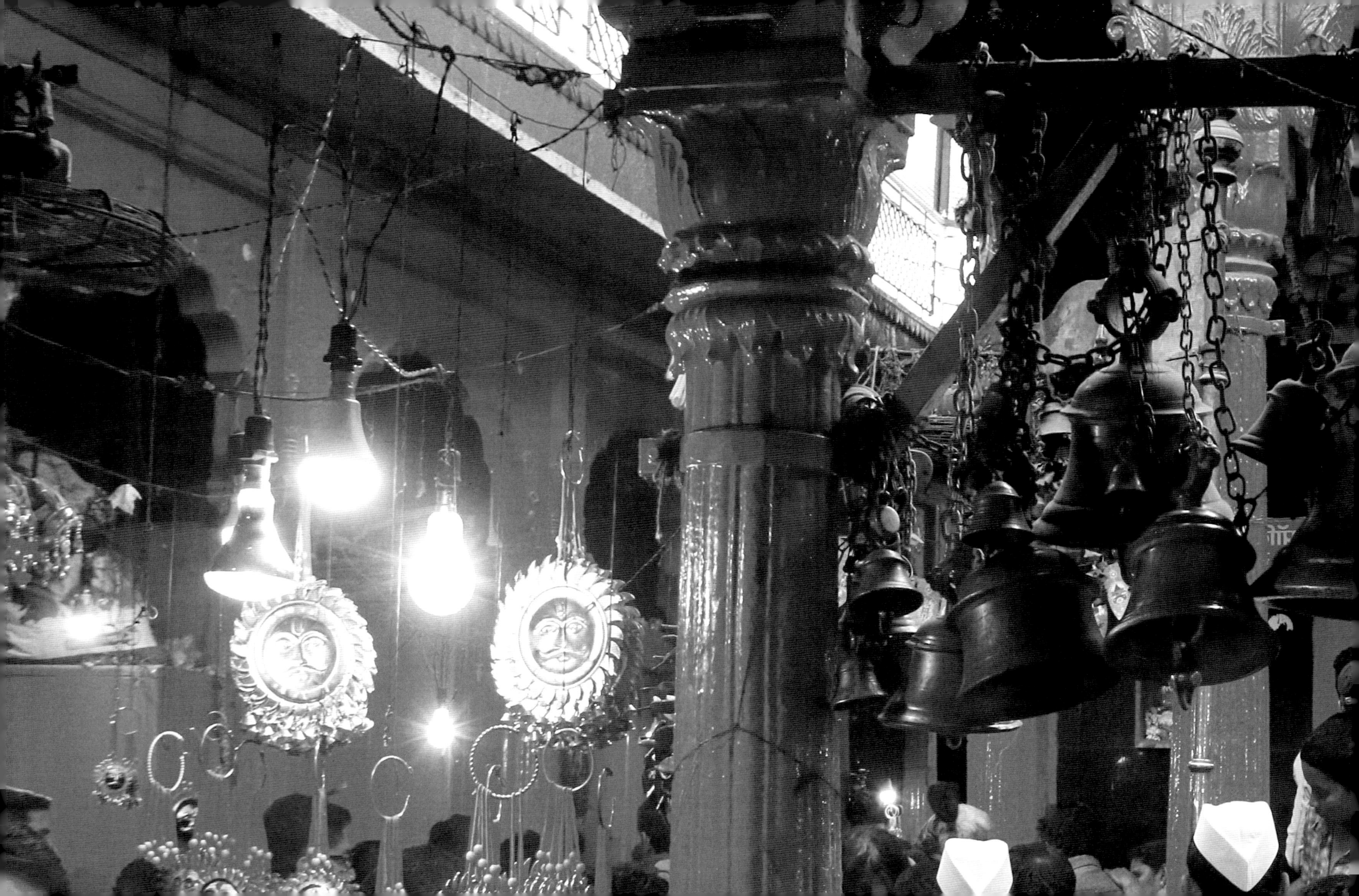

# Temples

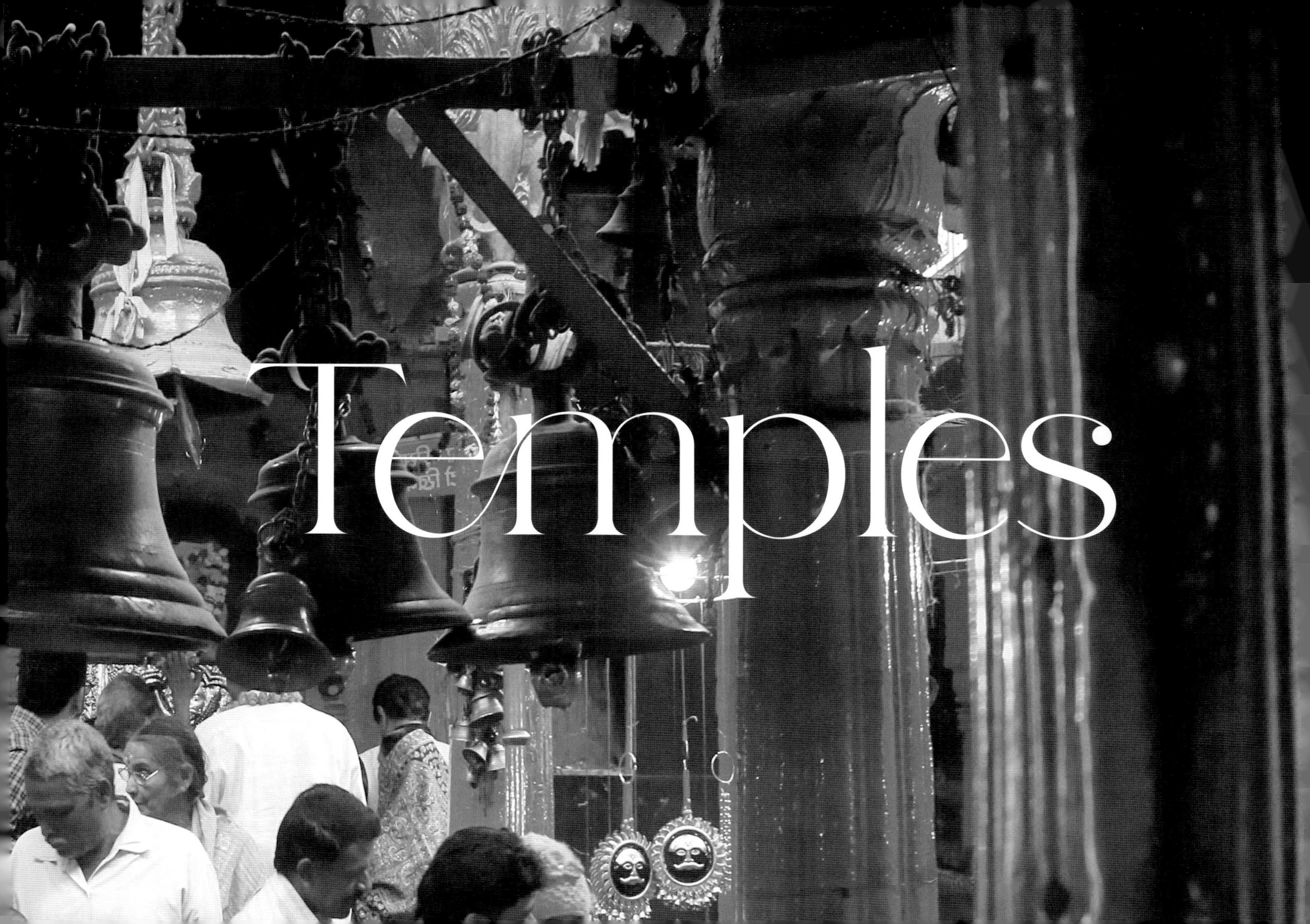

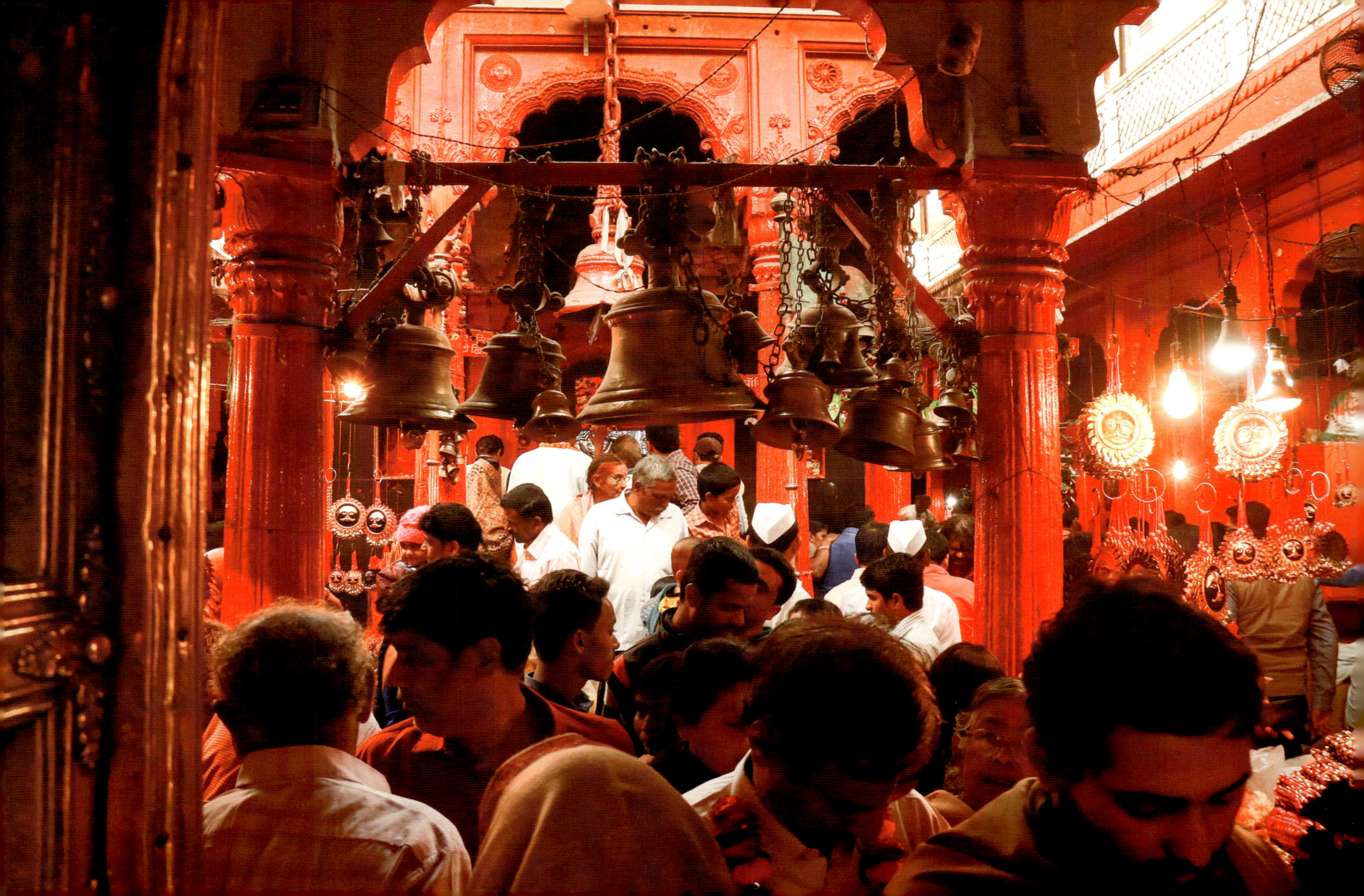

The Gatekeeper, Kaal Bhairav—Kashi ke kotwal. One needs to bow down to Him before embarking on the journey to the Vishwanath temple. It is here that seekers come to find freedom from the fear of Kaal, which denotes both Death and Time.

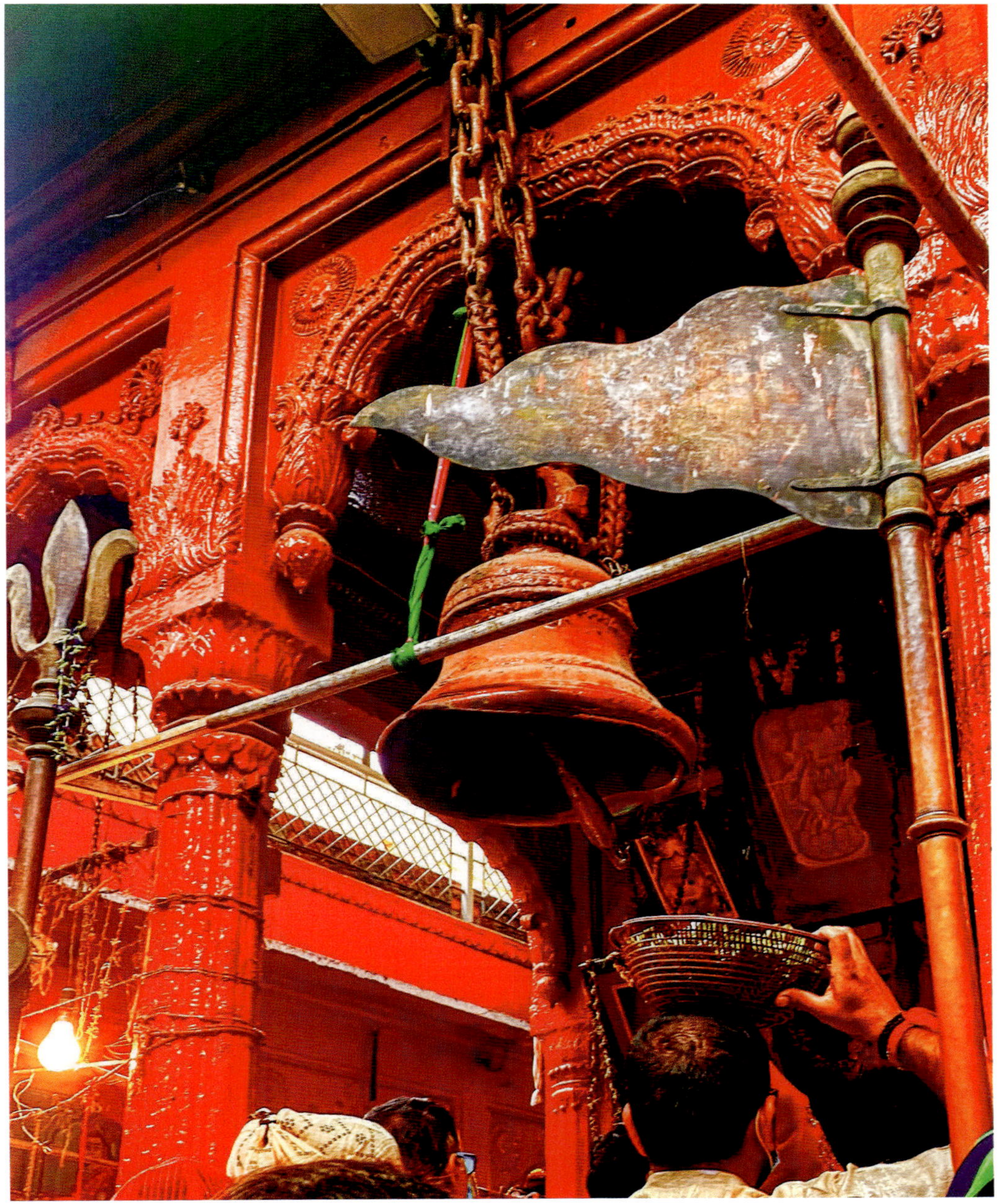

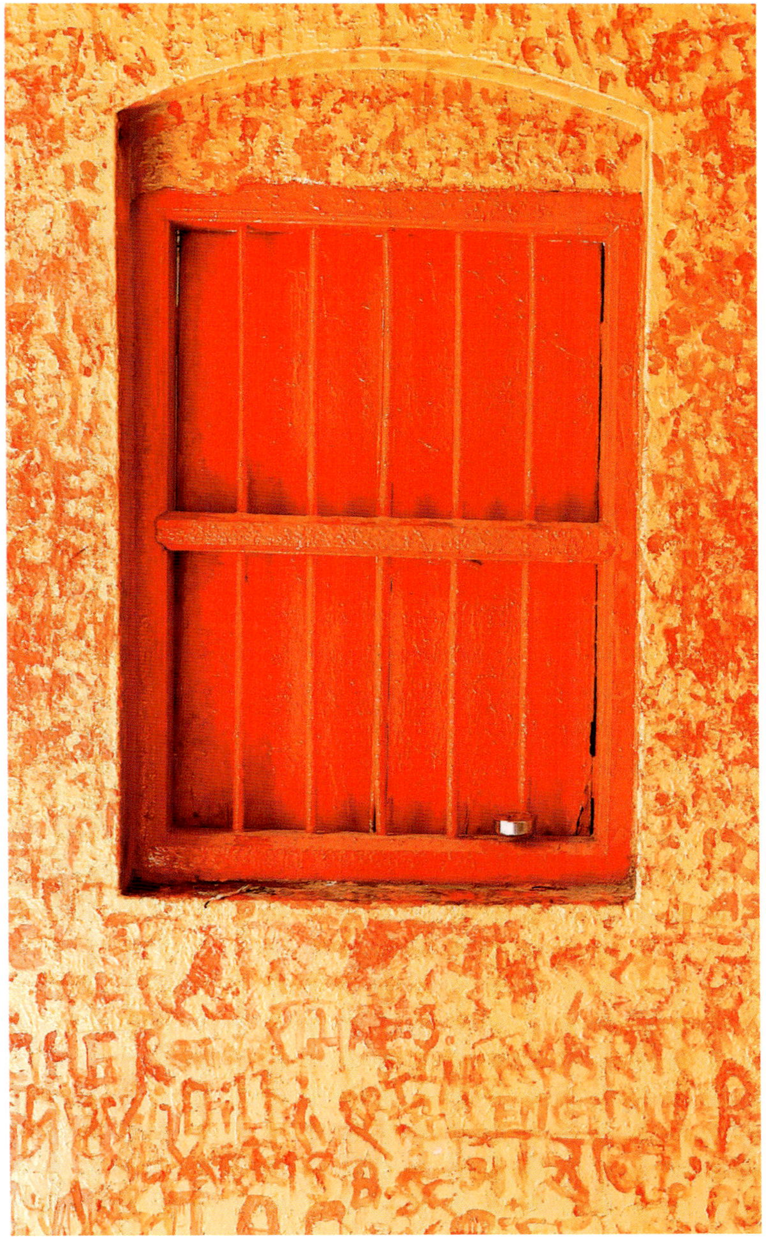

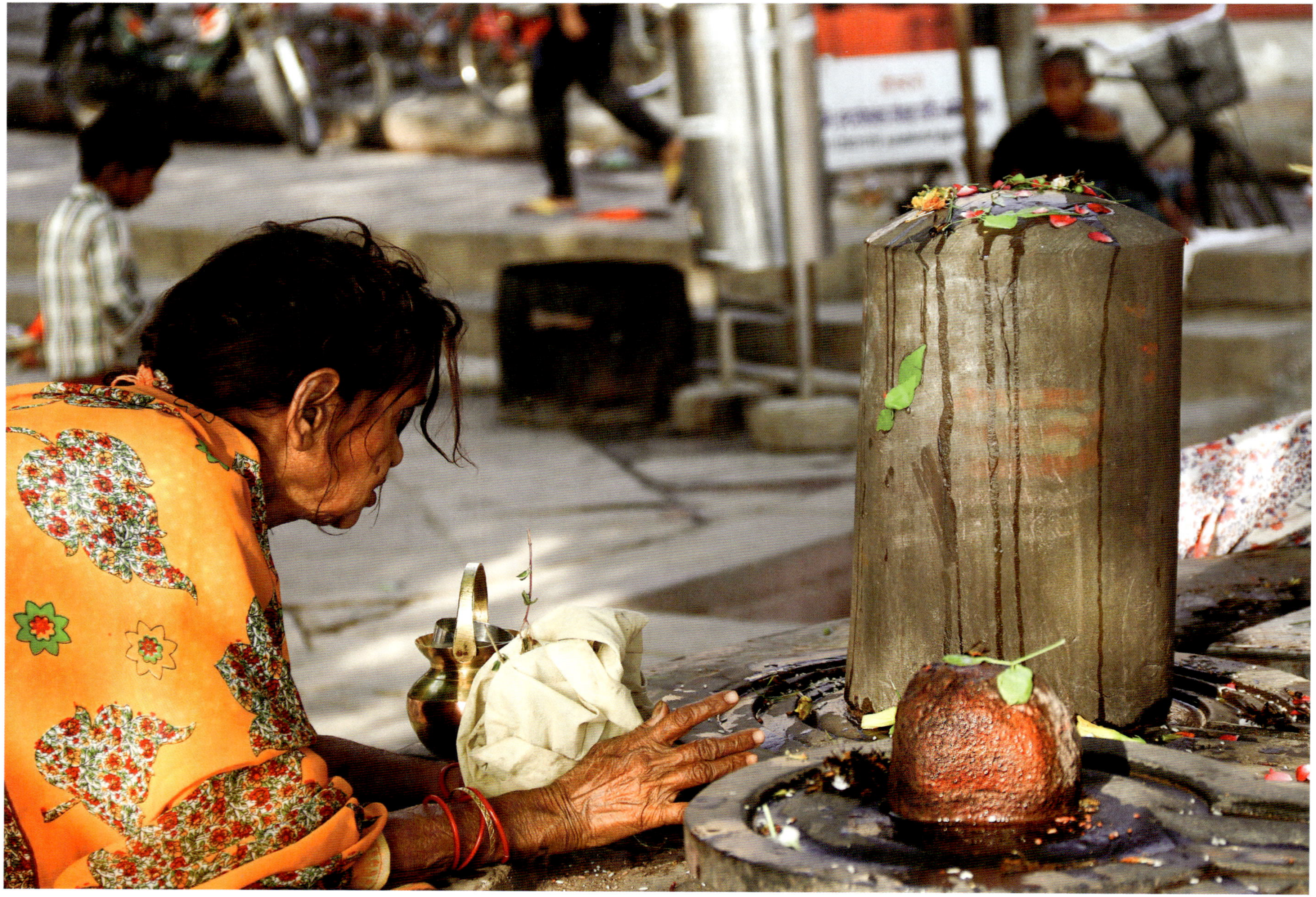

Surrender:
Empty the urn by
surrendering to
the Supreme and
then fill it up with
an abundance of
spiritual truths.

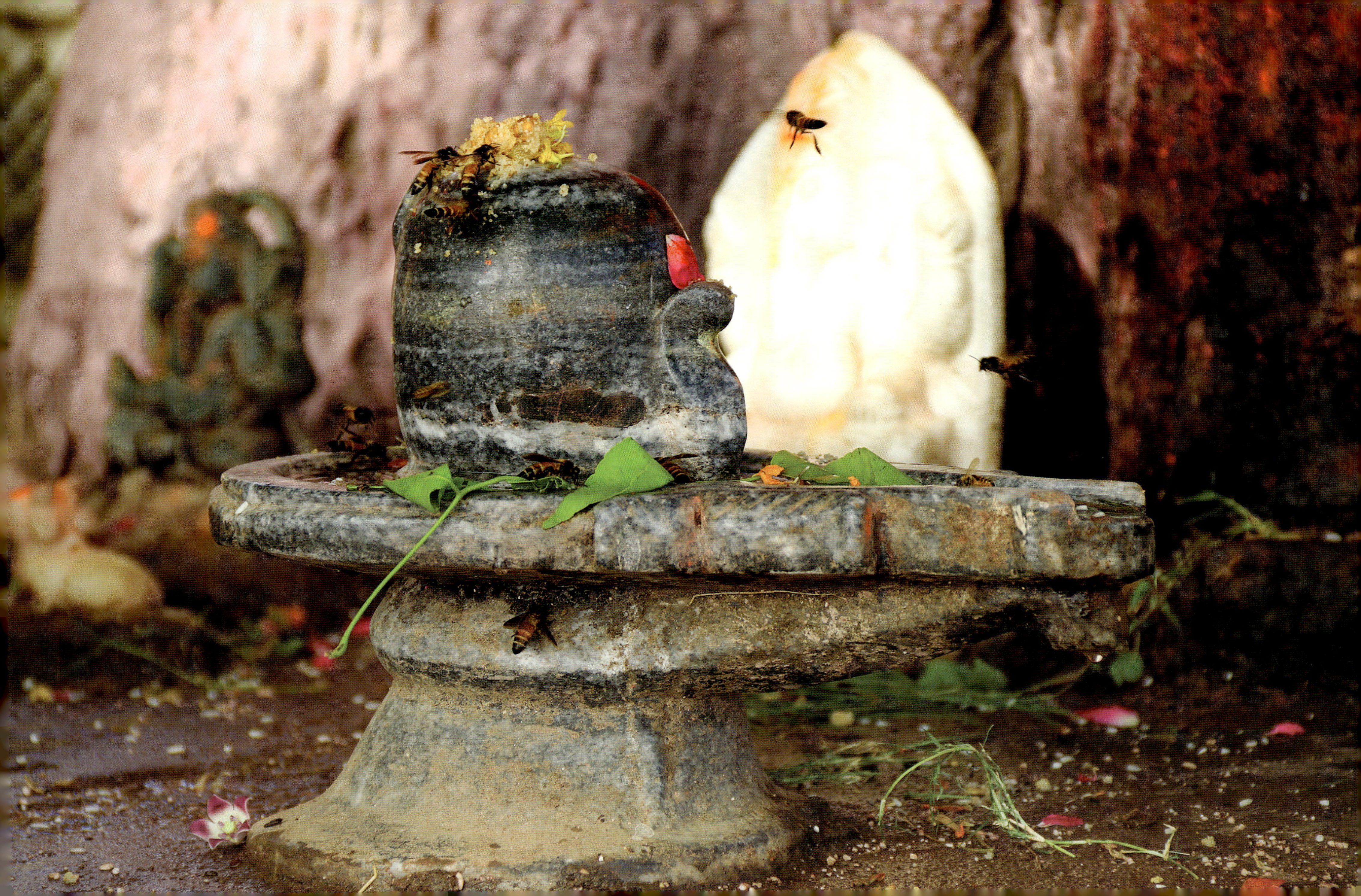

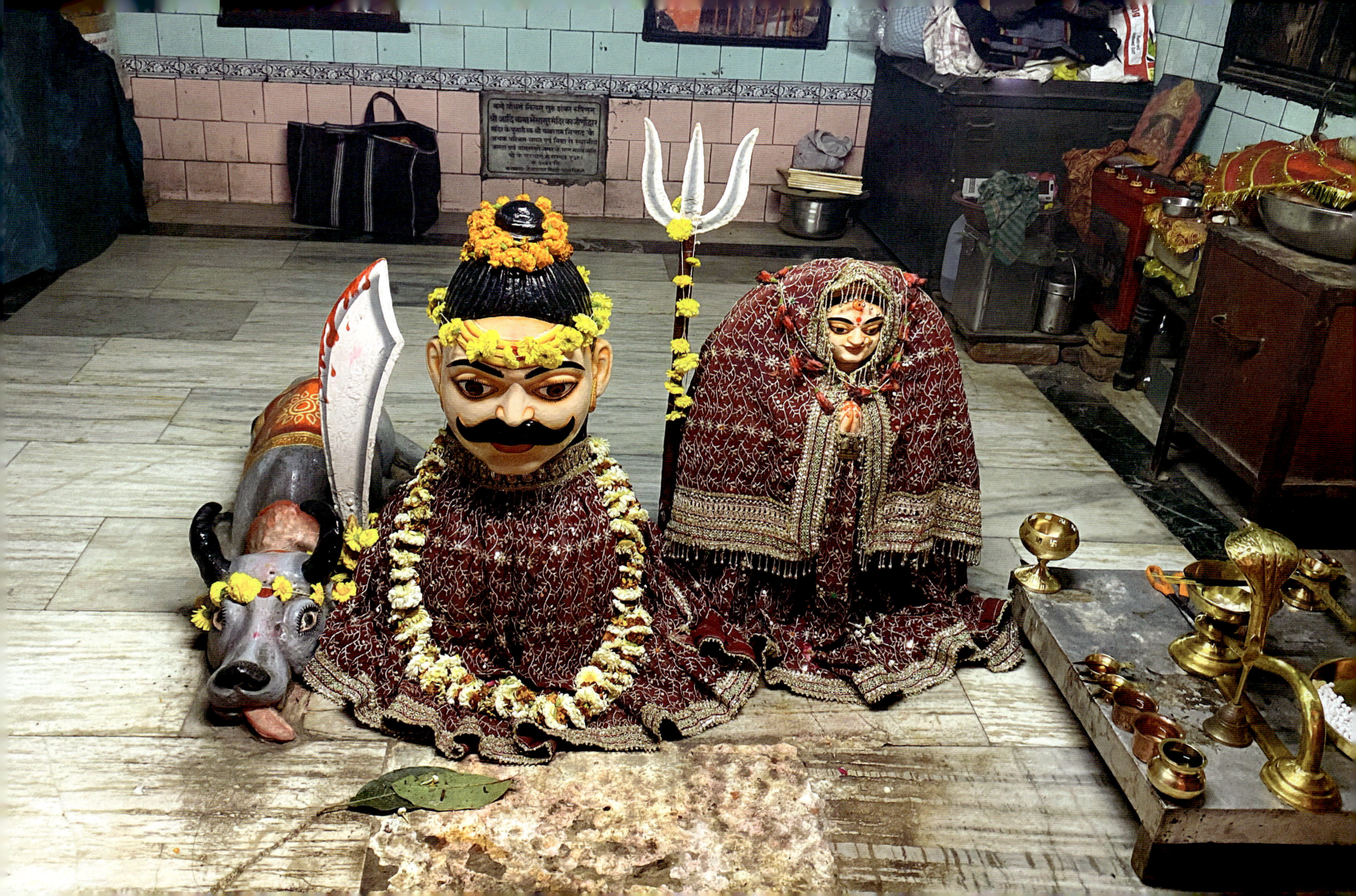

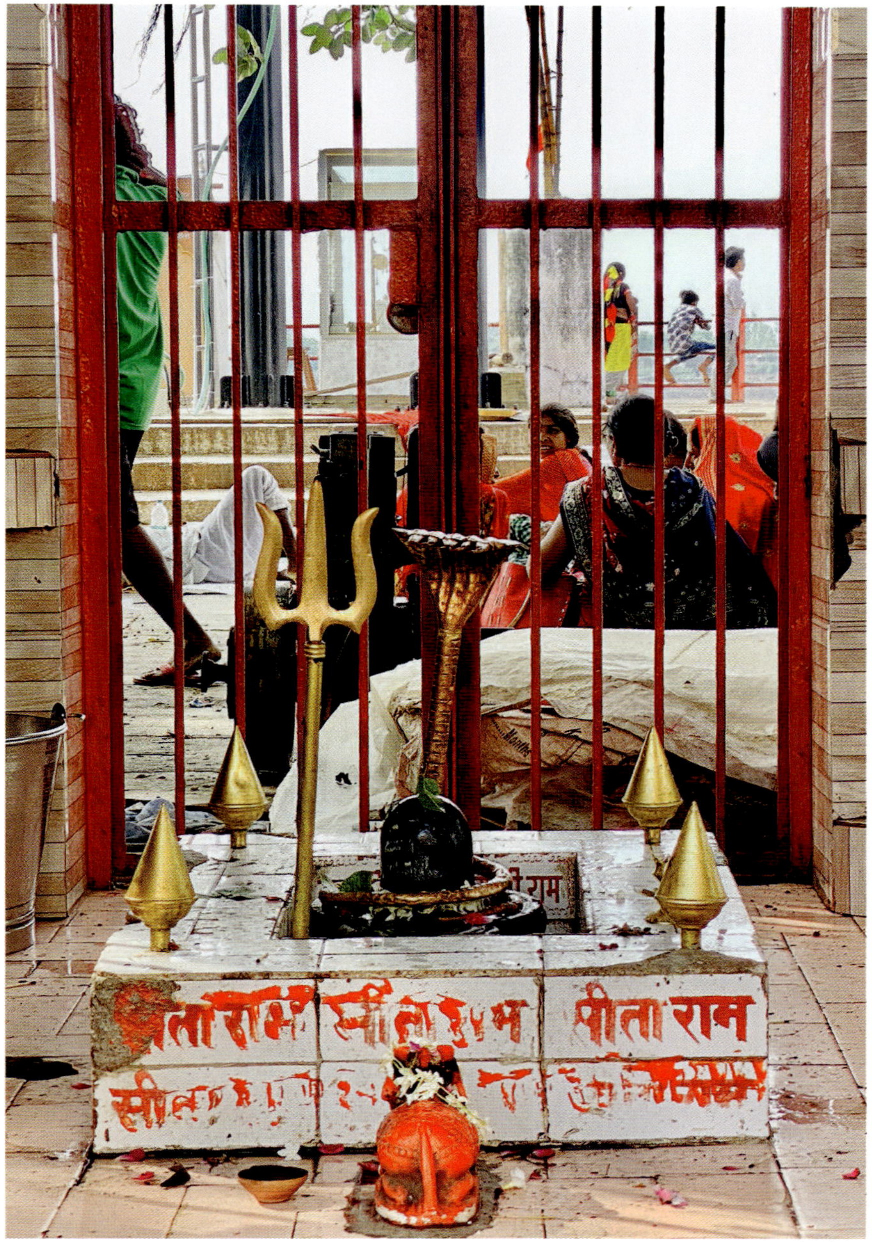


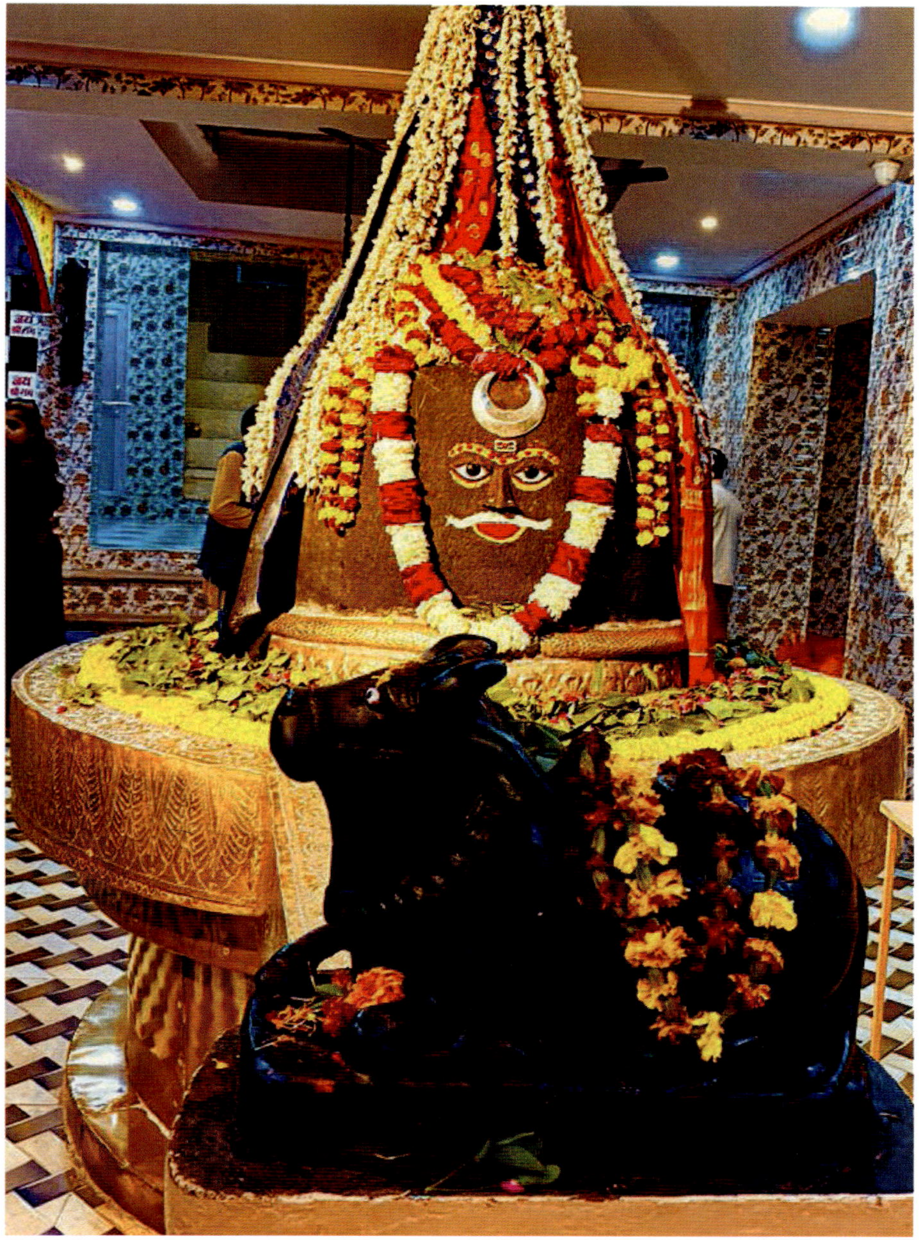

Benaras houses more than 3,000 temples and shrines—from the humble linga to the moustache-bearing inornate statue, He is a reflection of the soul that seeks Him.

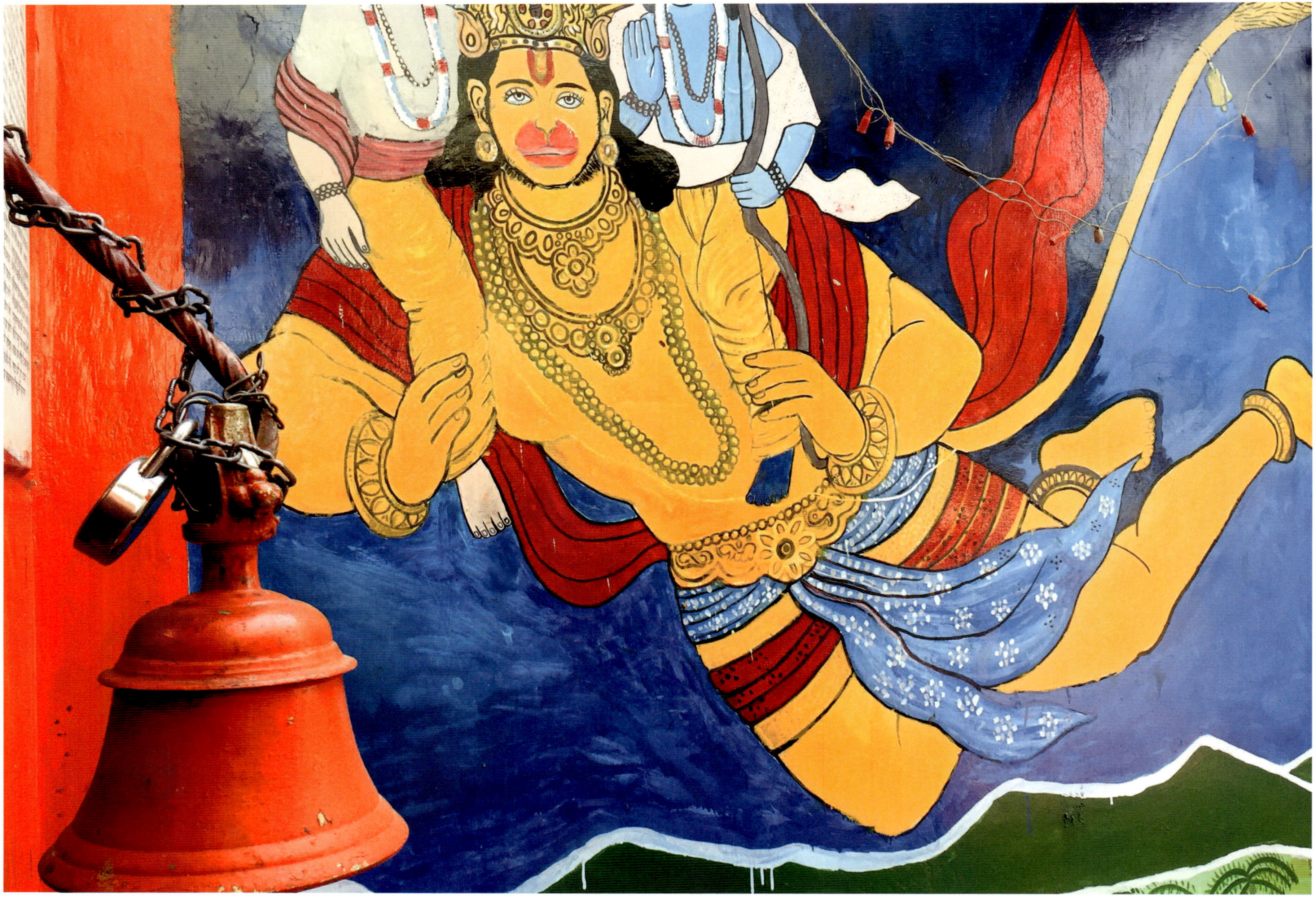

The two opposite faces of Rudra—Bhakti and Shakti. One depicting love and devotion, the other a destroyer of evil.

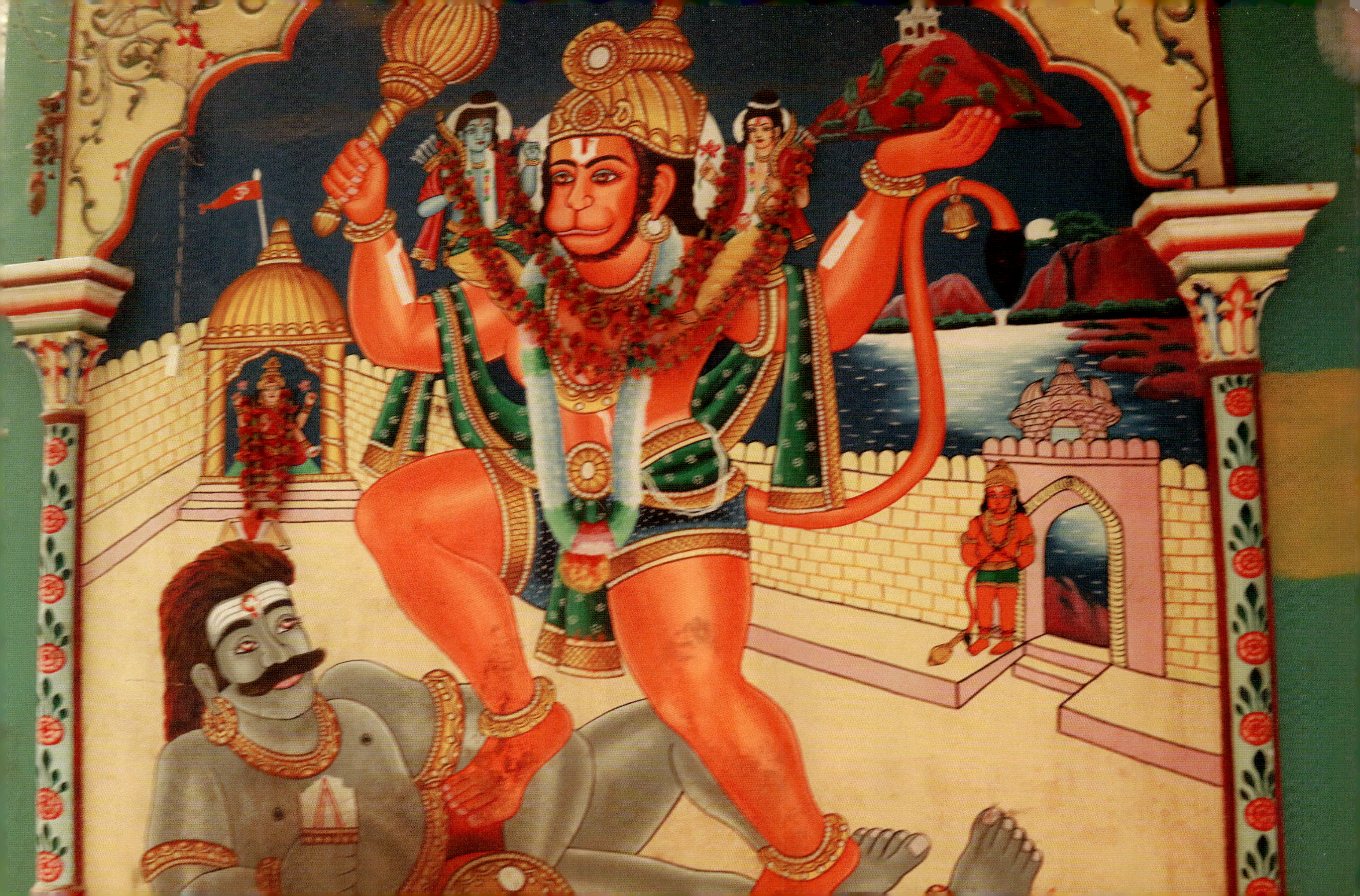

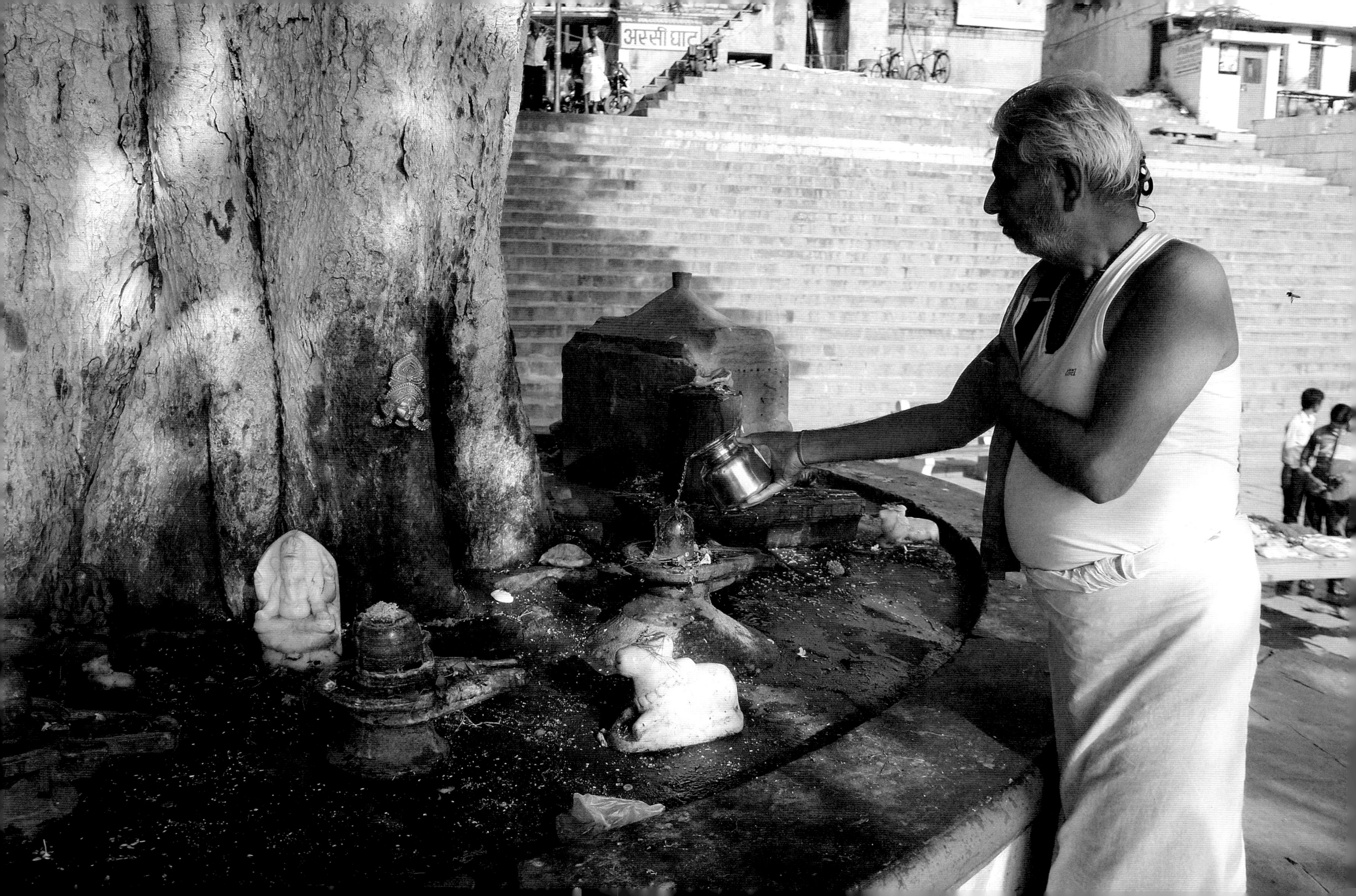
अस्सी घाट

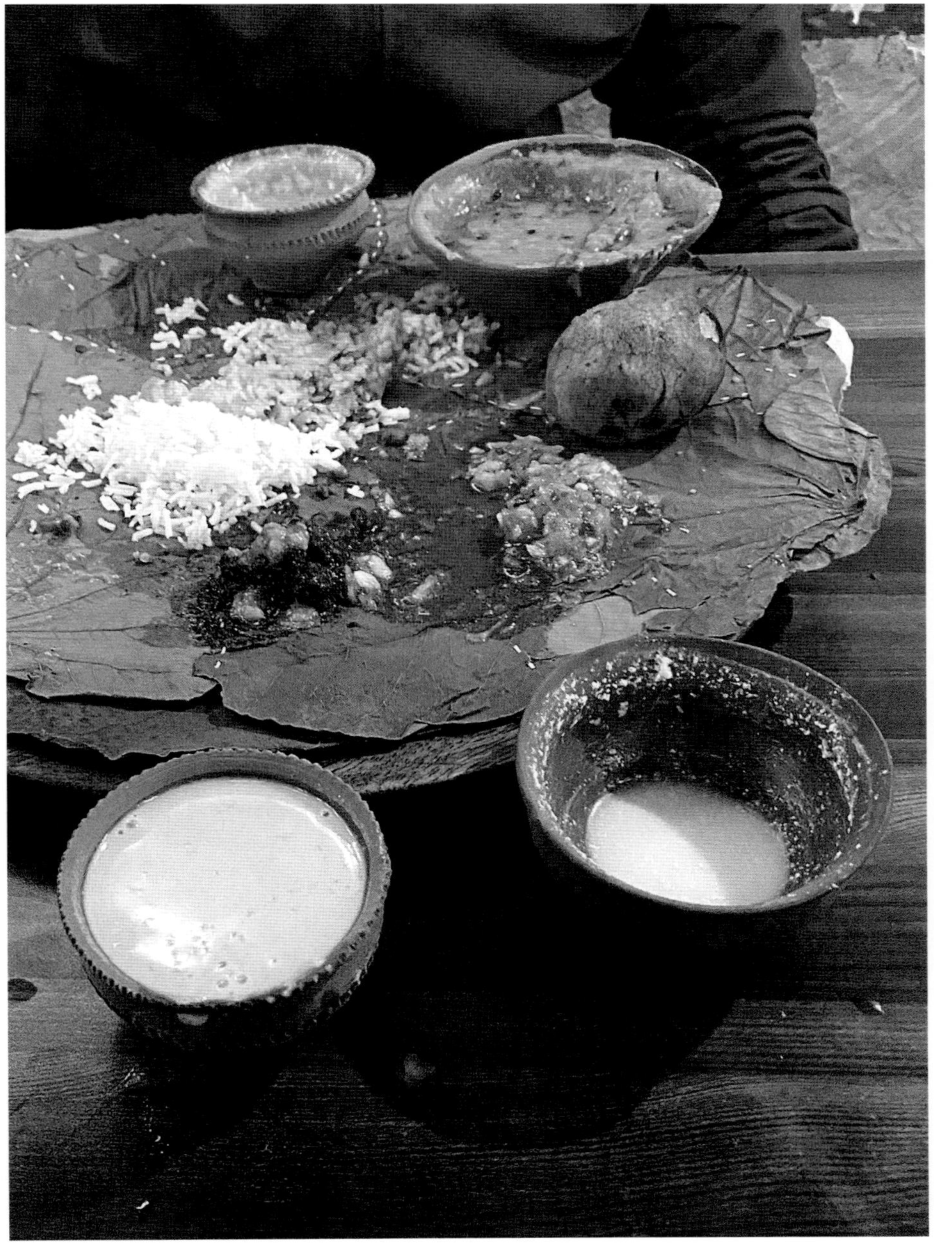

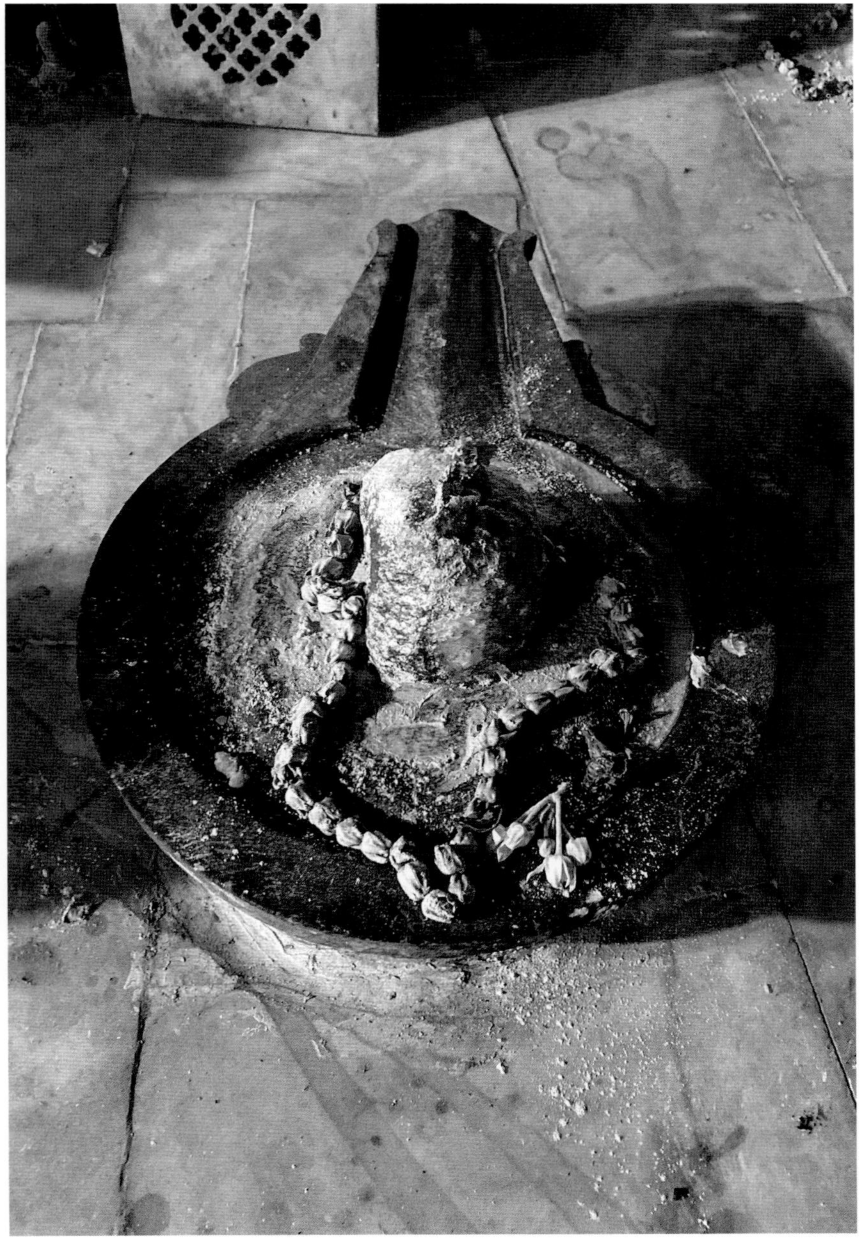

*Kan Kan mein Shankar*: Only faith can lead to the ultimate realization that God exists in the flowers and fruits you offer to Him, in the prasad you receive and even the ashes you rub on your forehead.

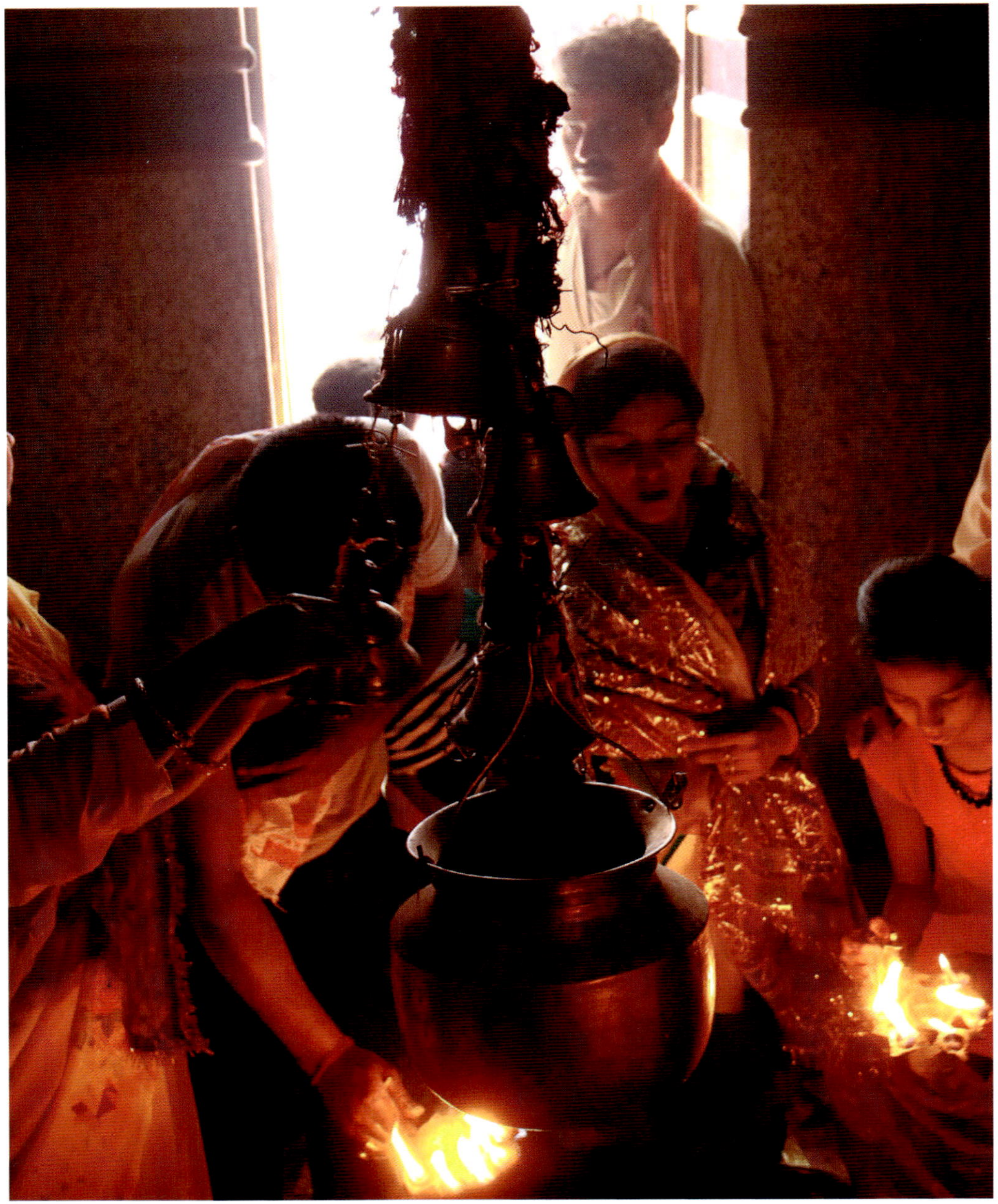

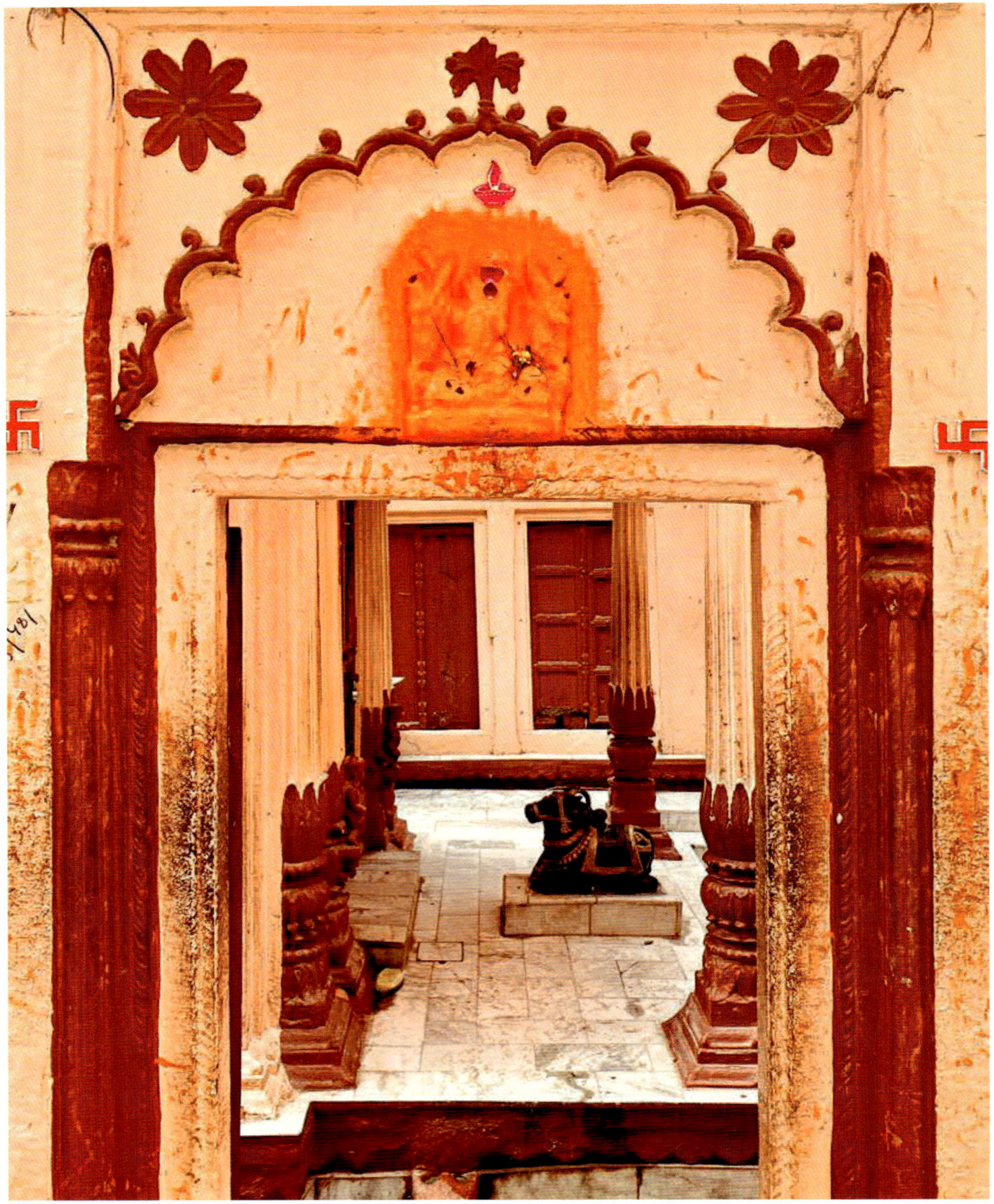

The temple door does not just lead you from one room to another, it is a spiritual threshold where one must leave all baggage, and enter only with faith.

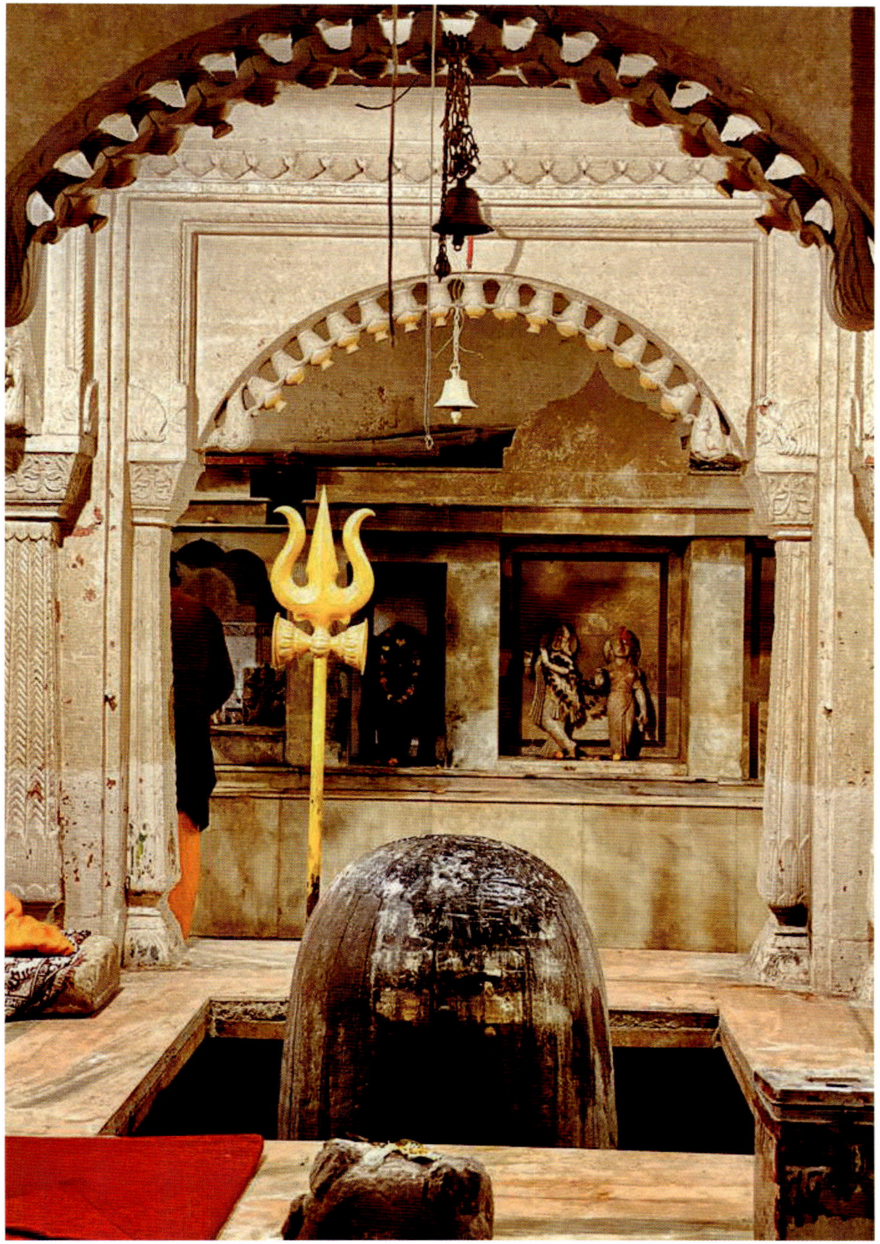

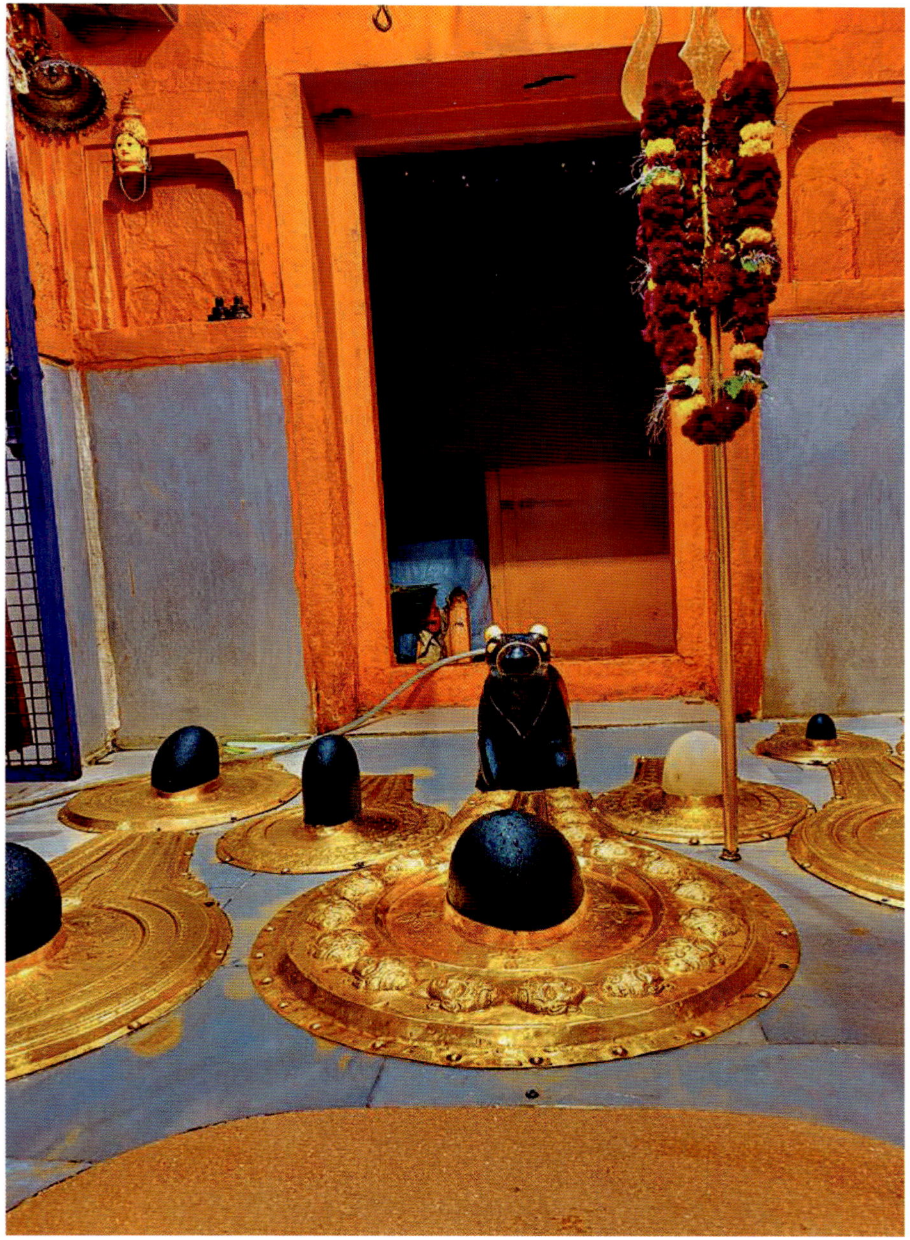

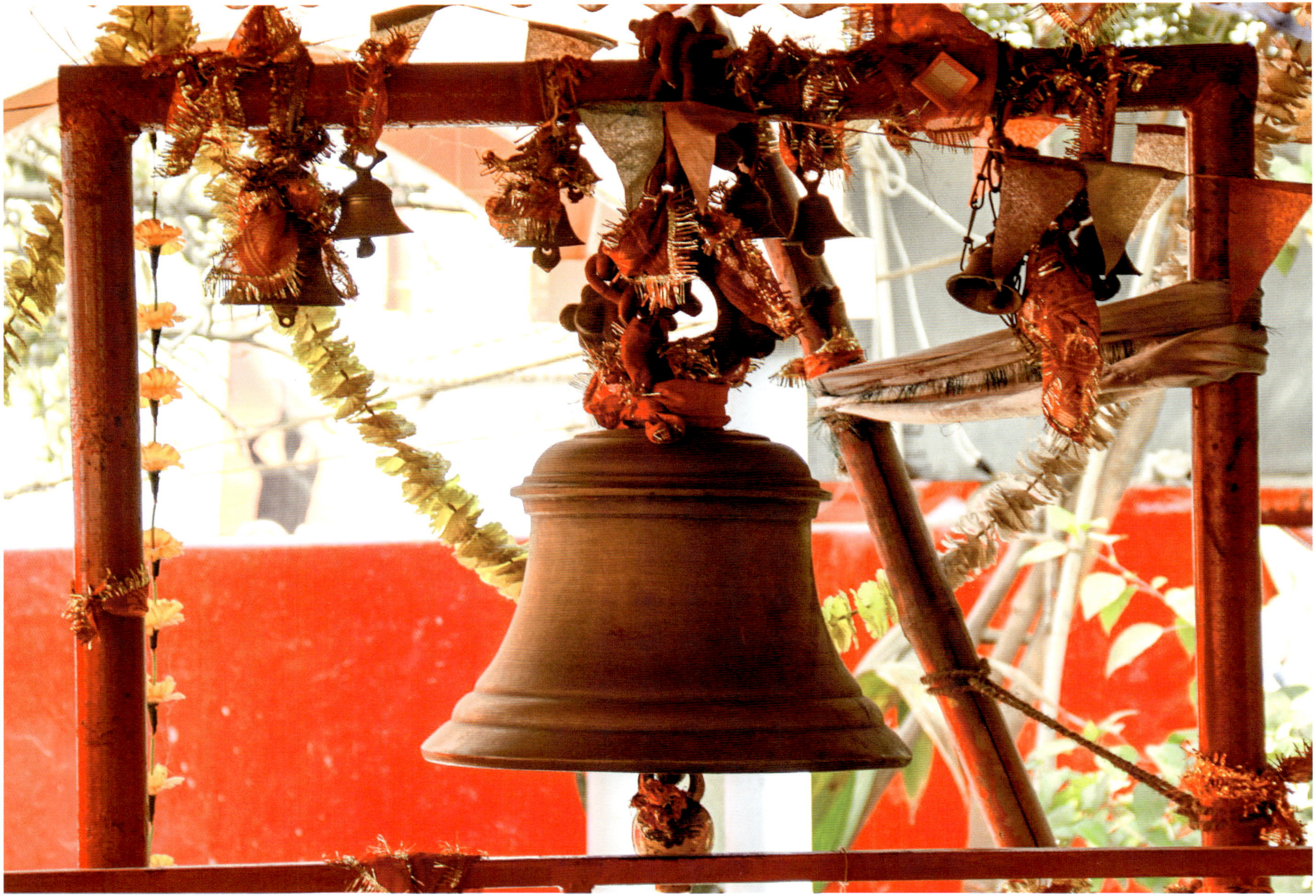

Ananta: Bells are a symbol of infinity that create the sound that marks the beginning and the end, and all that lies in between.

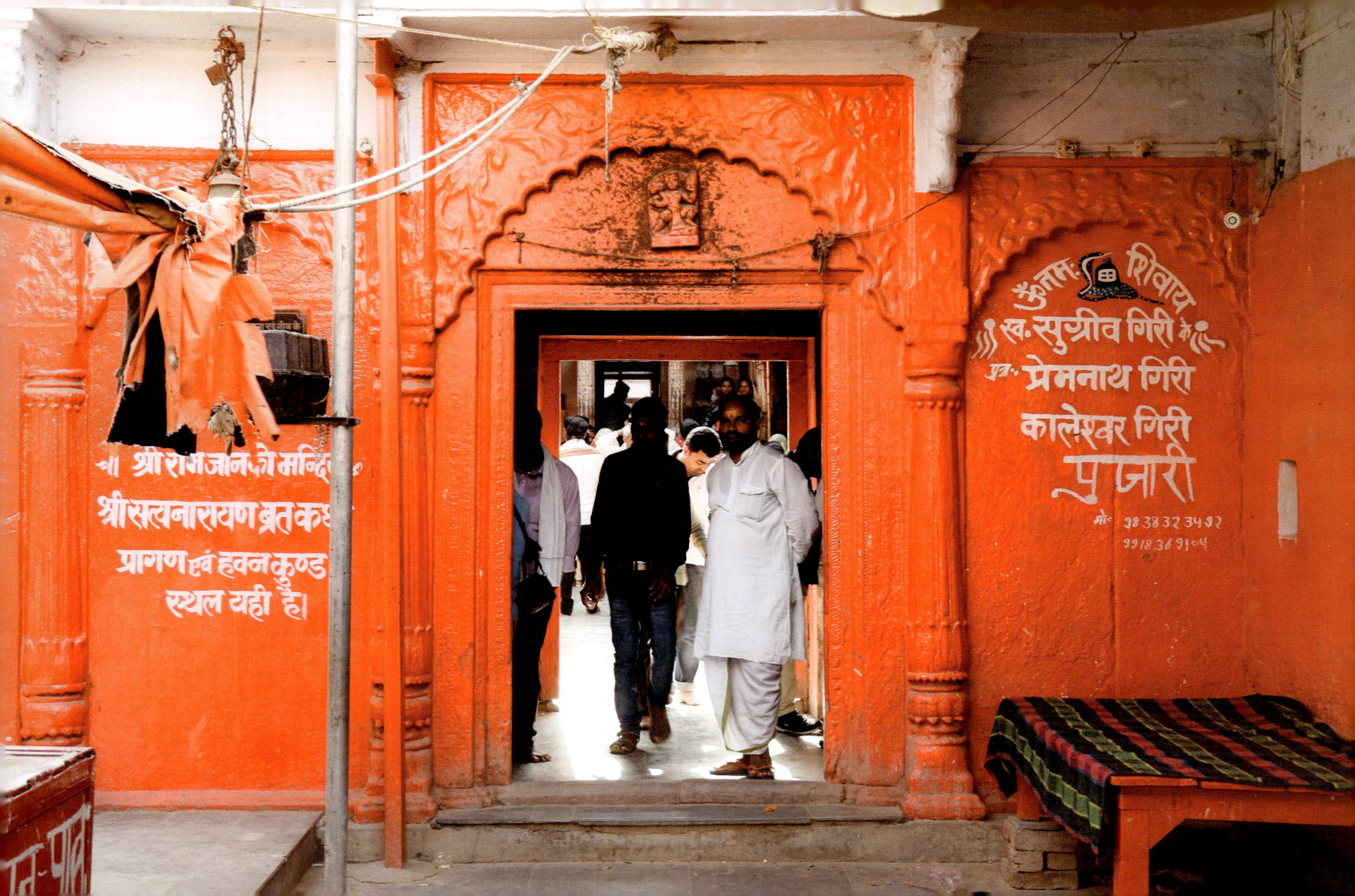
ॐ नमः शिवाय
स्व. सुग्रीव गिरि के
प्र. प्रेमनाथ गिरि
कालेश्वर गिरि
पुजारी
प्रागण एवं हवन कुण्ड
स्थल यही है।

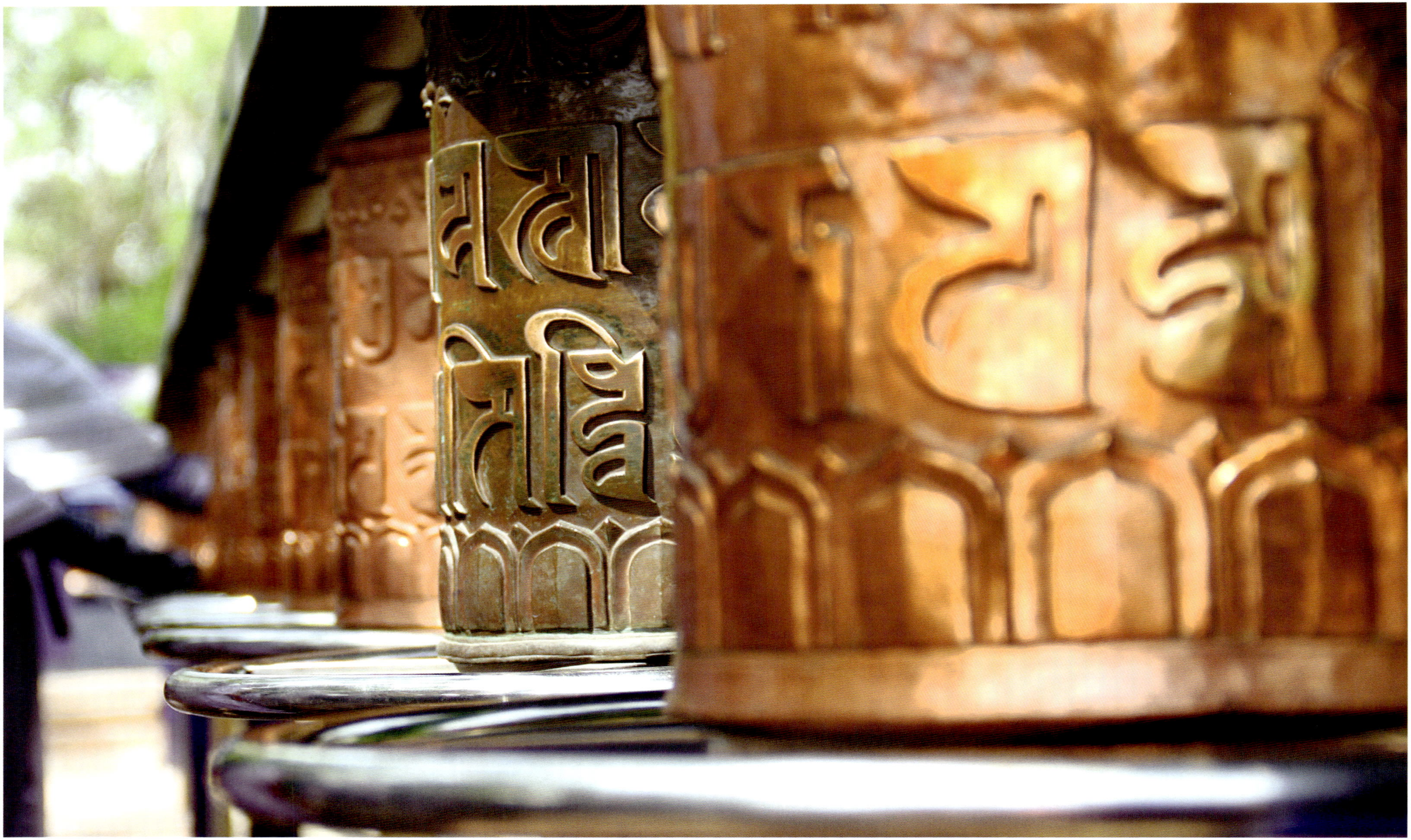

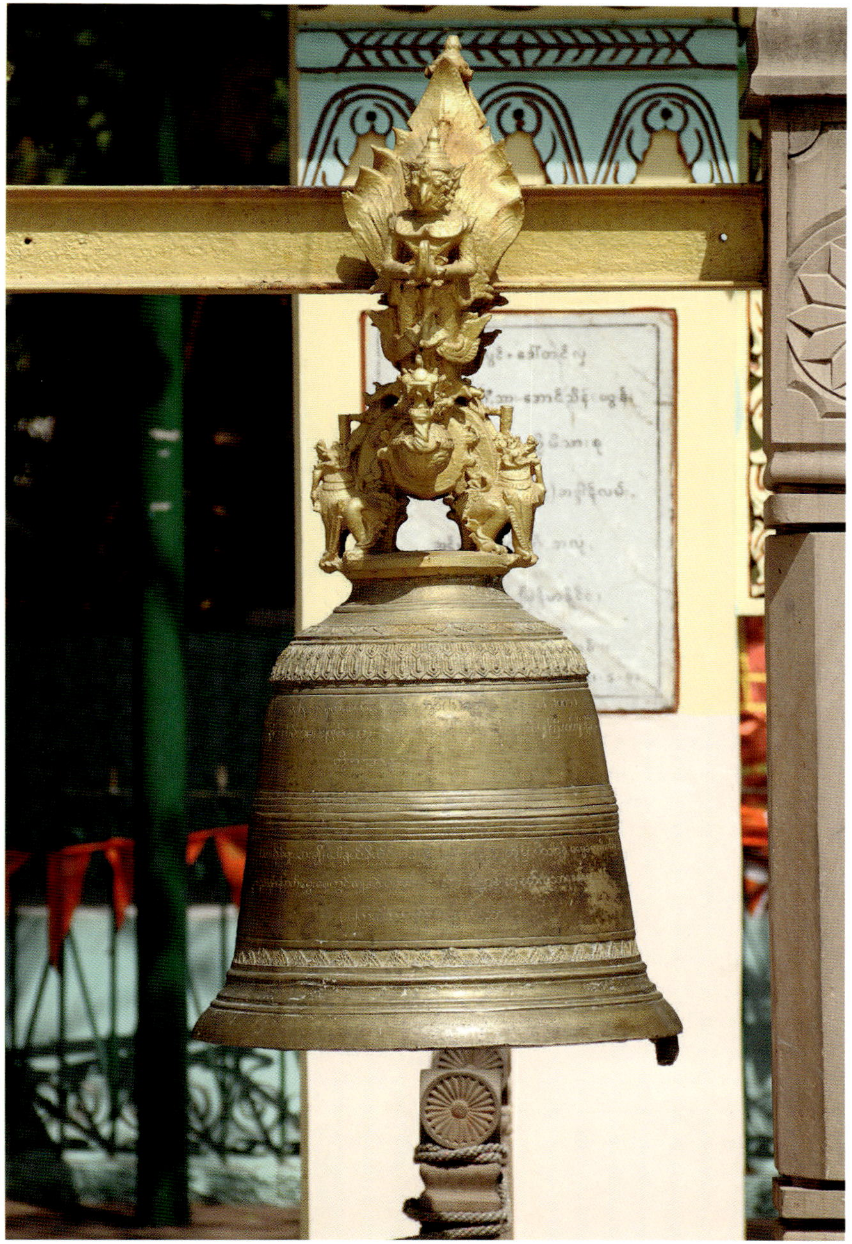

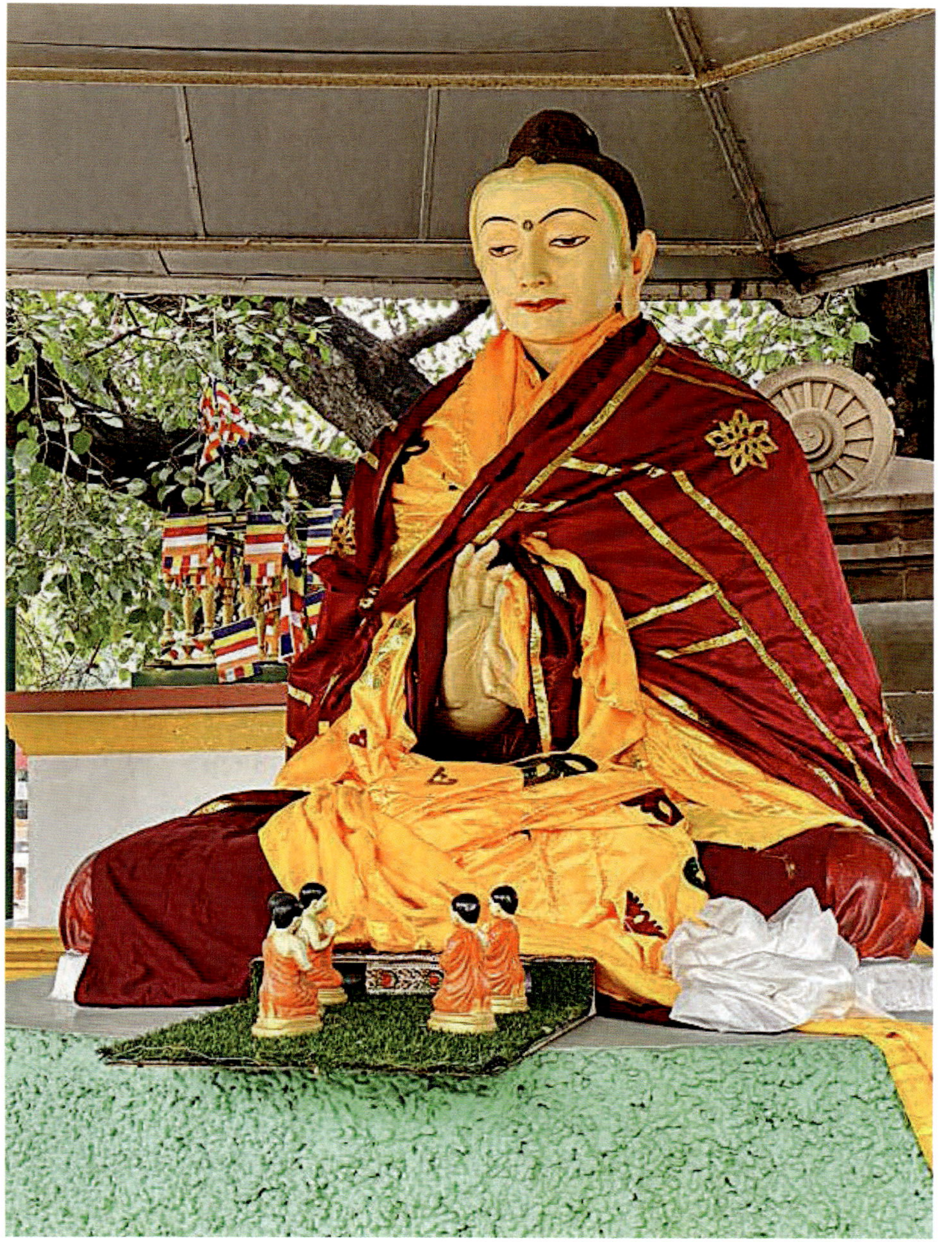

After centuries of Gautam Buddha's first sermon at Sarnath, one can still hear the vibration of his soul in the resounding sound of the sacred gong.

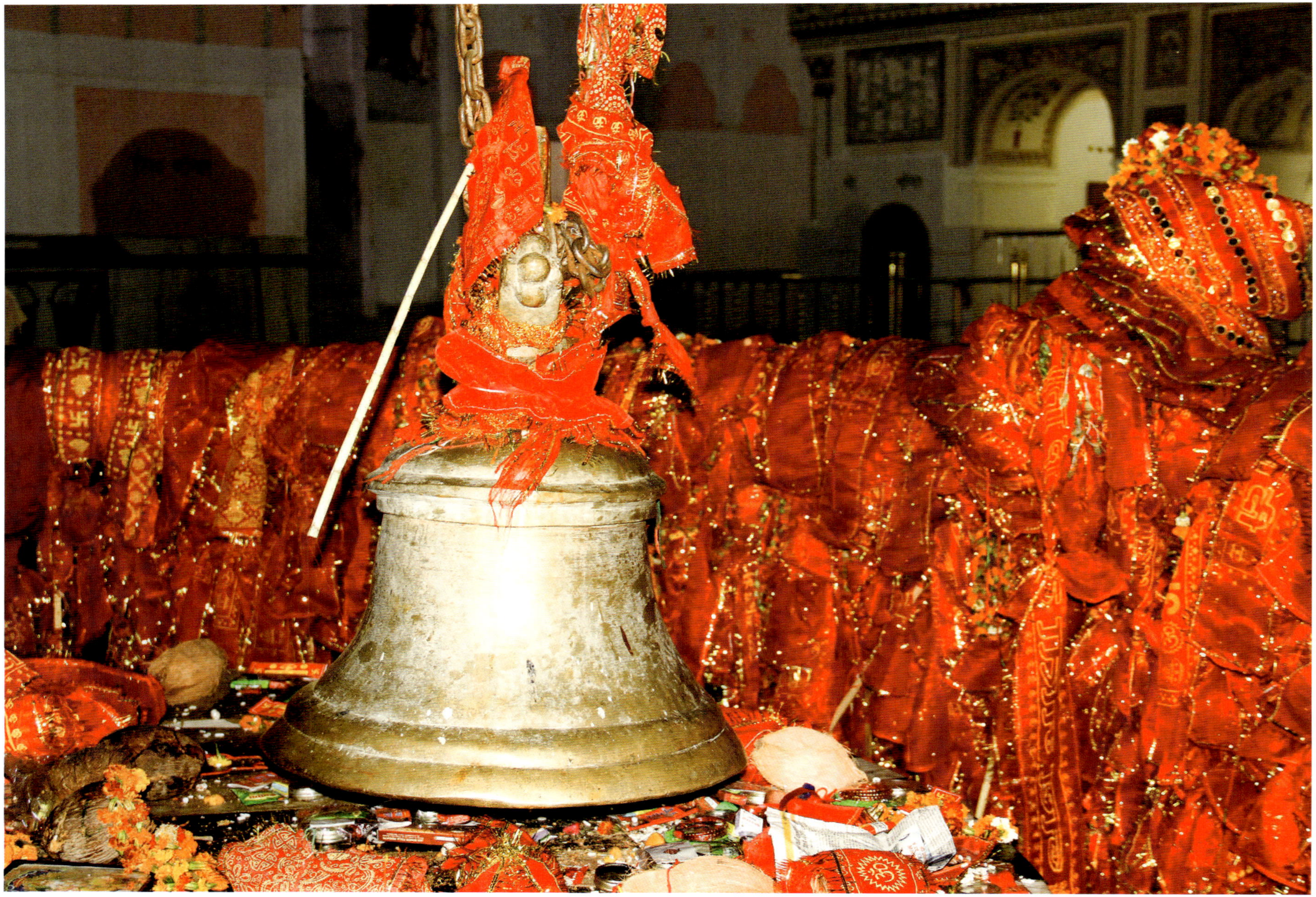

Millions of wishes wrapped faithfully in holy red cloth show the infinite nature of human desire—not all who come seek Moksha, some seek mere fulfillment.

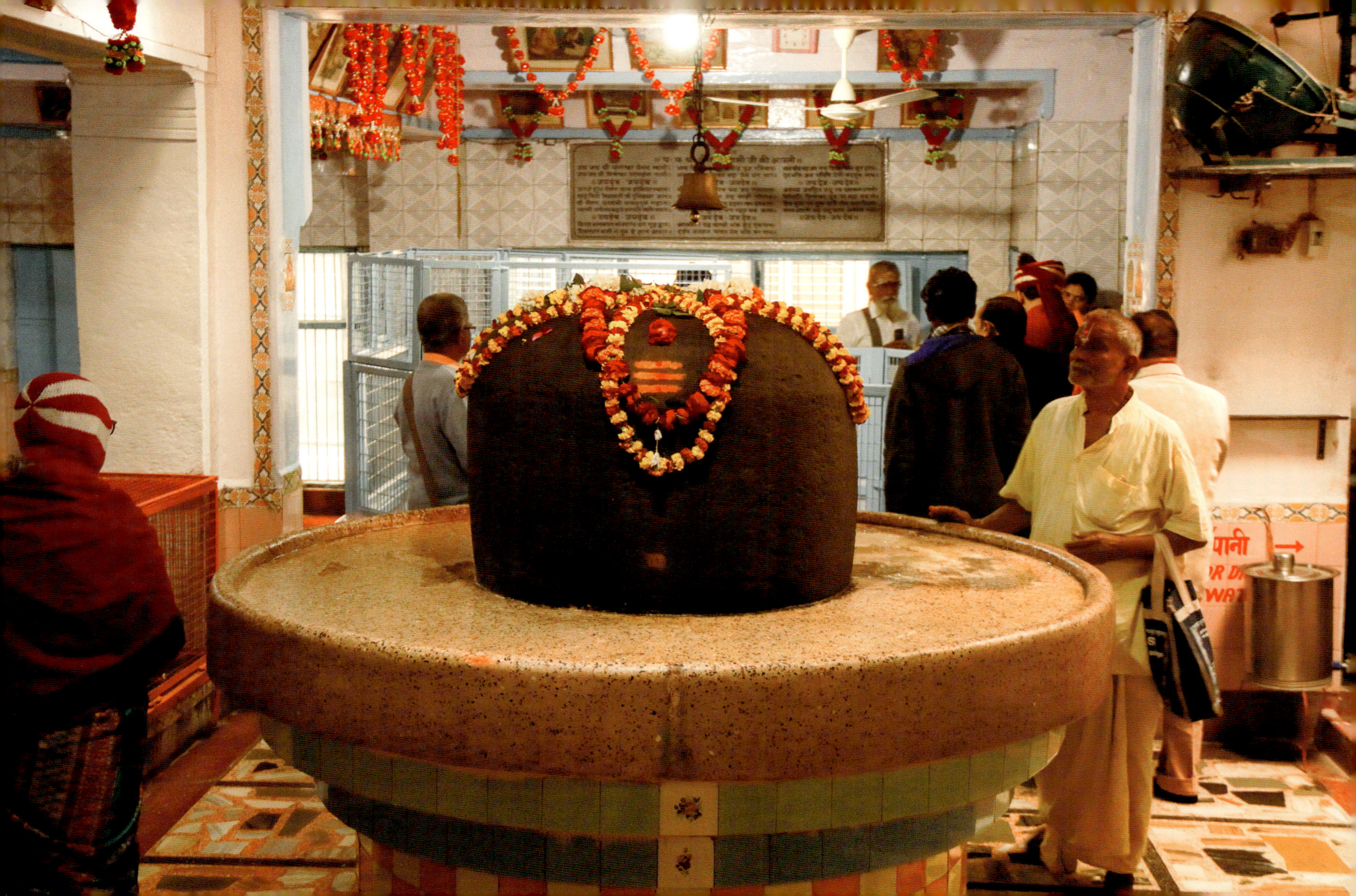
पानी

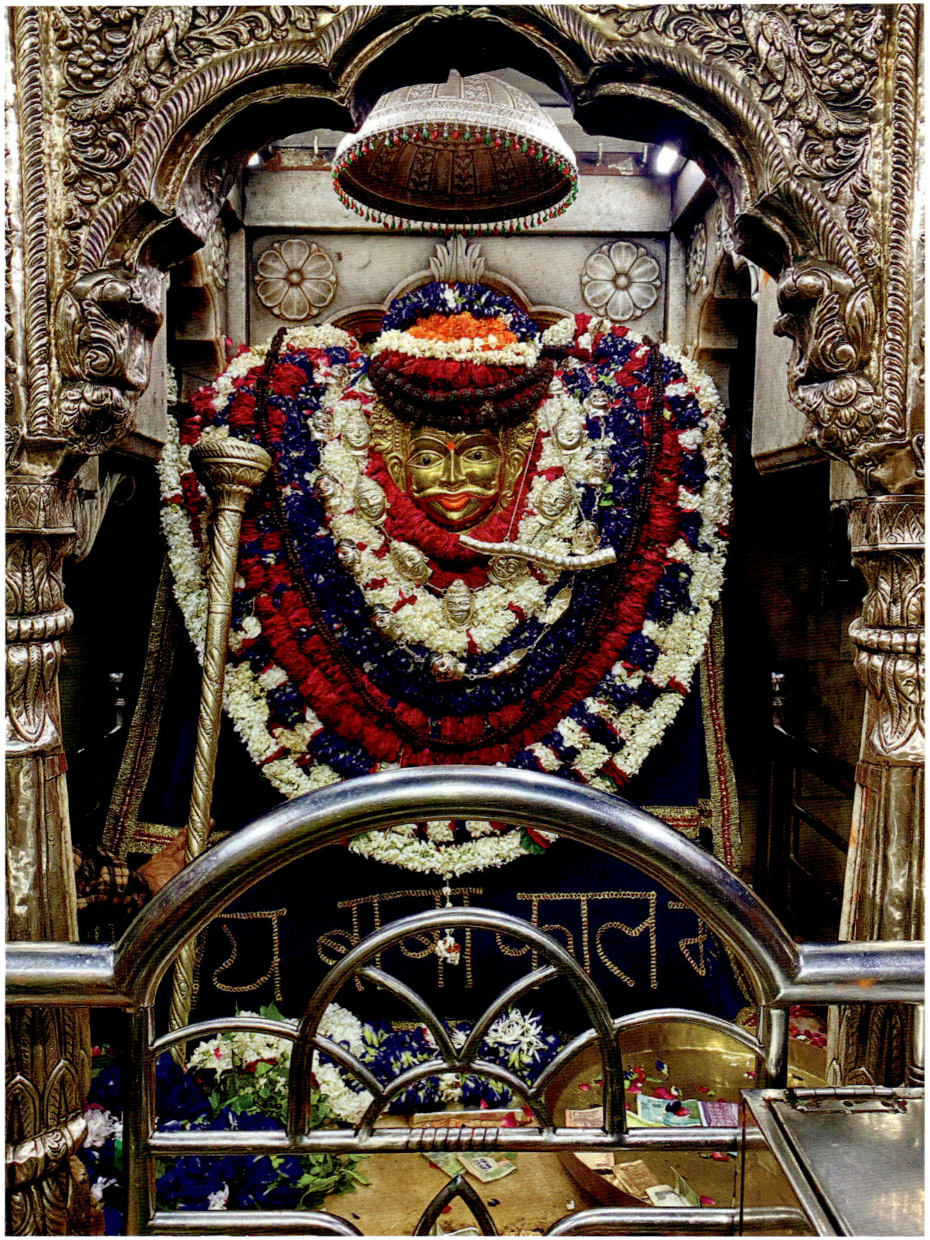

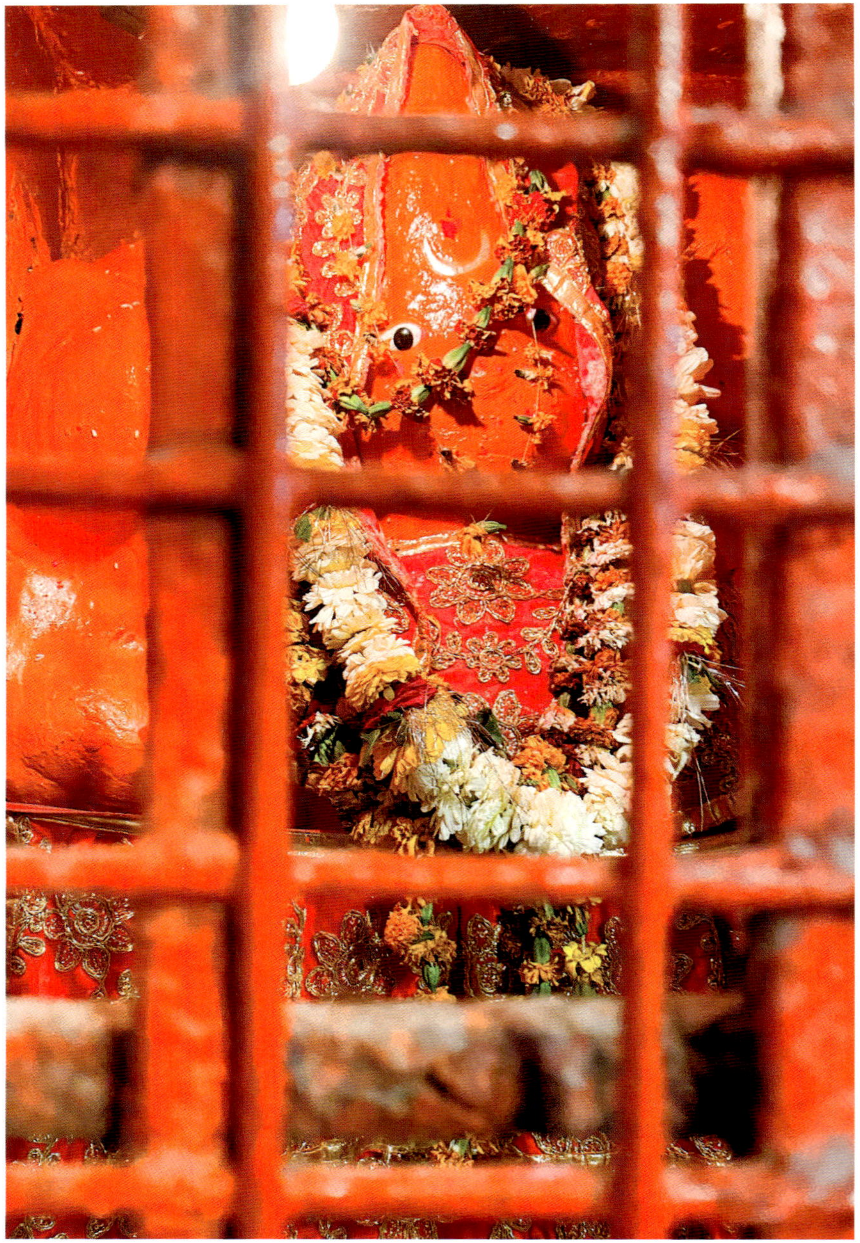

Rudra, Sarva, Pashupati, Ugra, Asani, Bhava, Mahadev and Ishaan are the eight forms of Shiva. His incarnations embody his primary forms as seen in the Dandapani, Pind, the Mangalmurti and the Sankatmochan rupa.

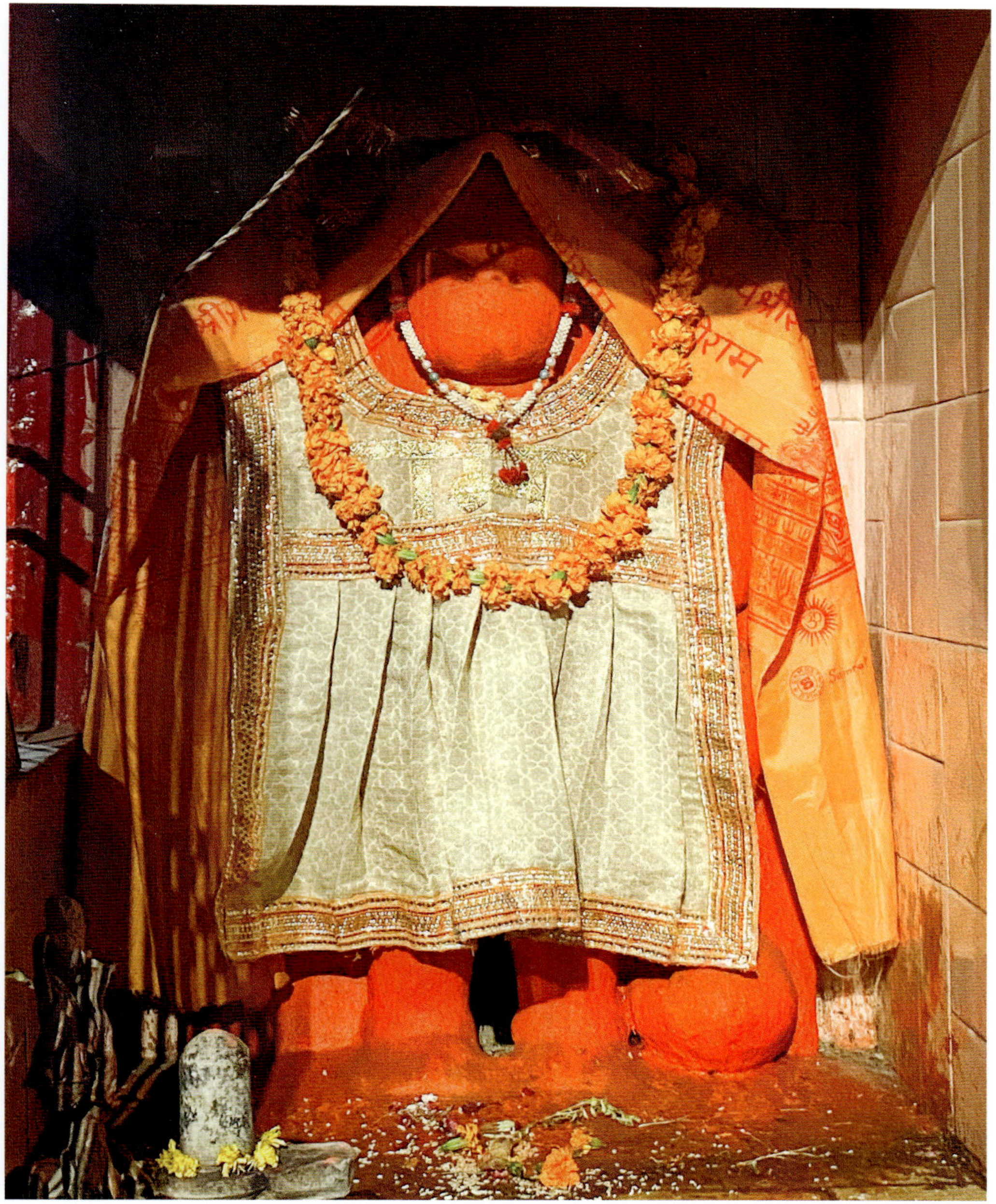

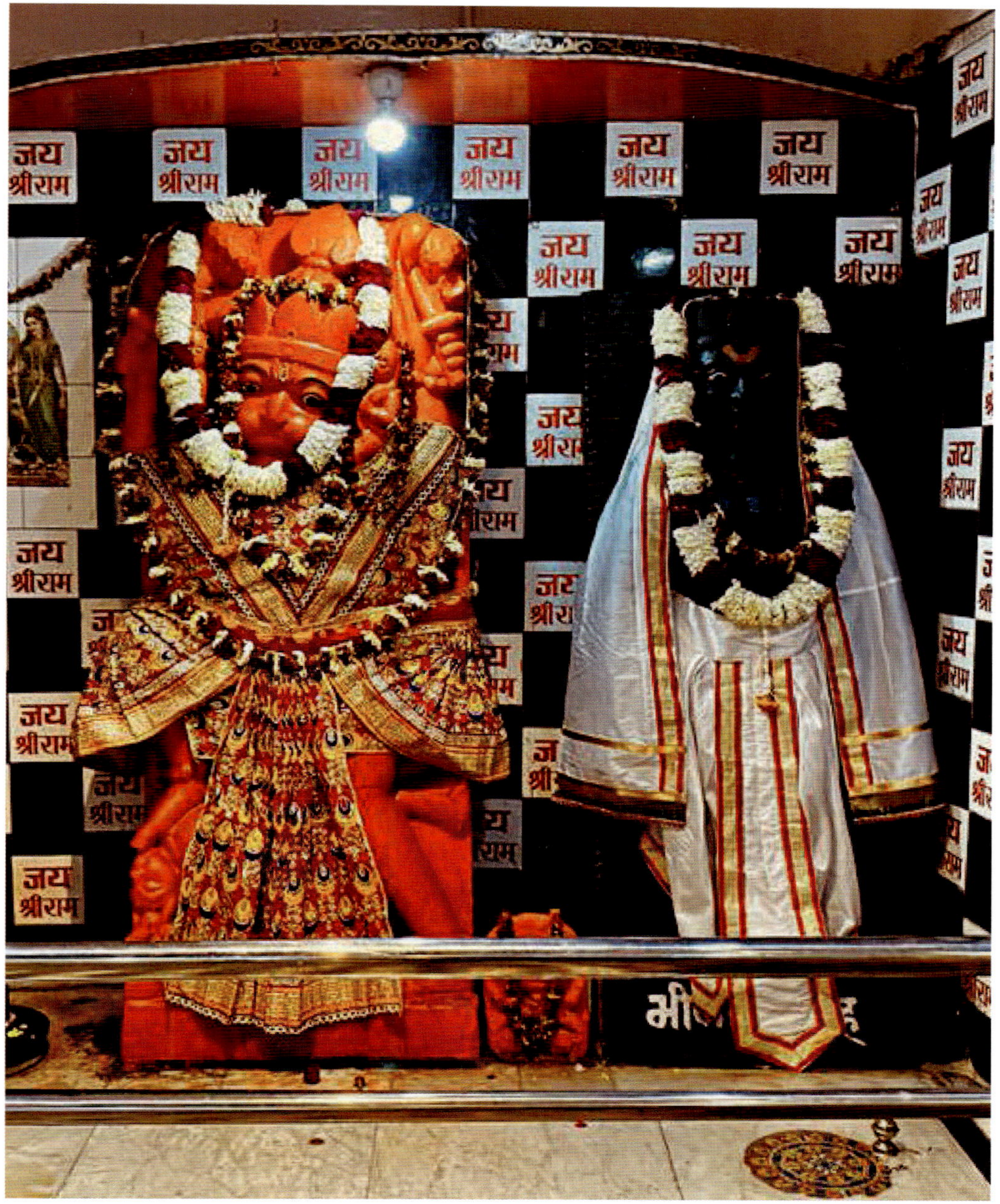
जय श्रीराम
जय श्रीराम
जय श्रीराम
जय श्रीराम
जय श्रीराम
जय श्रीराम
जय श्रीराम
जय श्रीराम
जय श्रीराम
जय श्रीराम
जय श्रीराम

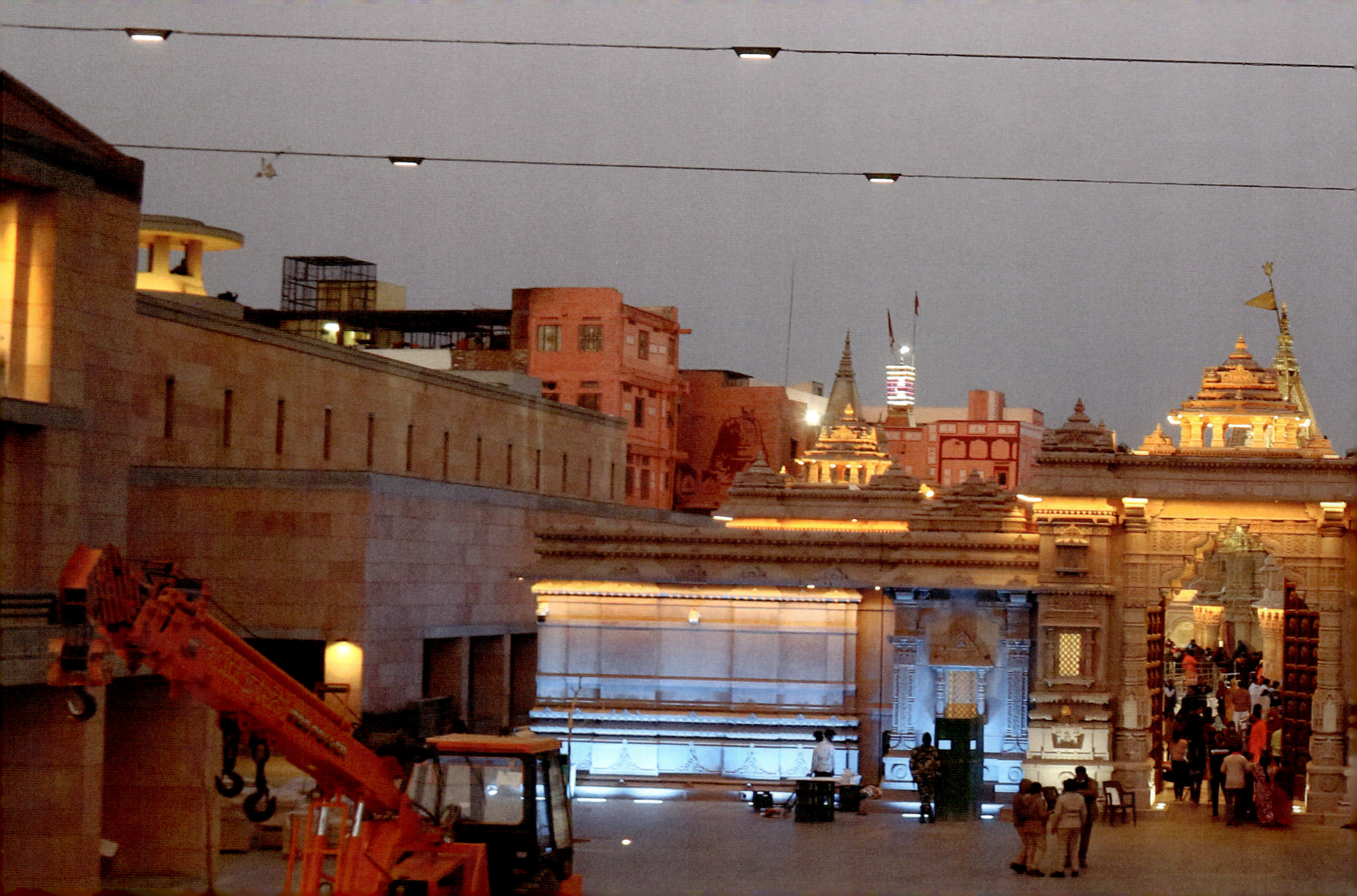

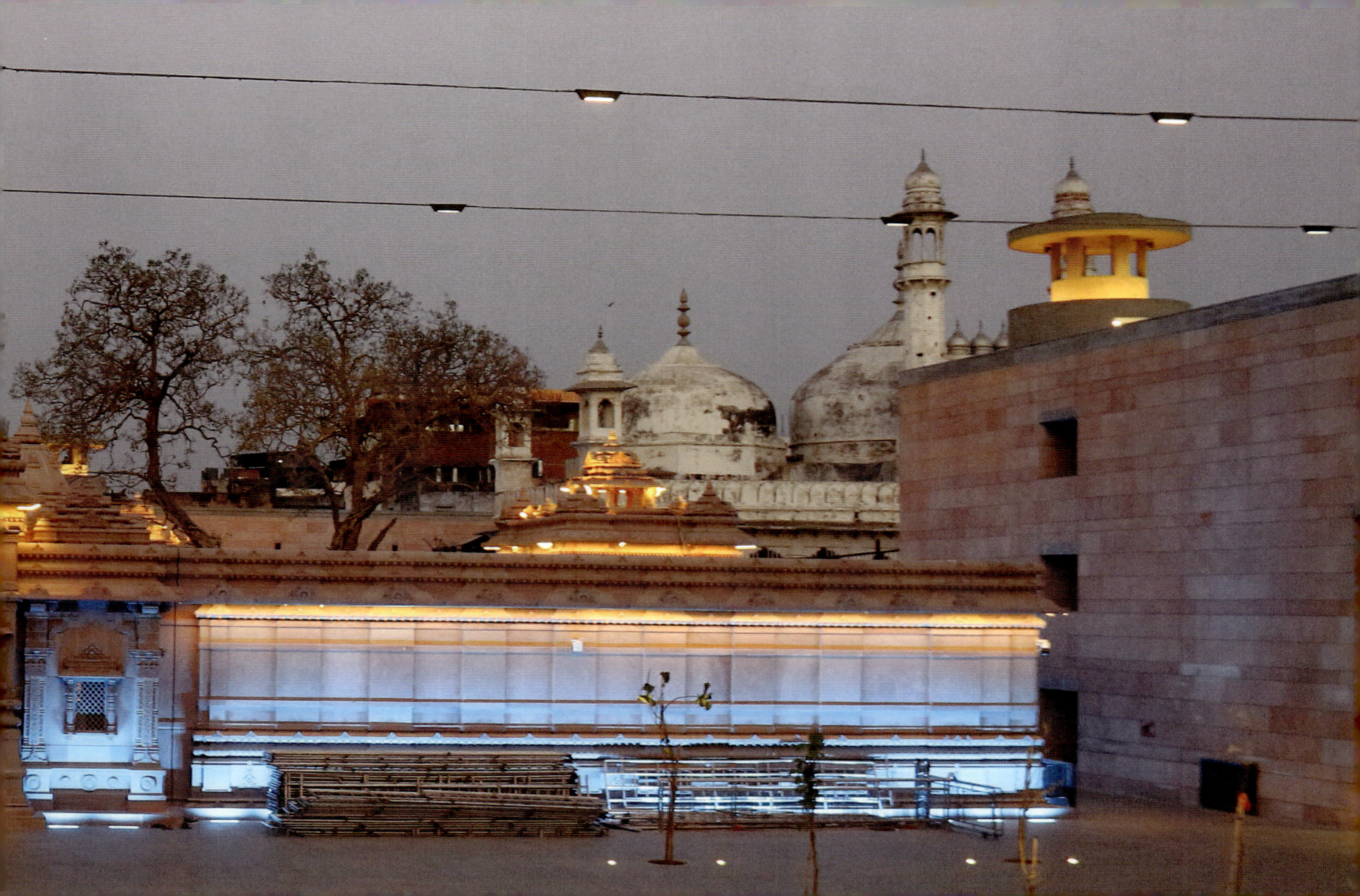

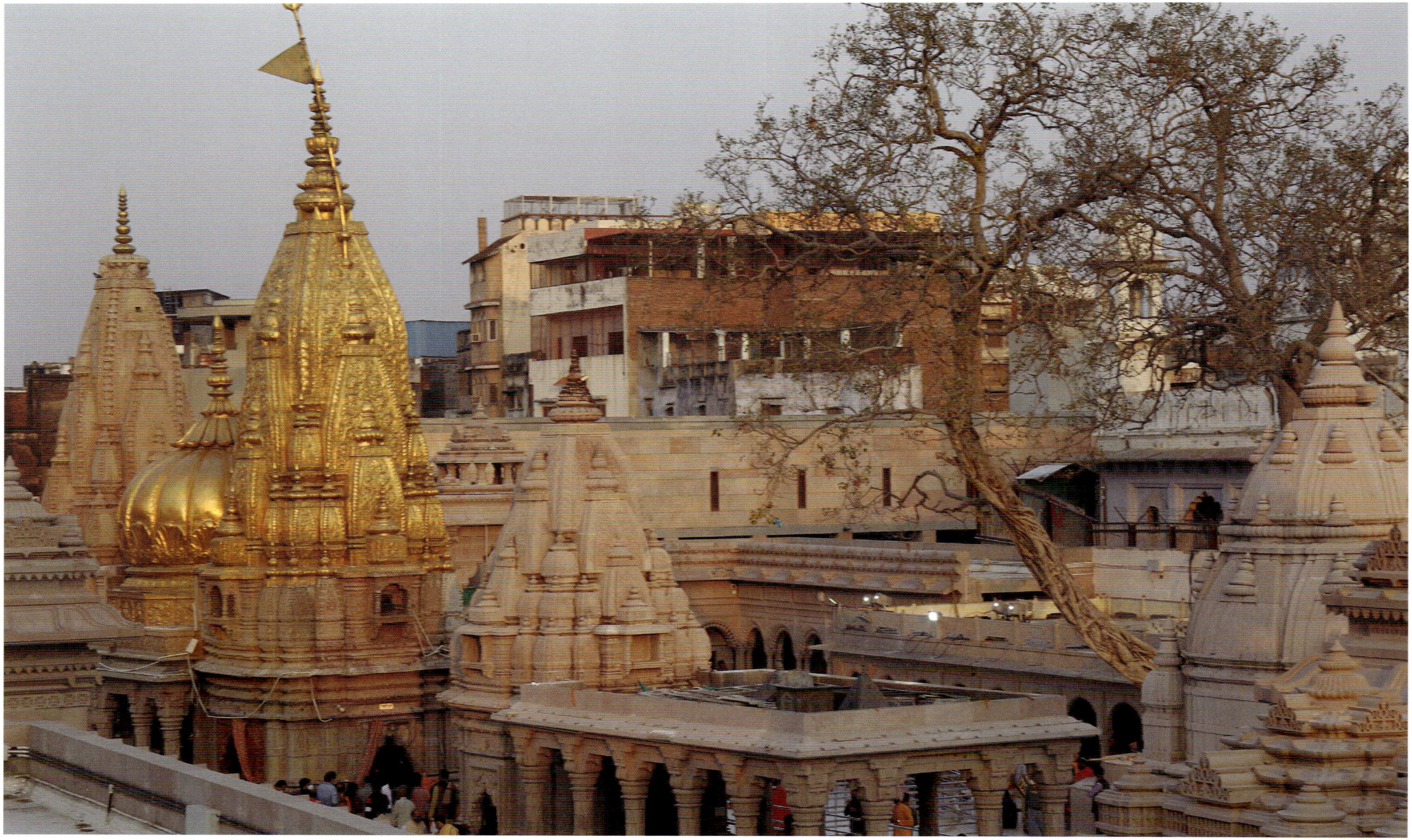

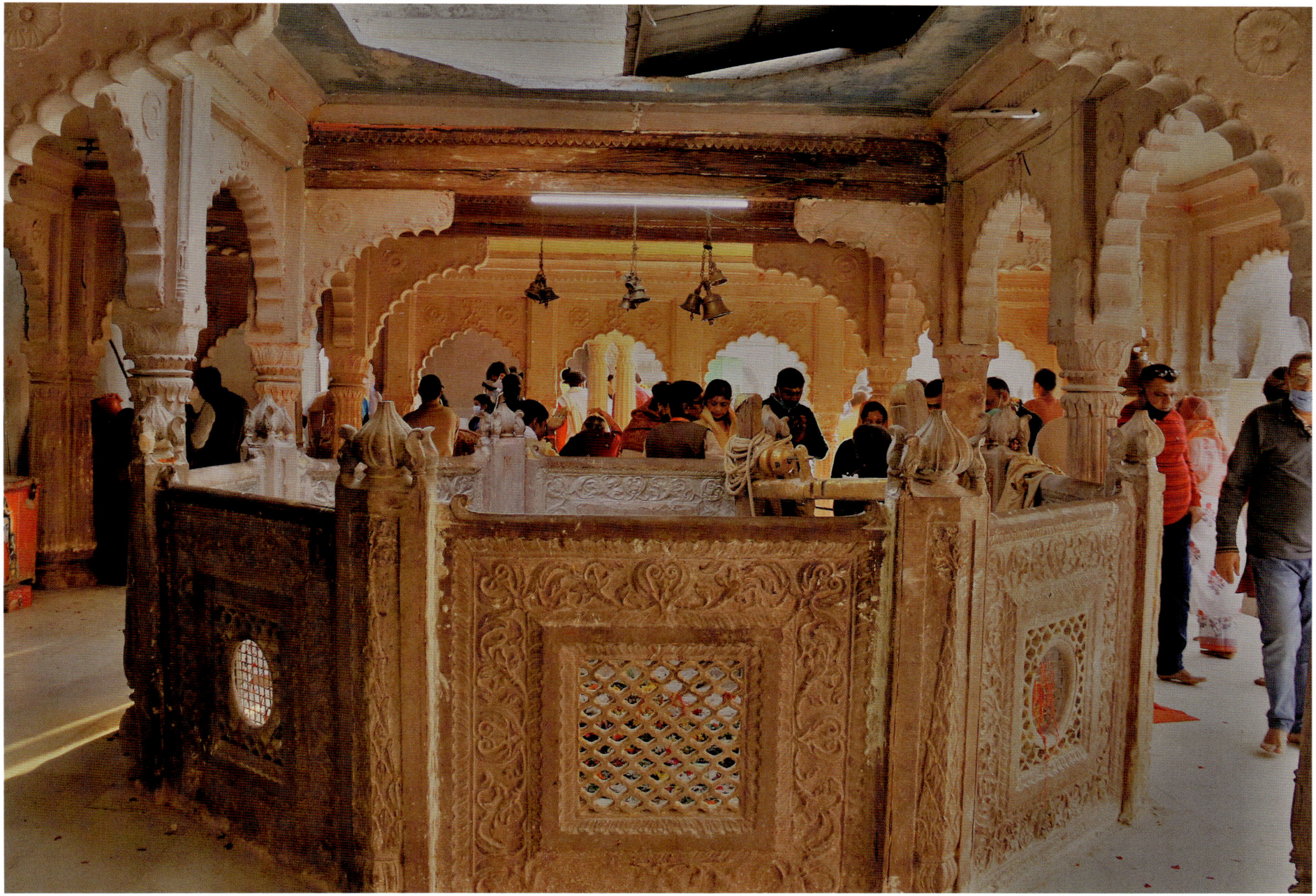

Gyan Vyapi: Located at the entrance of the Vishwanath temple, the 'well of knowledge' with water as sweet as nectar is said to have been the hiding place of the linga which was later resurrected by Maharani Ahilya Bai.

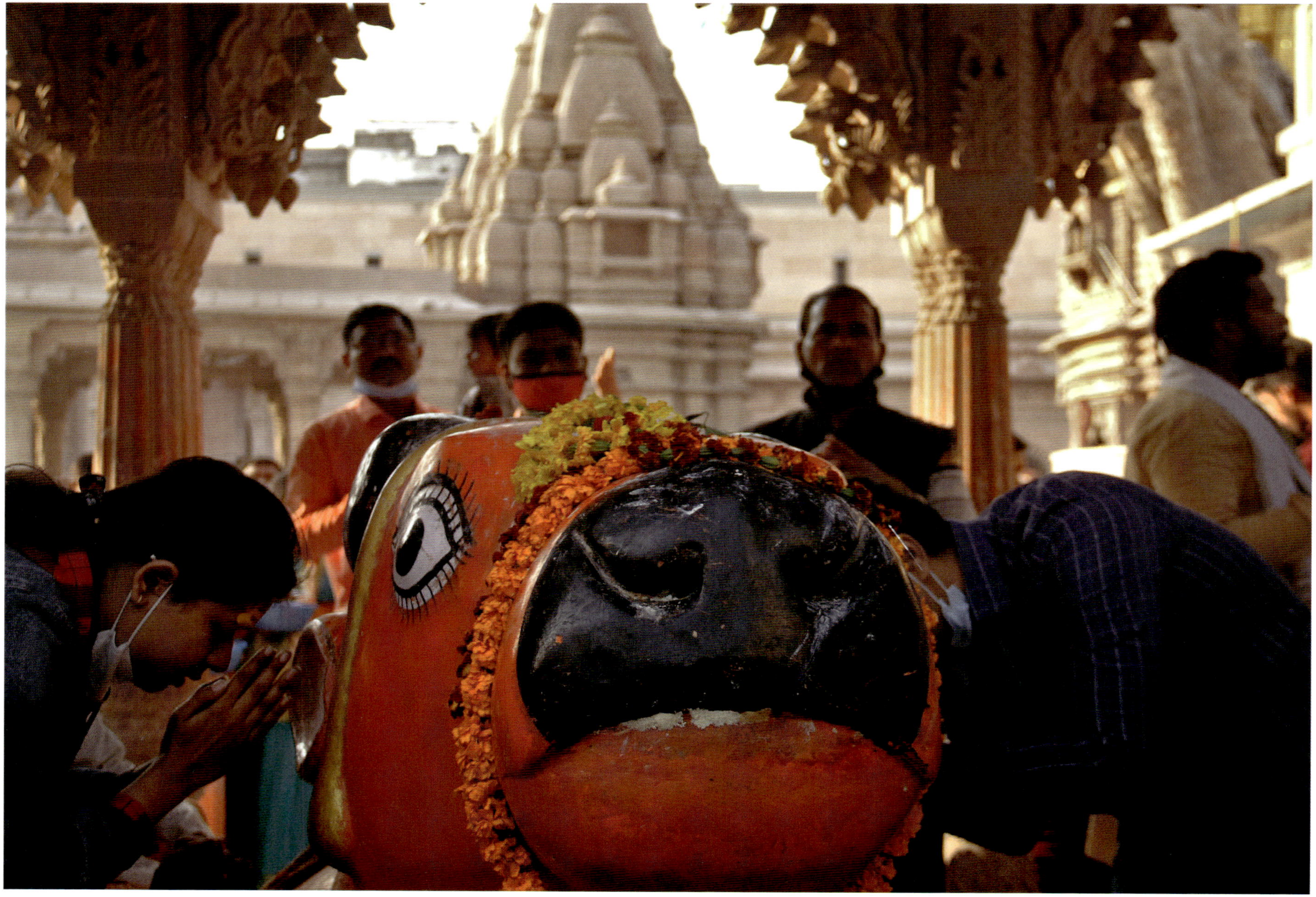

Nandi, the sacred bull, gatekeeper and vehicle of Lord Shiva. Worshippers whisper their wishes into his ear as they prepare to enter the sanctum sanctorum, hoping that if their intent is pure, he will convey their message to Mahadev.

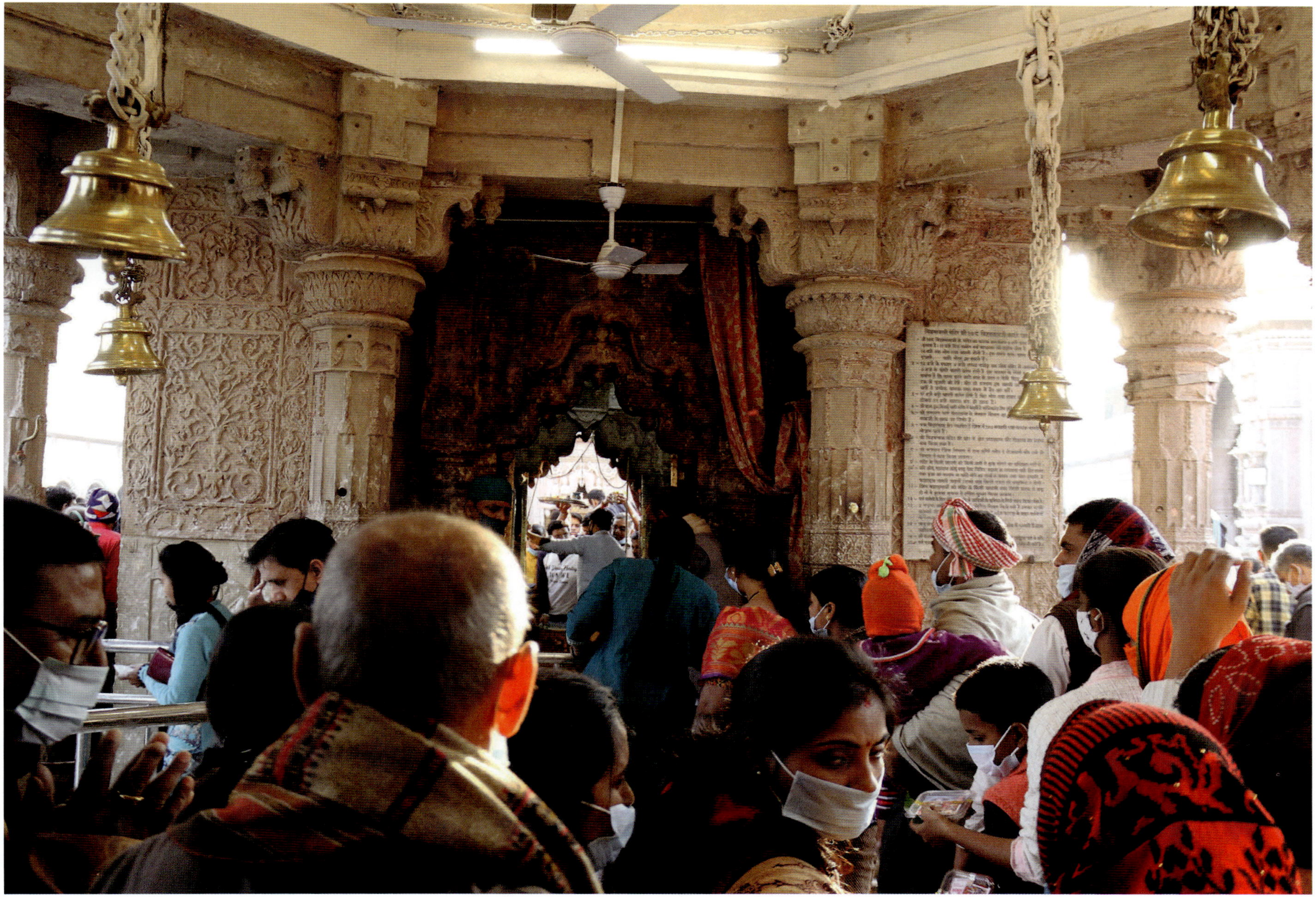

Mandapa: The peripheral space leading to the centre of the universe. Bhakts assemble here waiting to catch just a glimpse of the divine. The air smells of curiosity, anxiety, expectations, anticipation, respite and devotion.

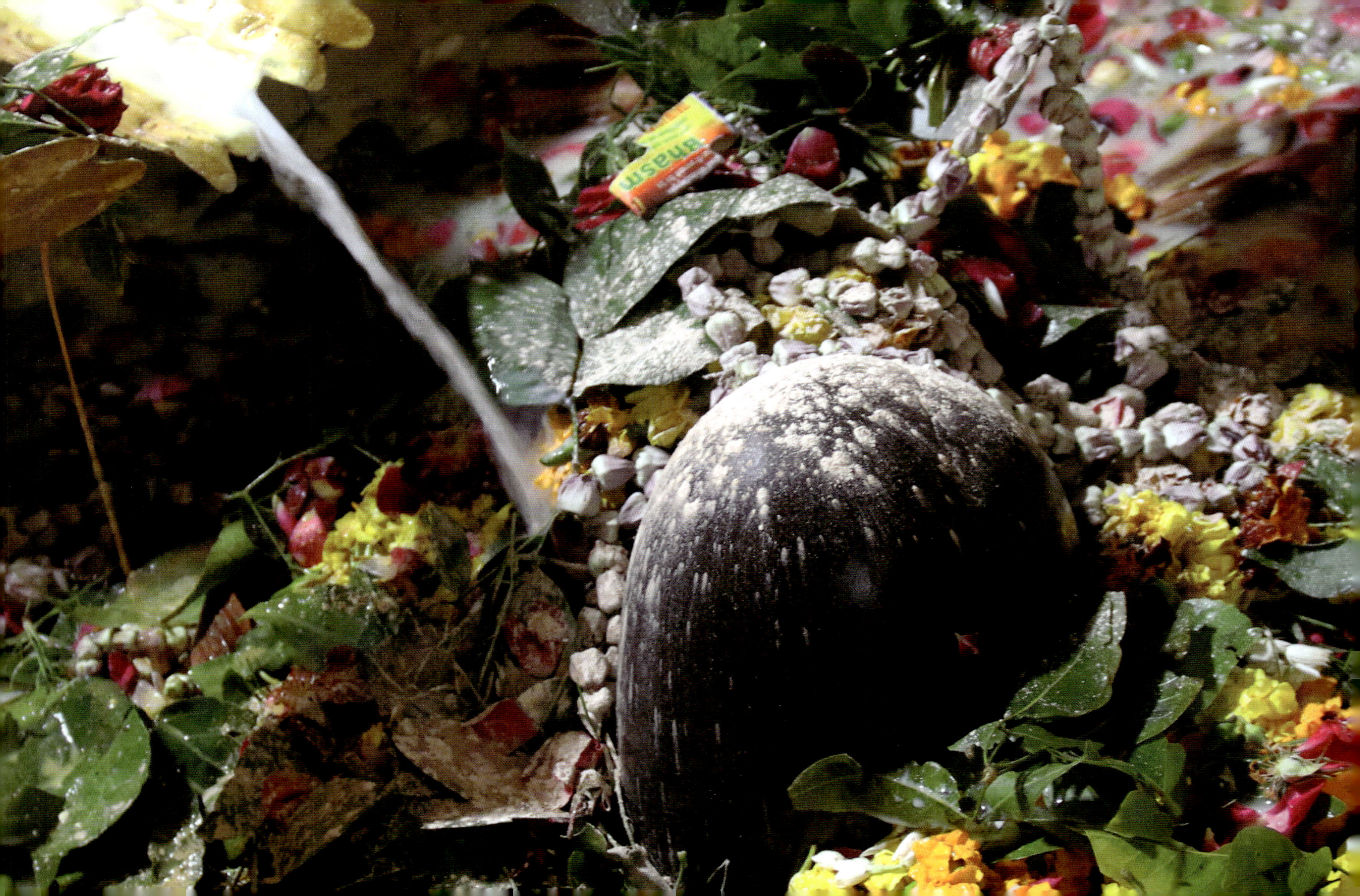
bhasm

Garbha Griha: The linga, a symbol of the divine generative energy, sits on the yoni, while the Trishul pulsates with such energy that it rearranges one's physical, astral and causal body in alignment.

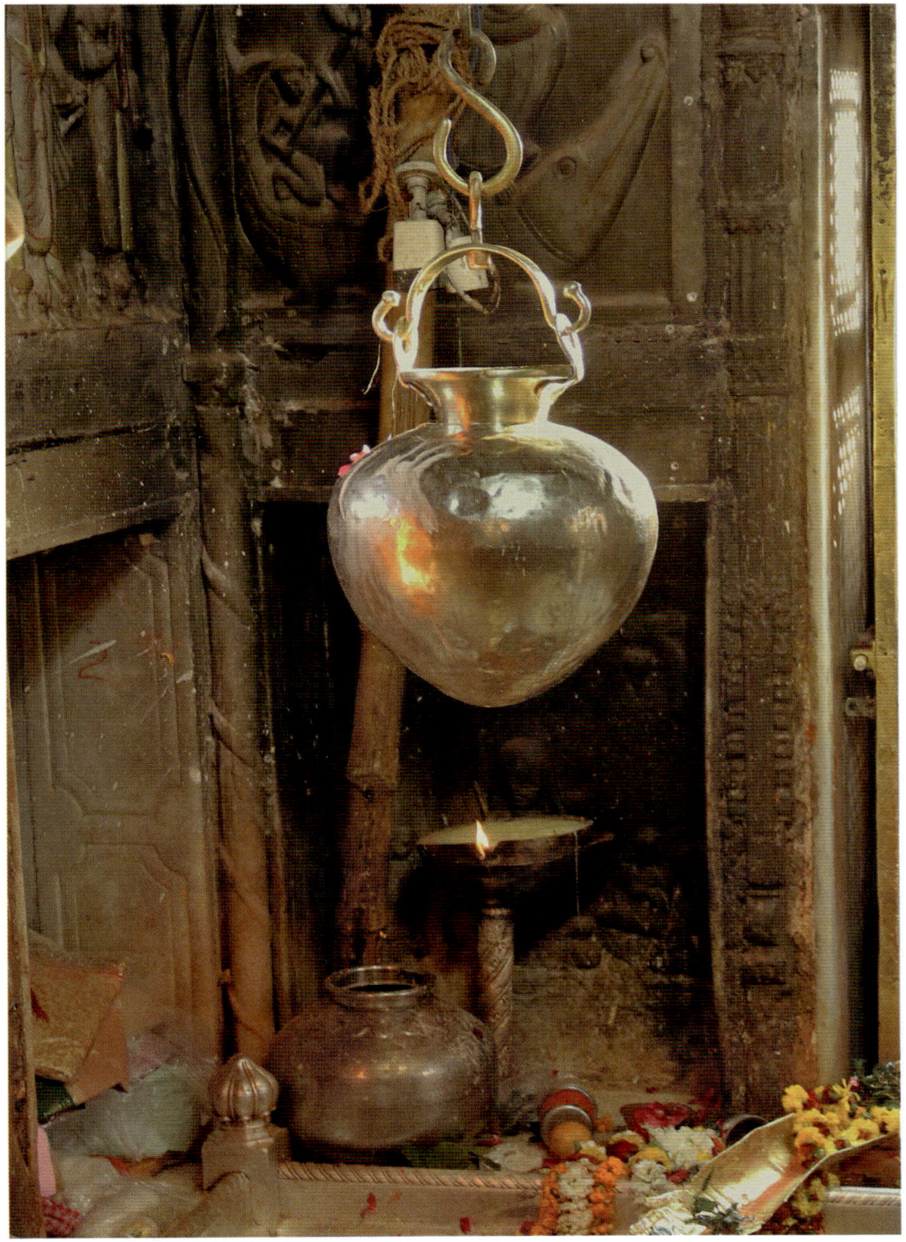

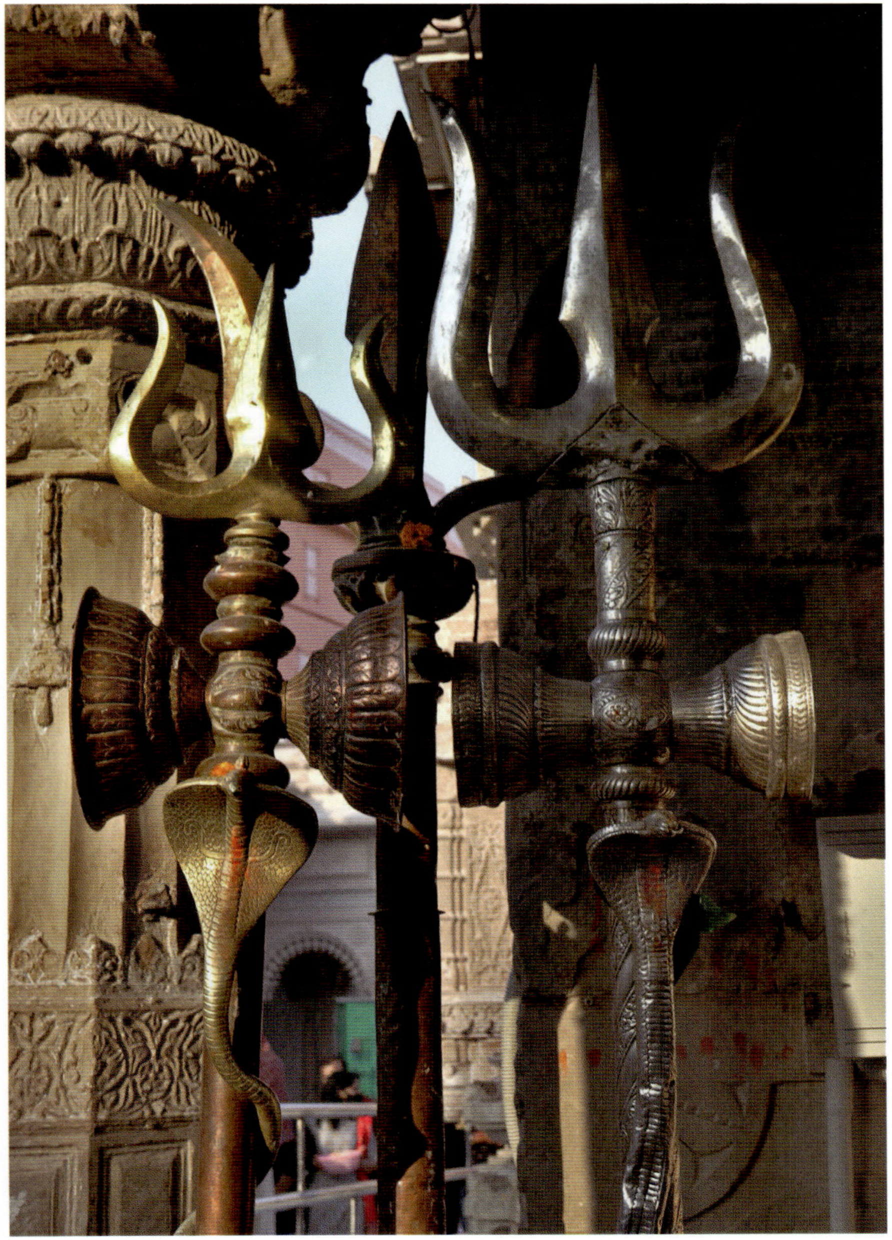

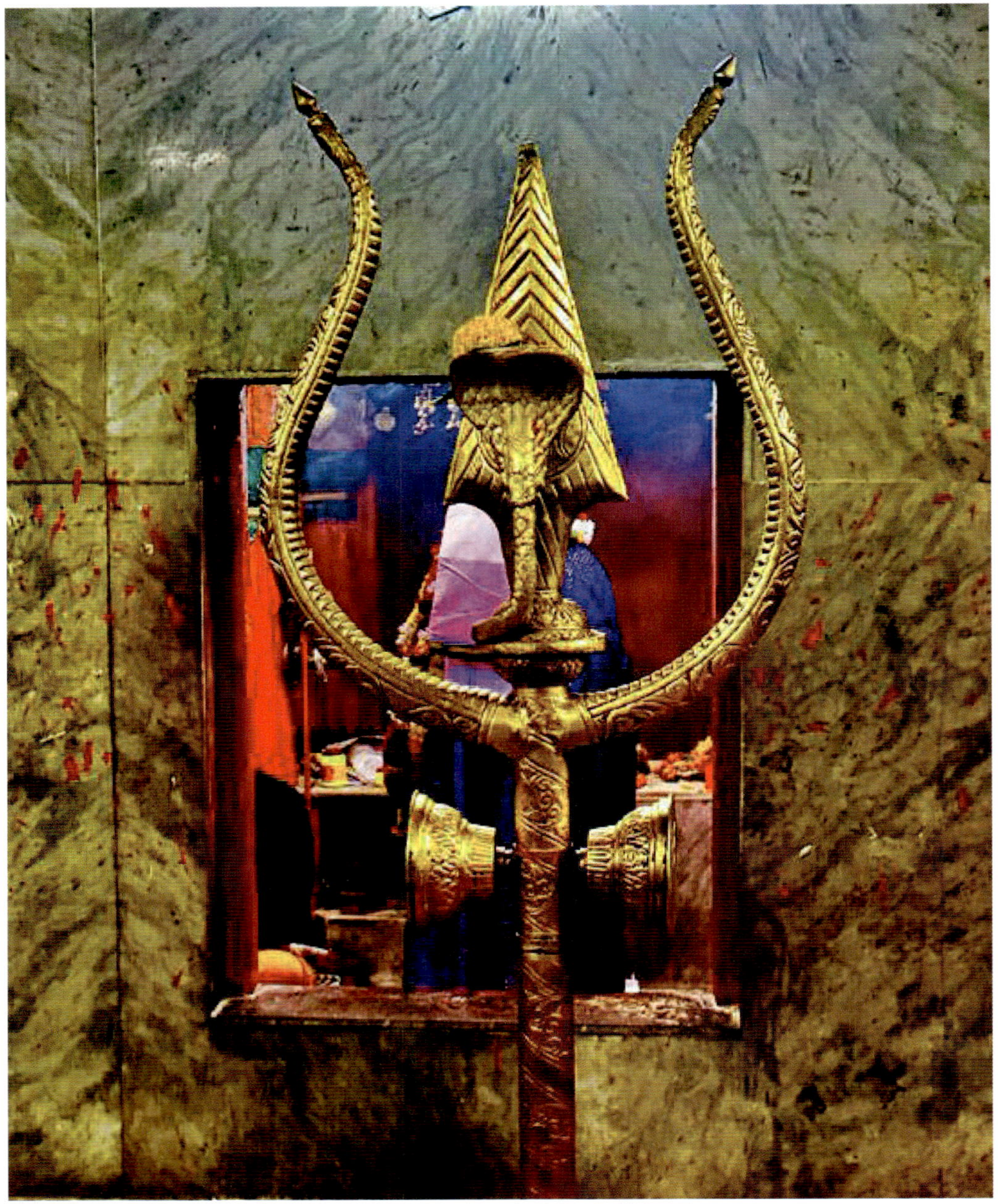

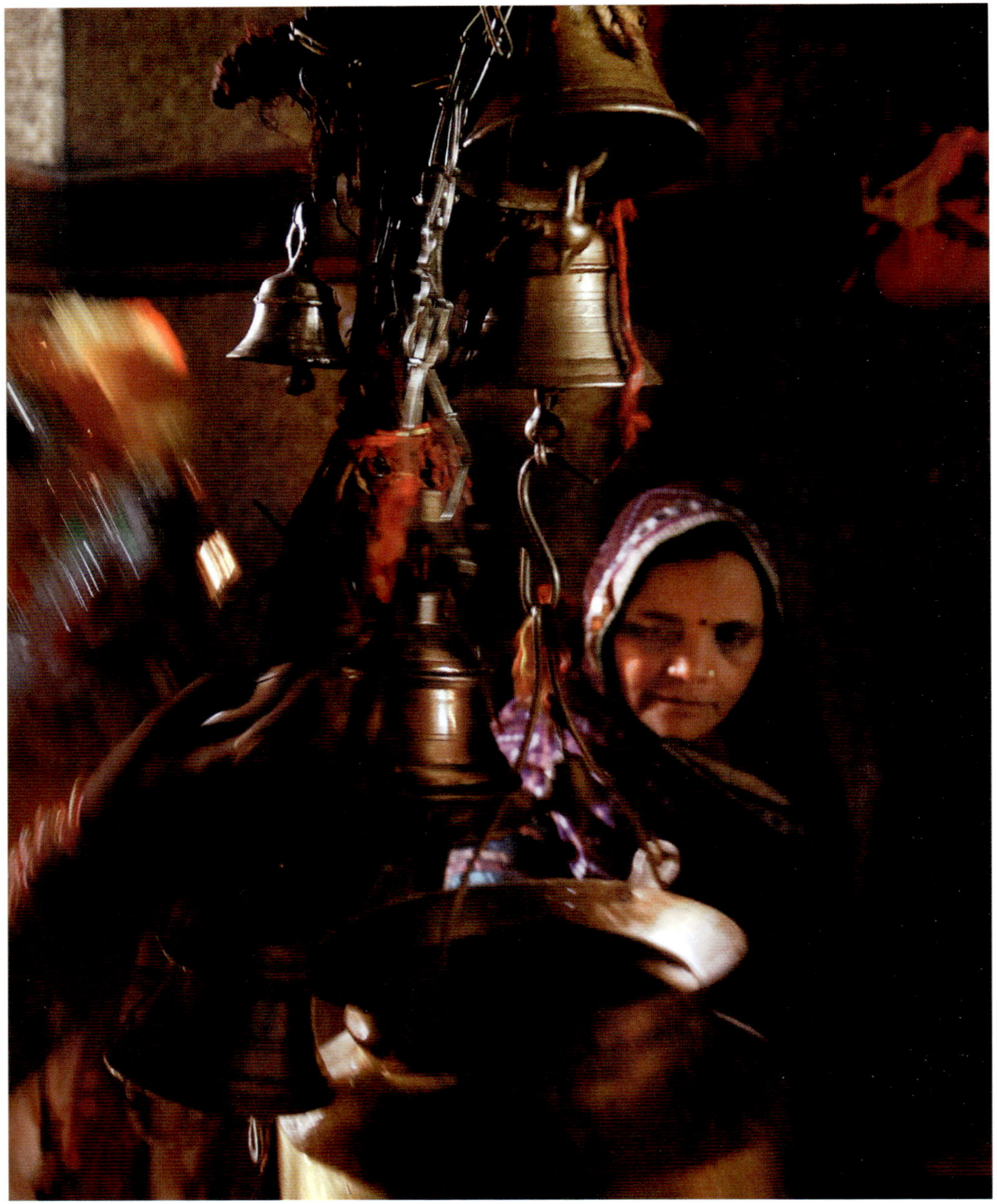

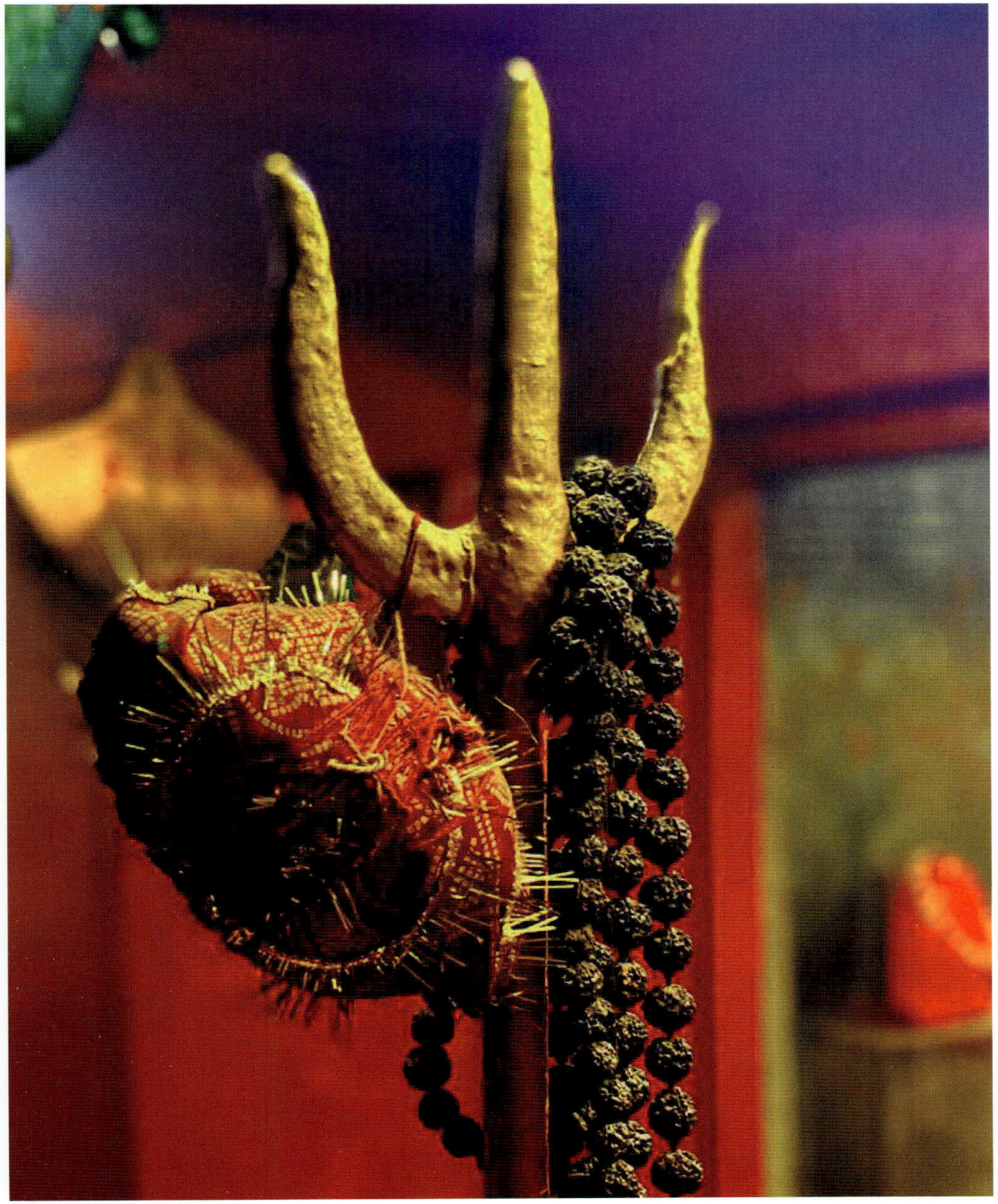

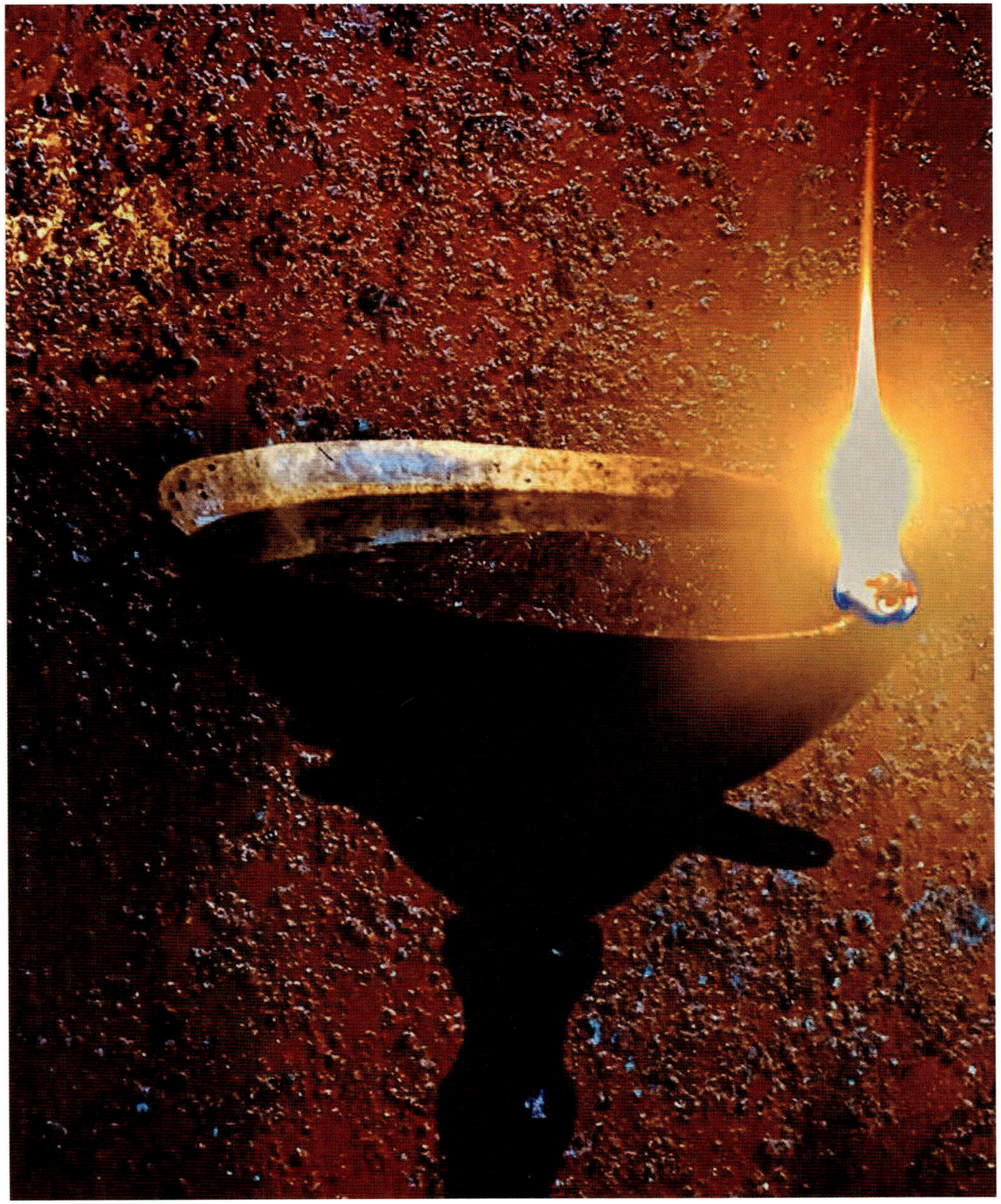

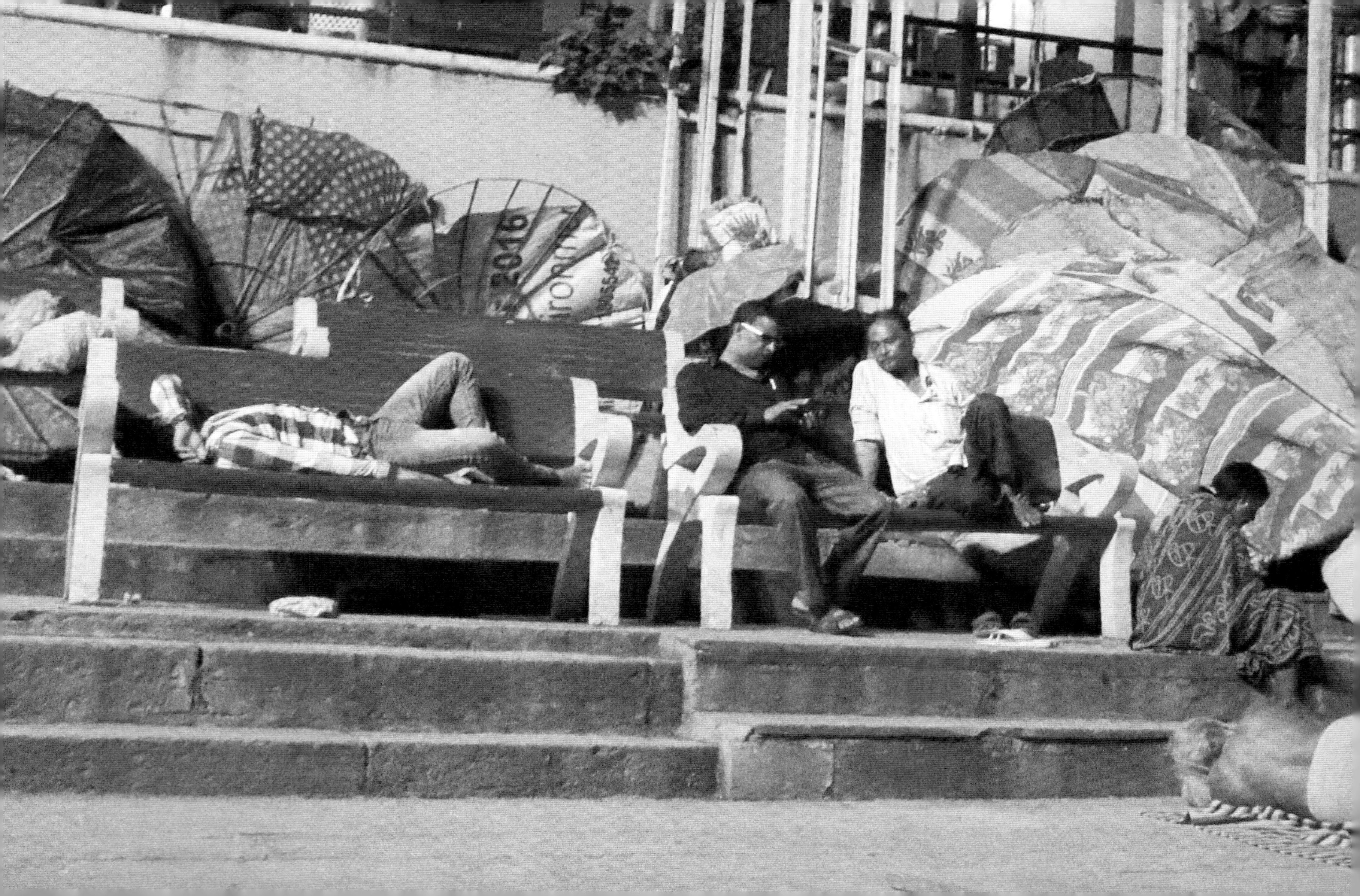

# Streets

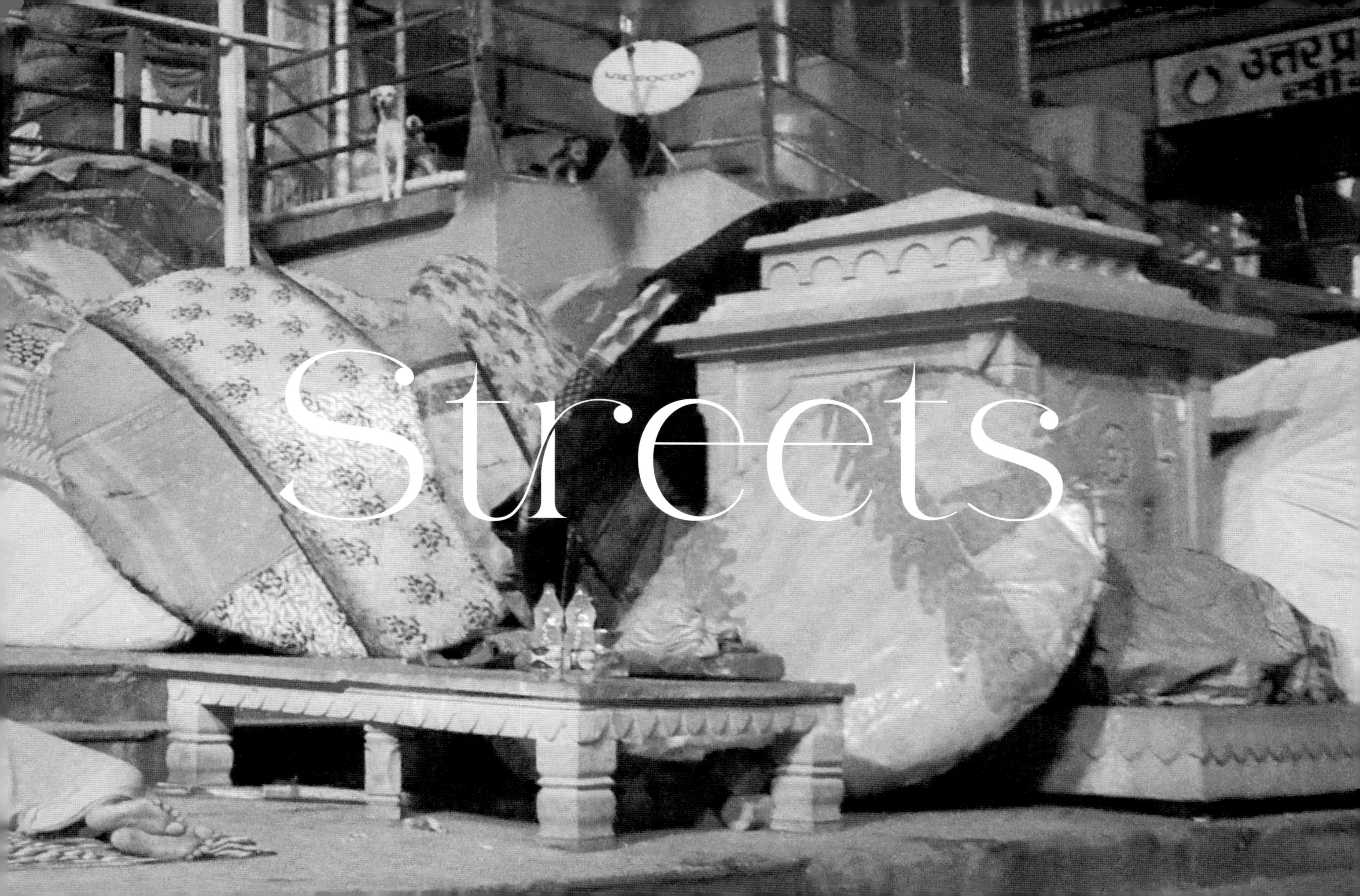

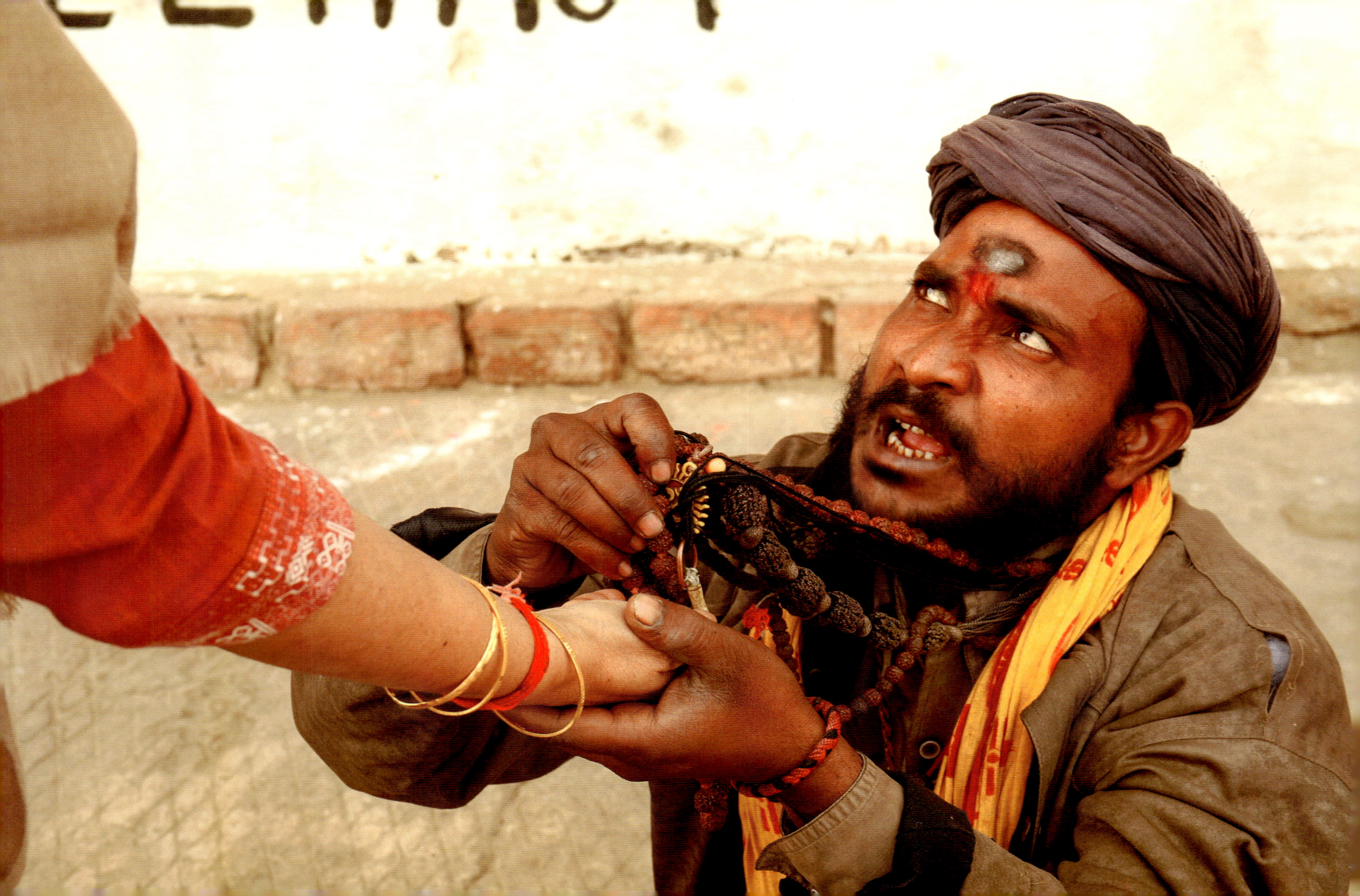

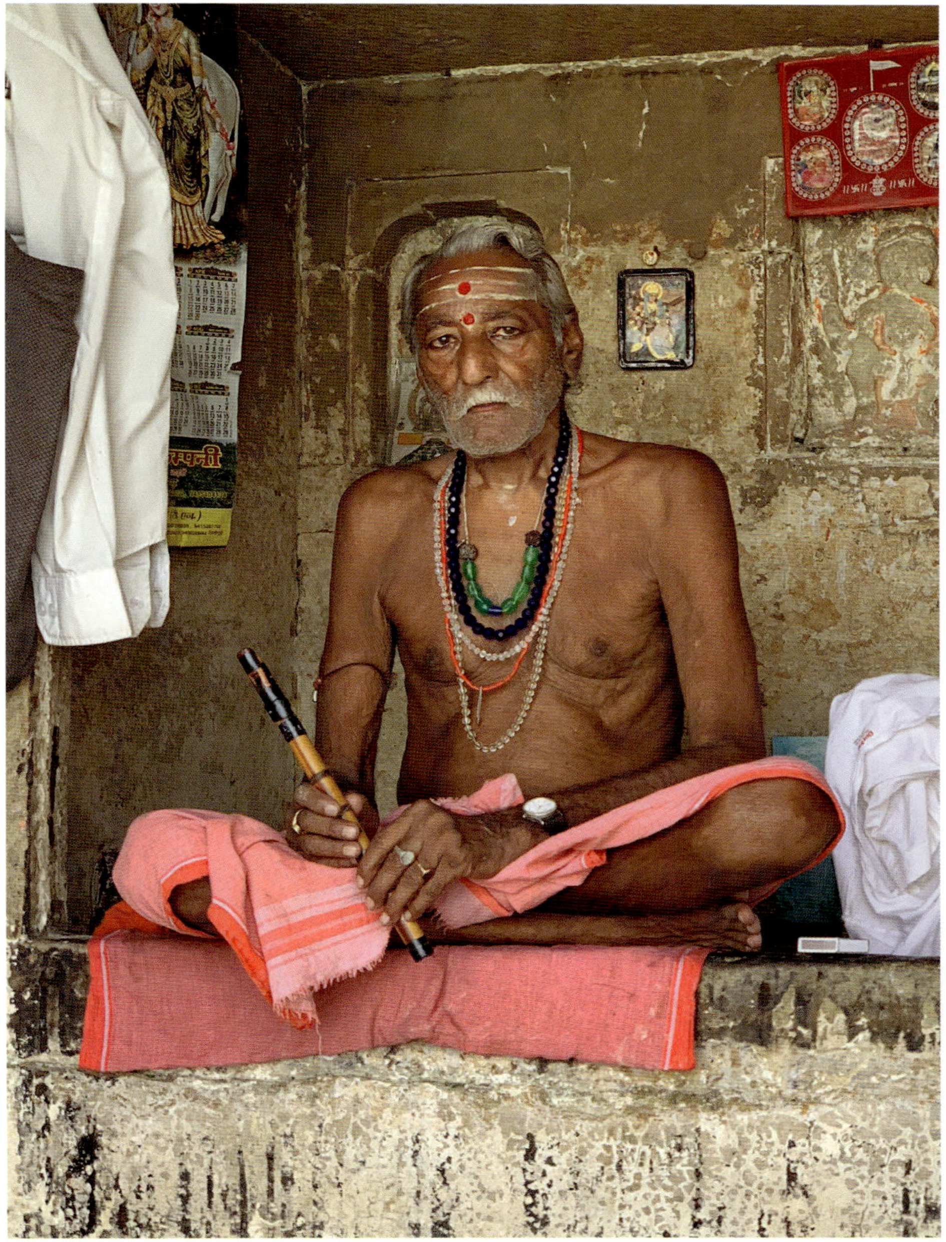

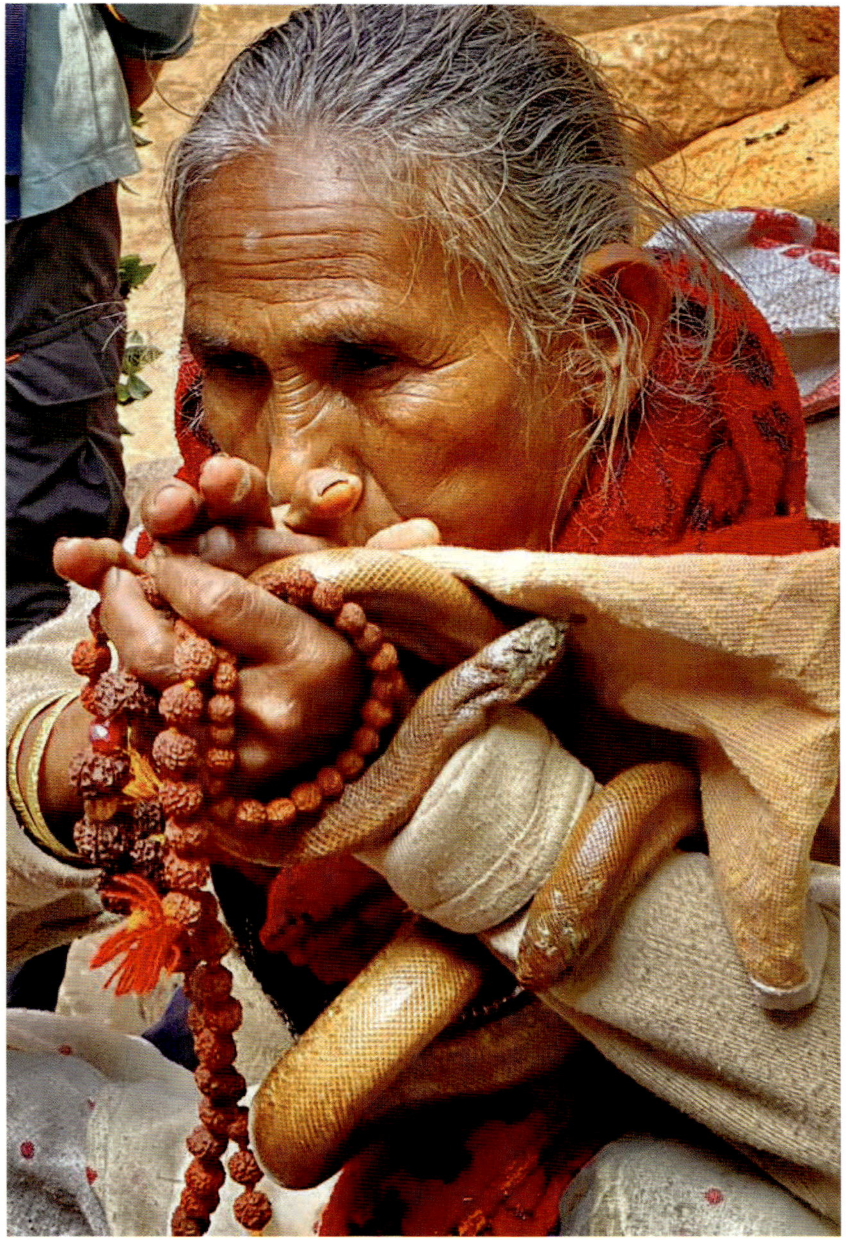

Sadhus dot the steps of the ghats like multicoloured stones as the sun, a ripe tangerine, ripples over the golden blue waters.

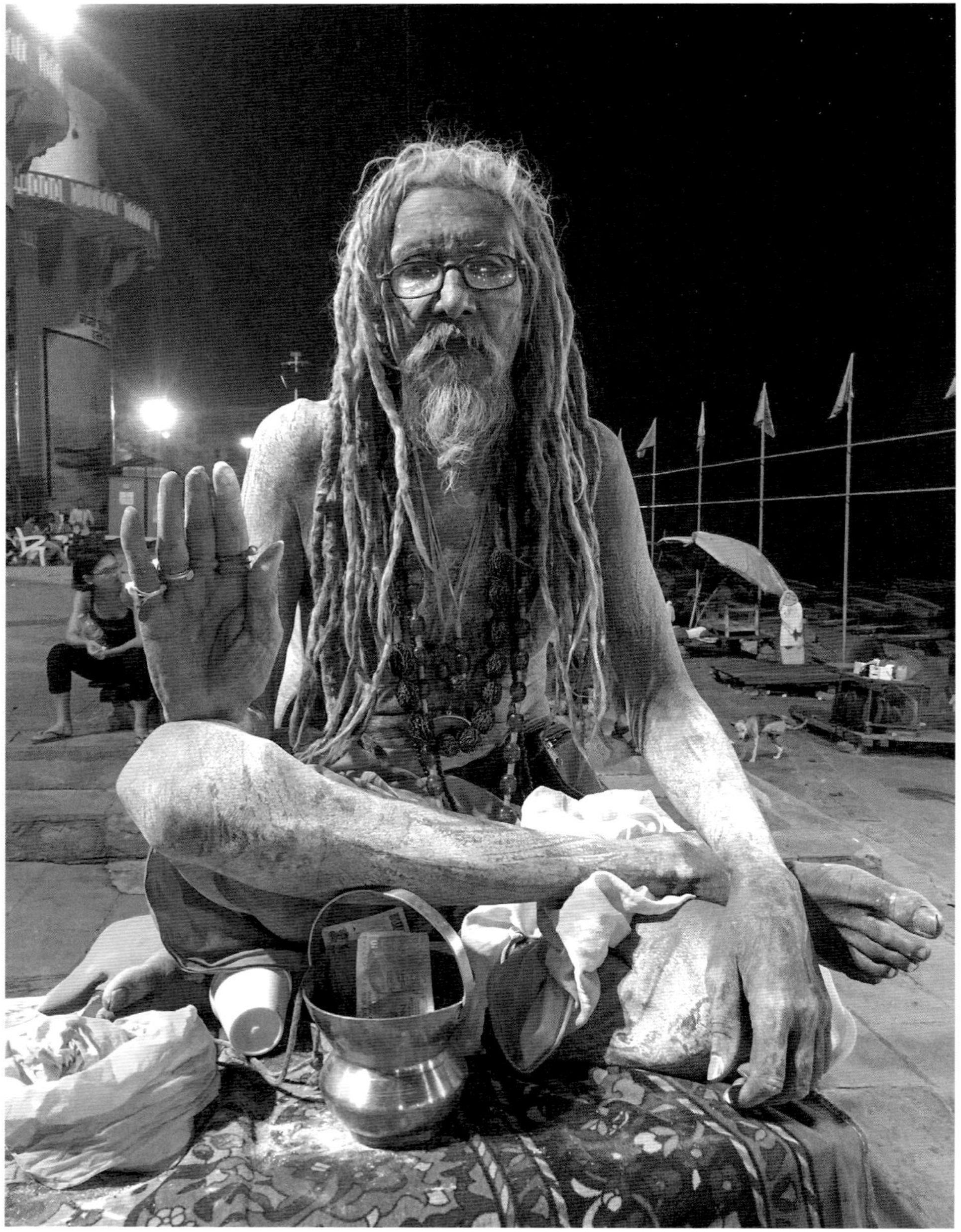

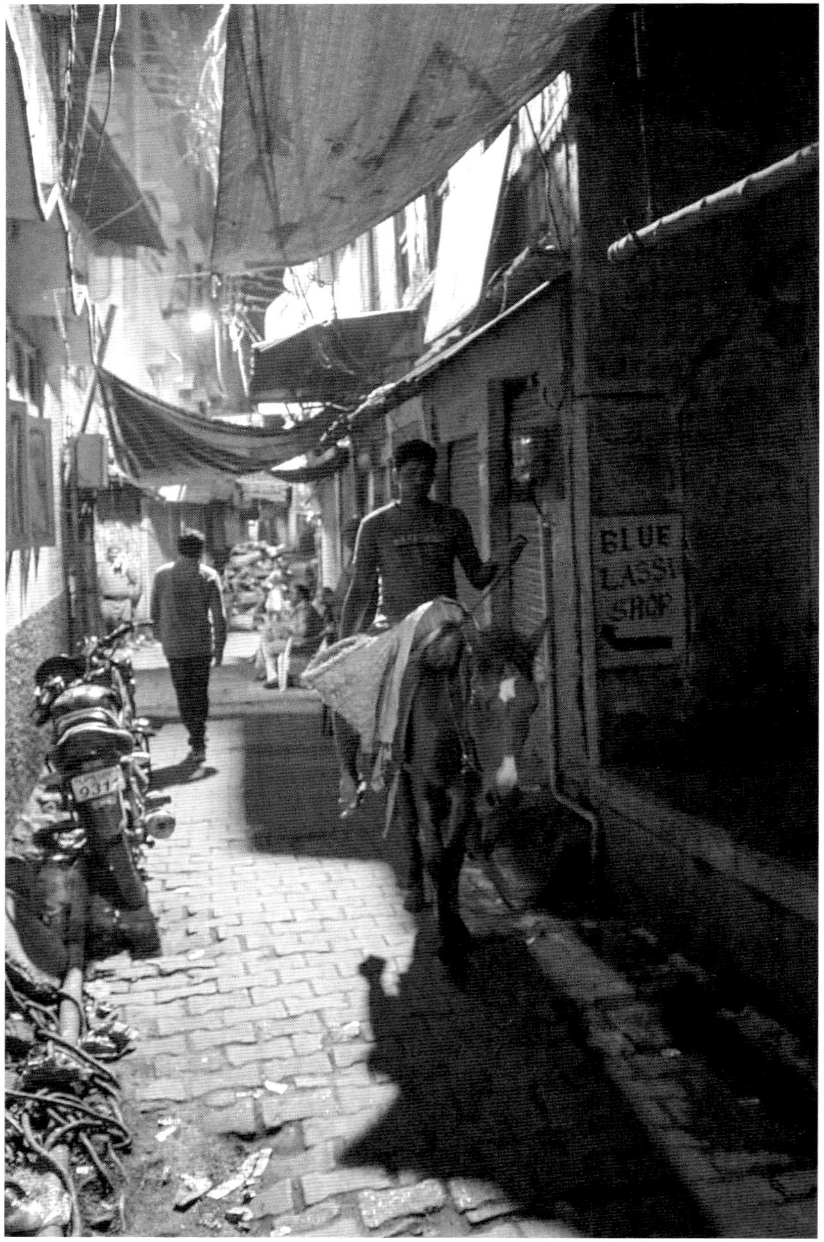


Sansar and Vairagya, the ceremonial and the crematorium, peacefully co-exist on the streets of Kashi.

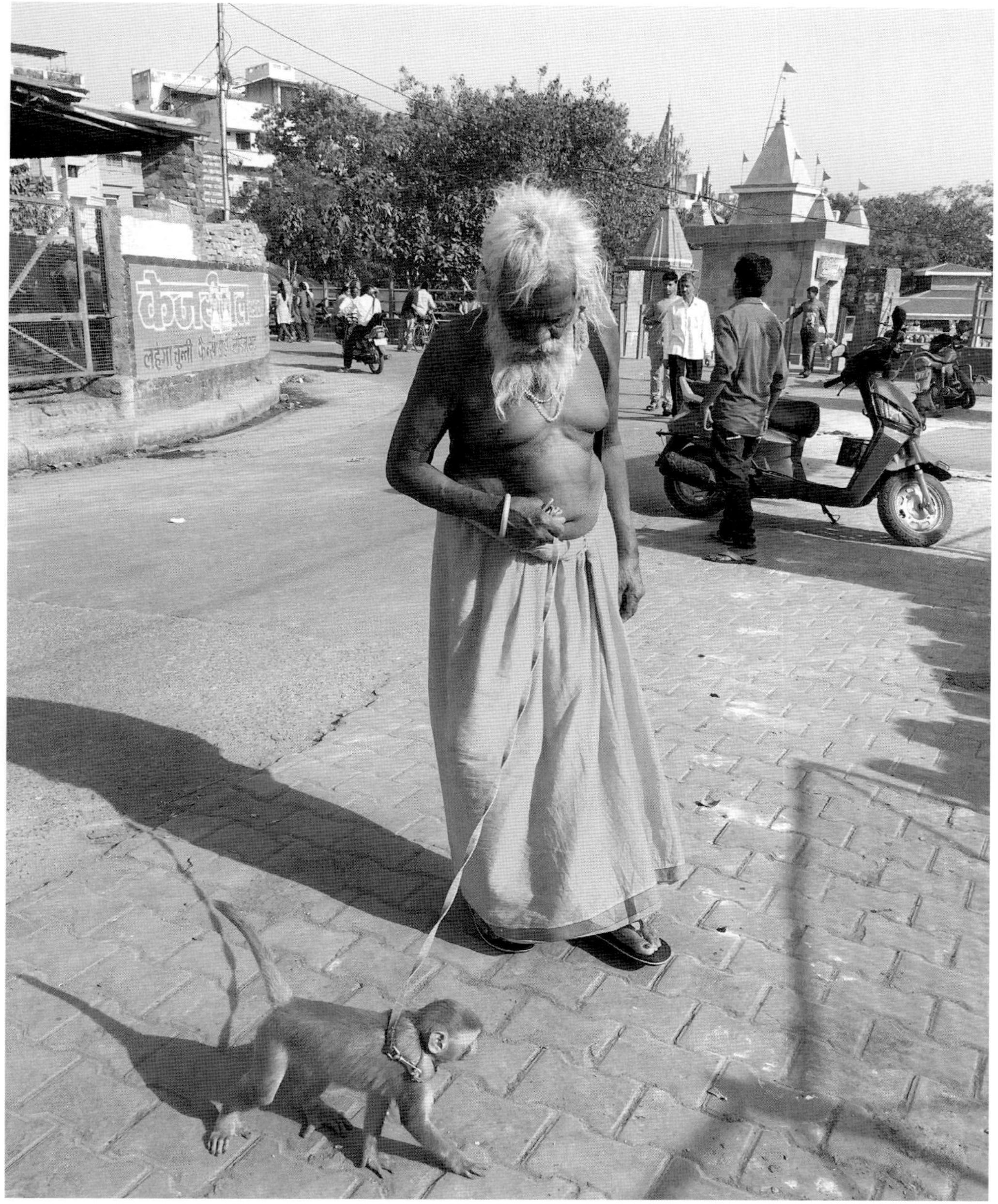

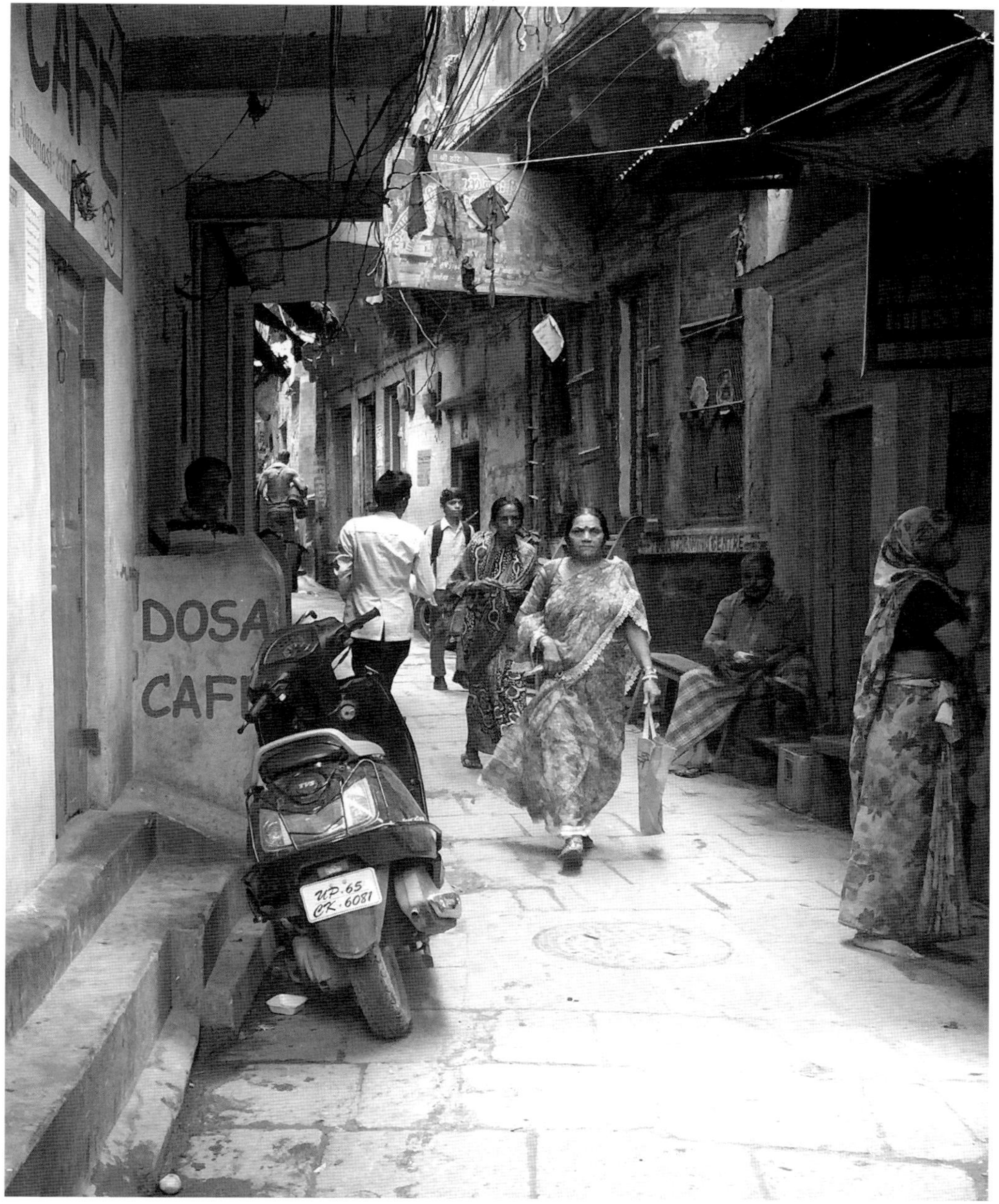
DOSA
CAF
UP 65
CK 6081

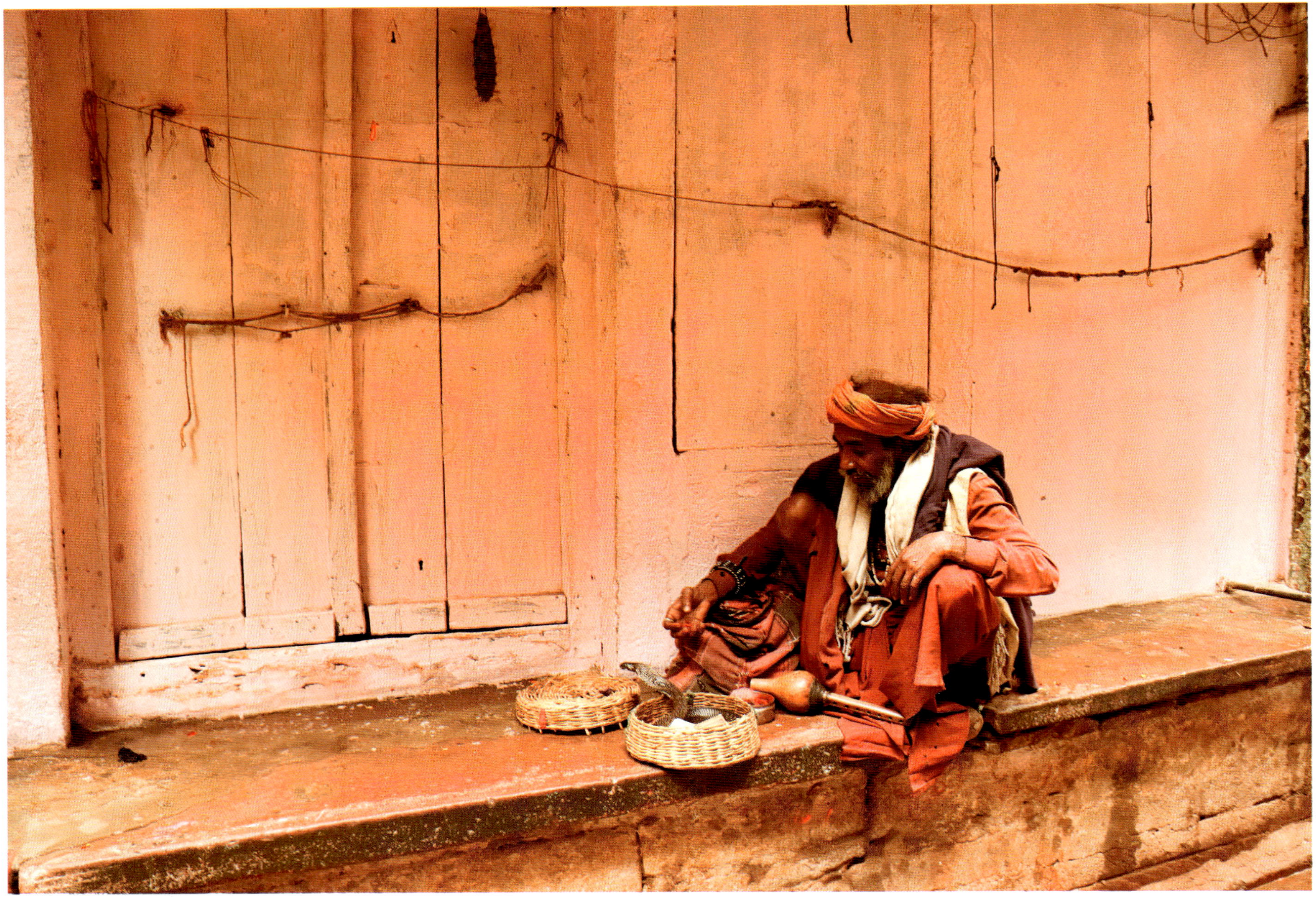

Benaras charms the soul, gets under your skin and catches you unawares. It is something that cannot be fully expressed but only felt by the lone self.

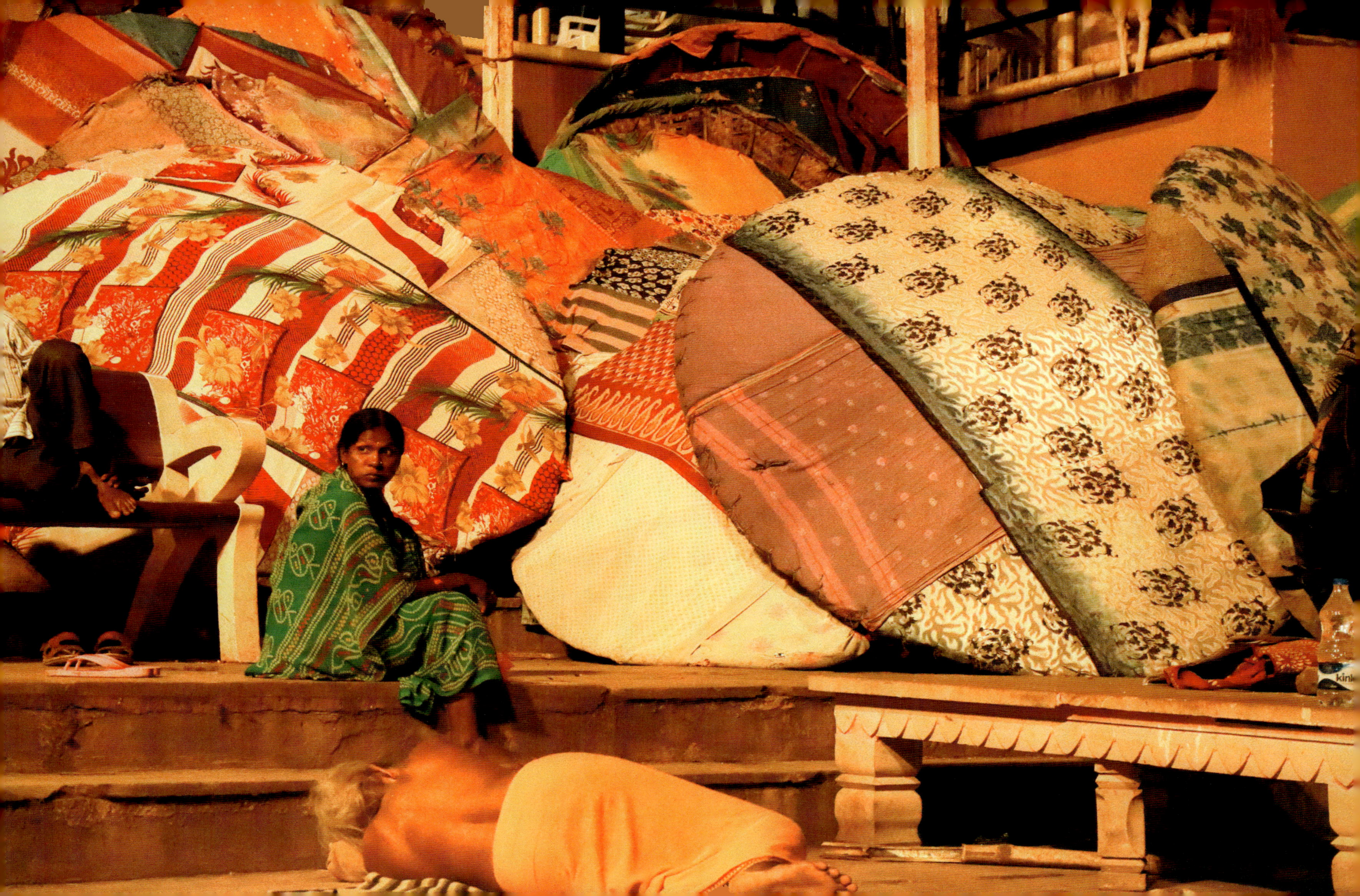

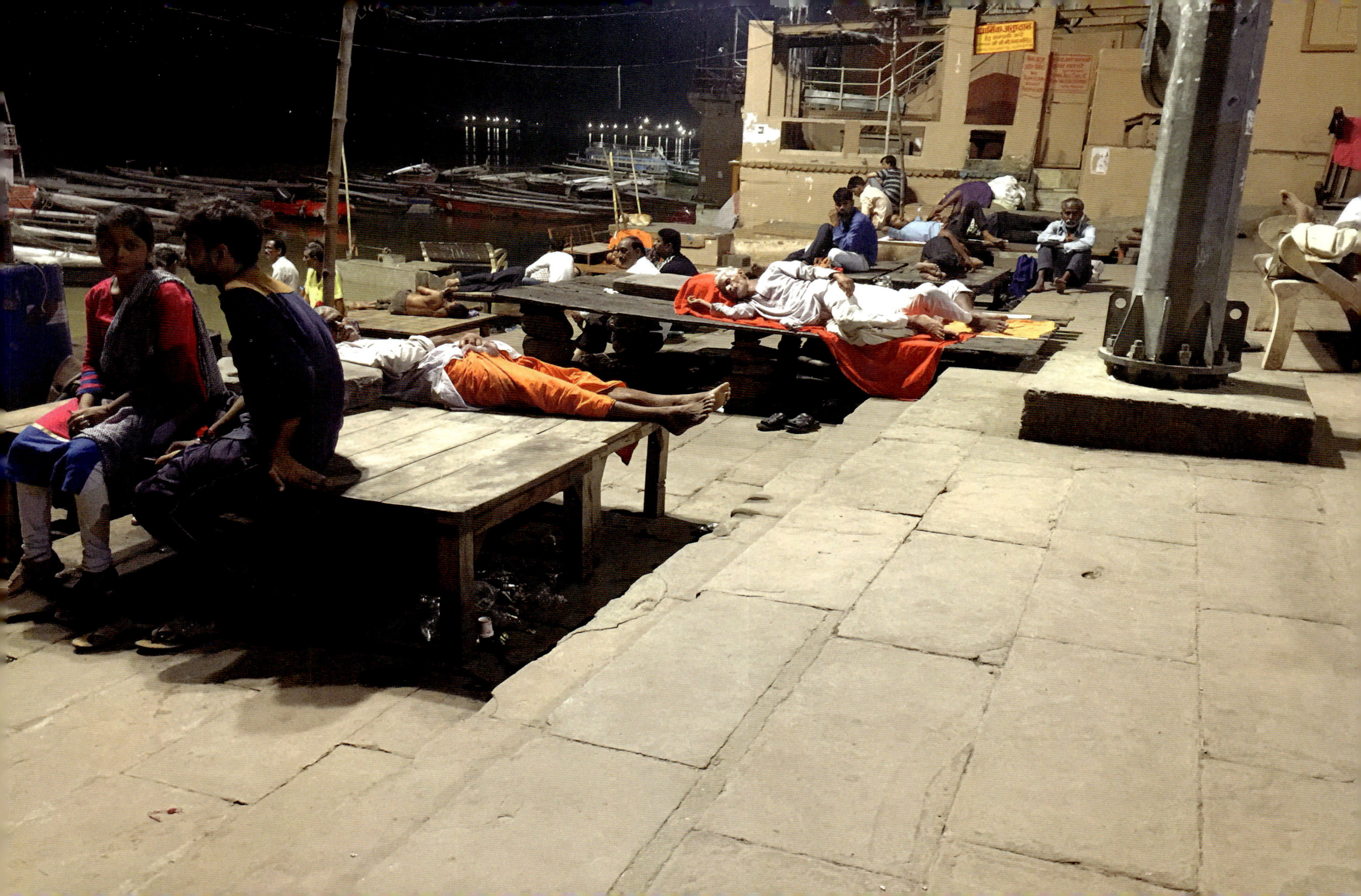

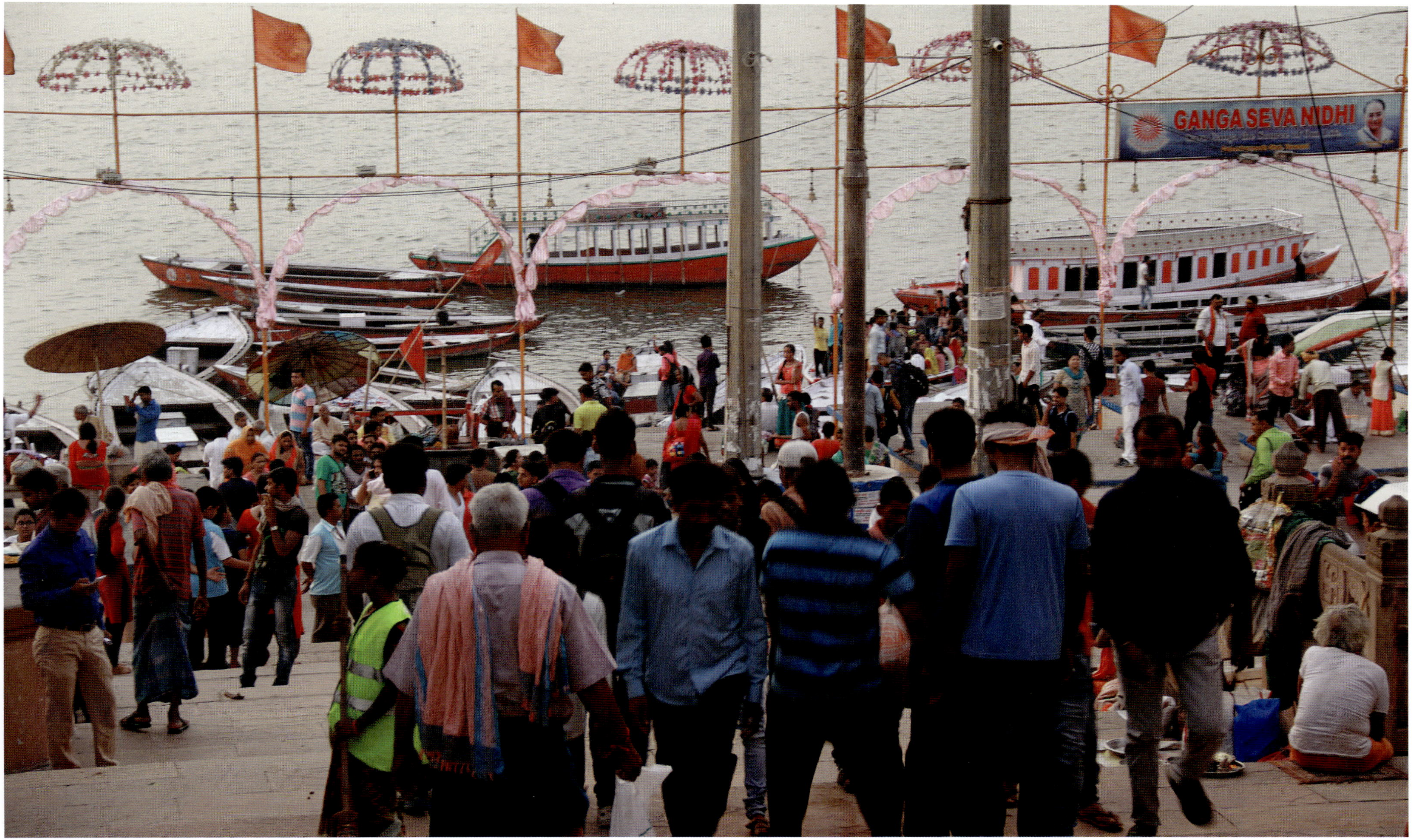
GANGA SEVA NIDHI

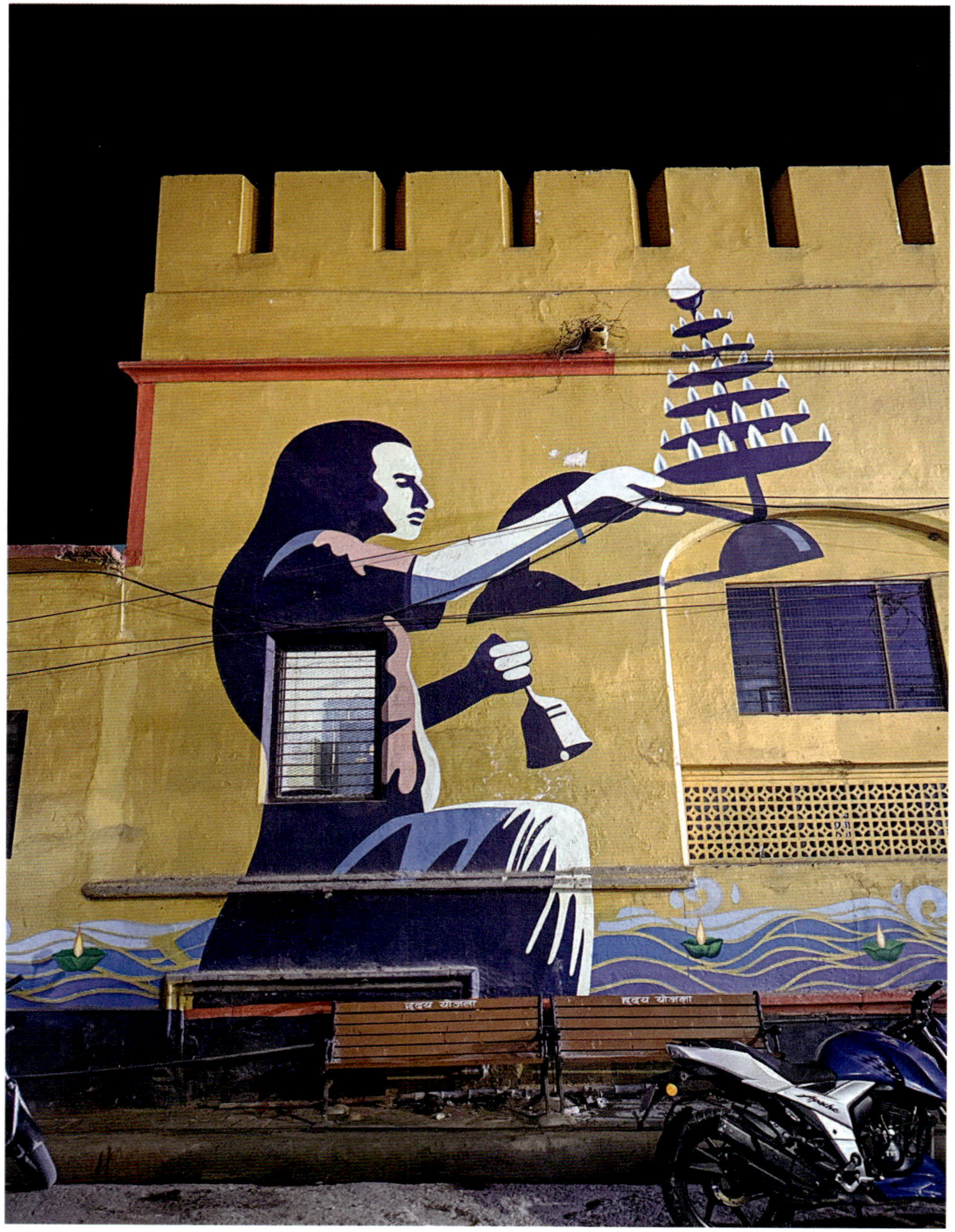

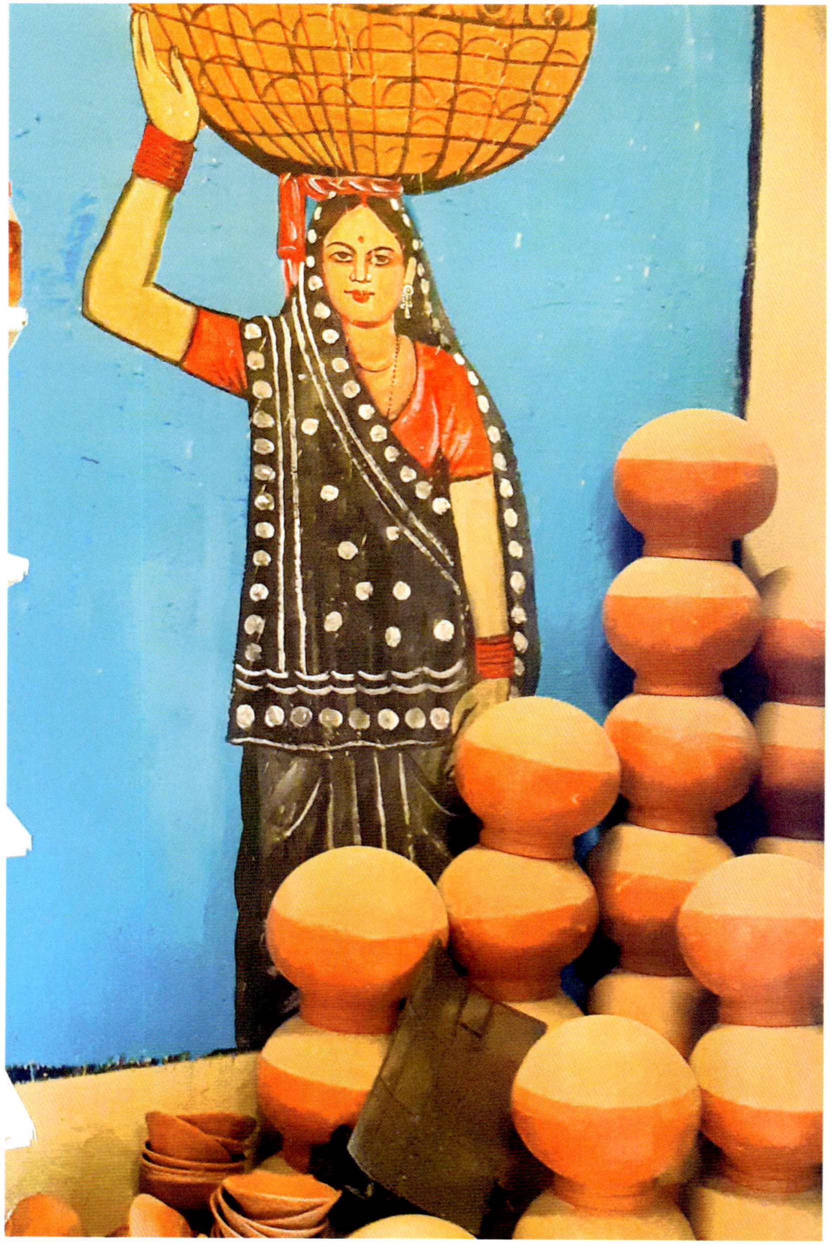

Other than the roots and fruits of spirituality, other tangents bring you back again and again to this wholesome city.

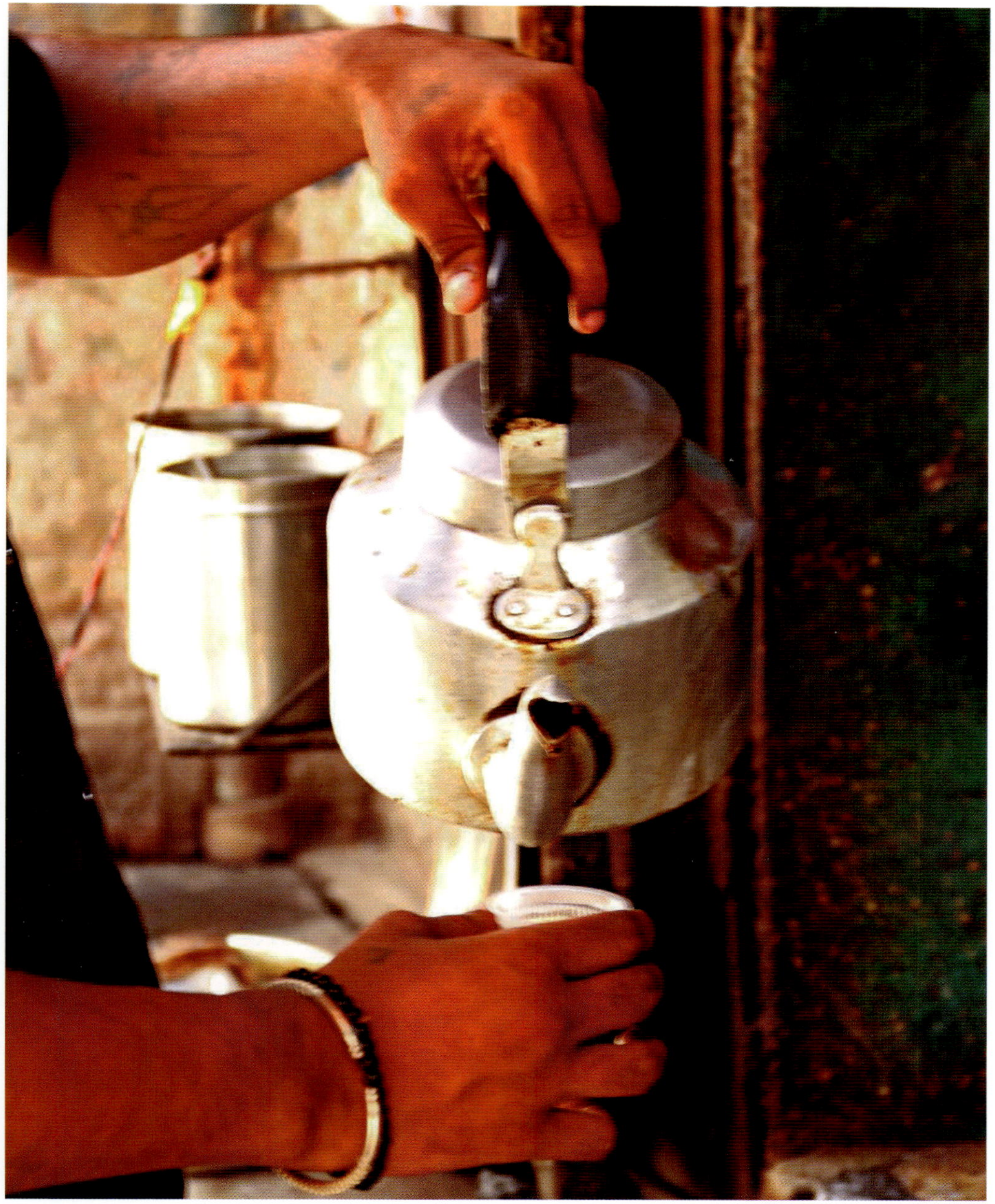

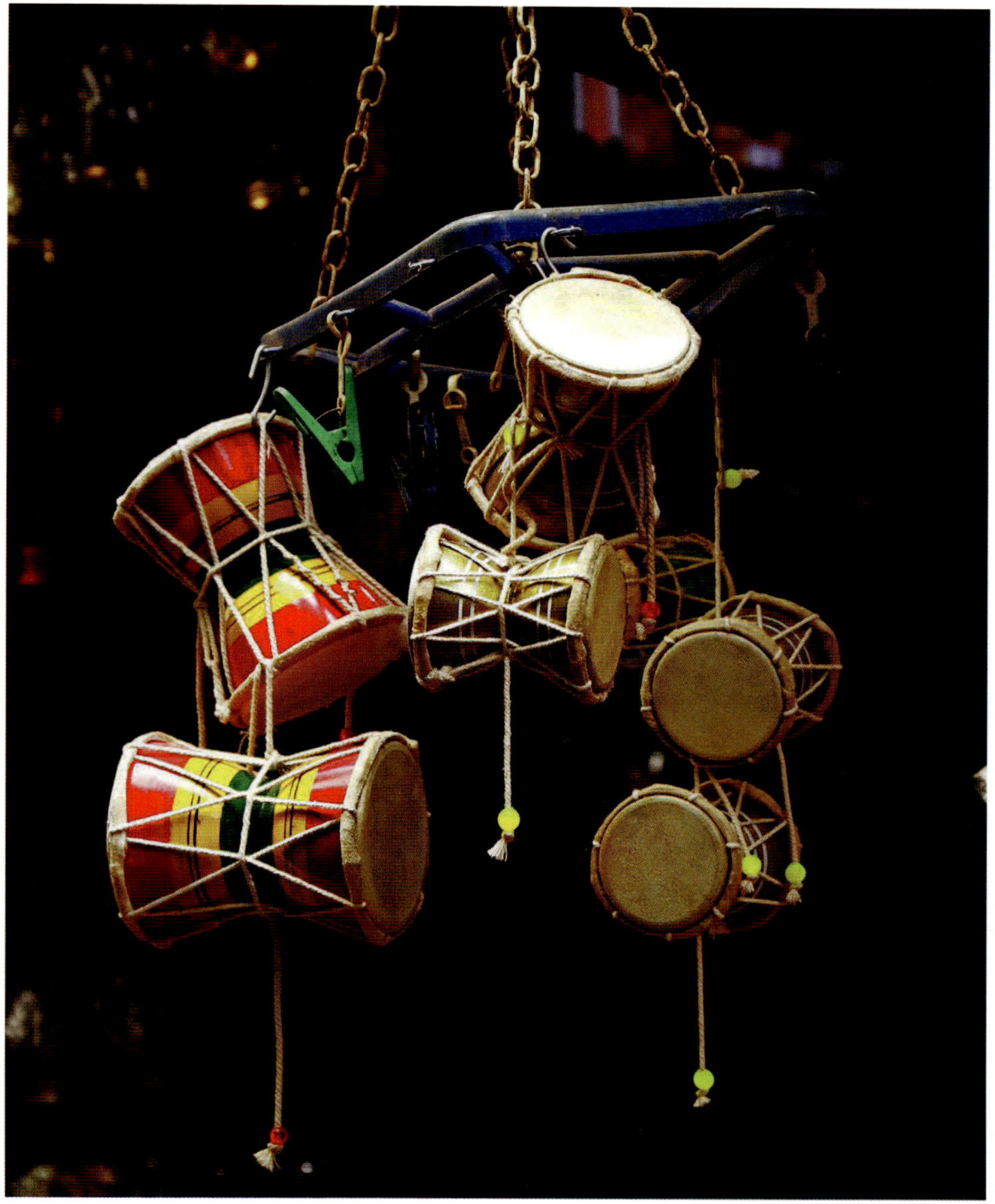

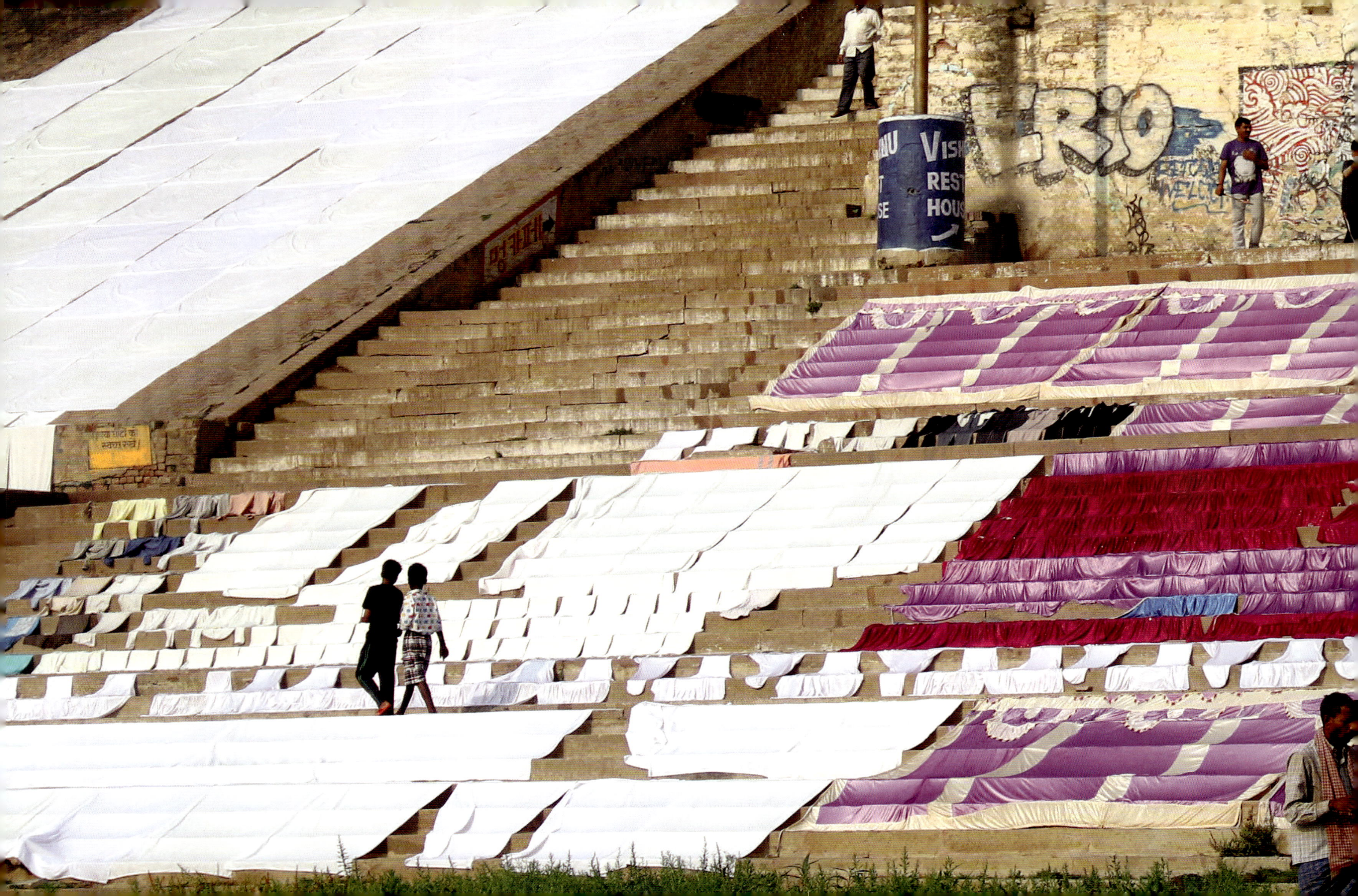

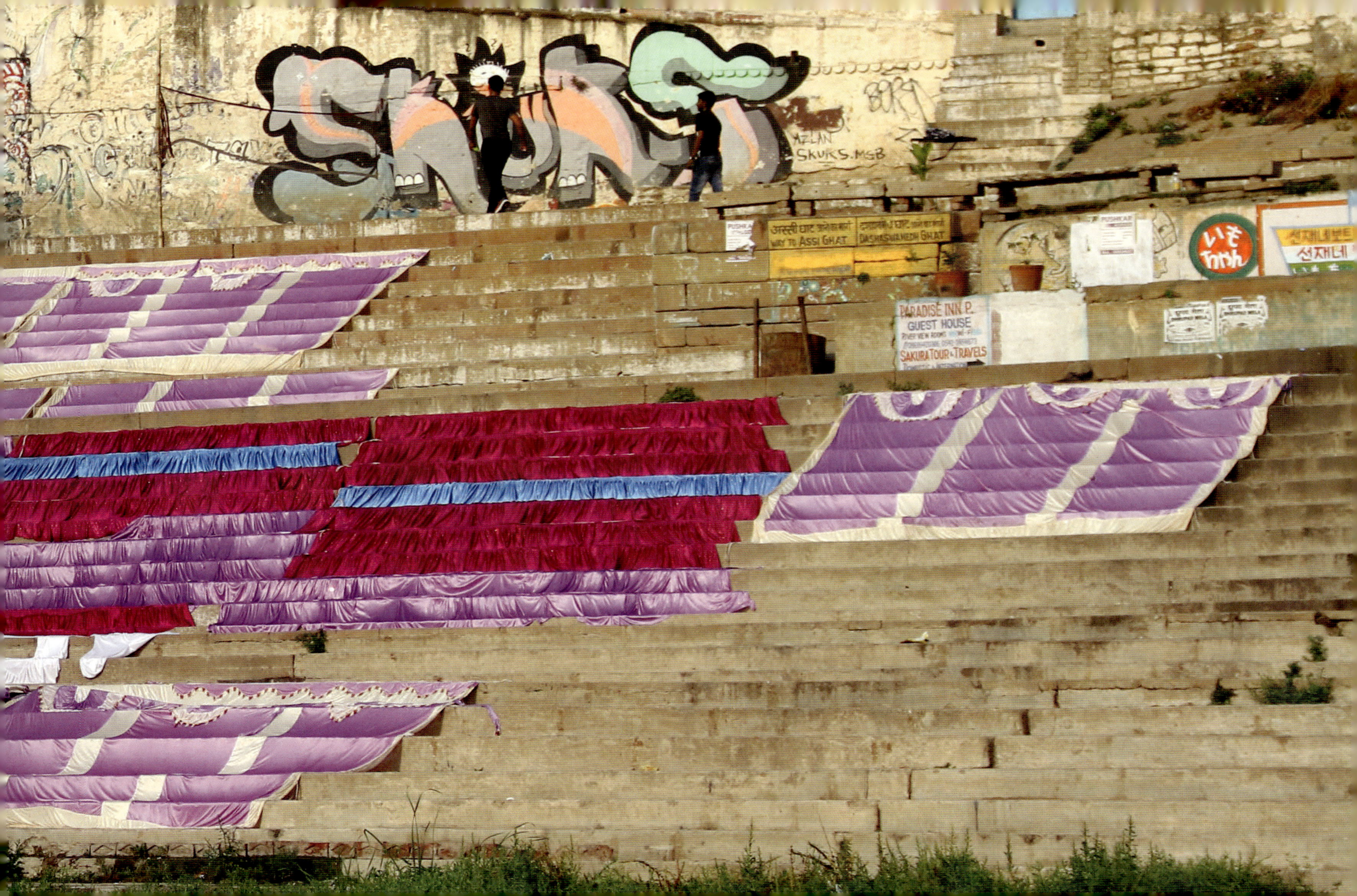
AZLAN
SKUKS.MSB
WAY TO ASSI GHAT
PARADISE INN P.
GUEST HOUSE
SAKURA TOUR & TRAVELS

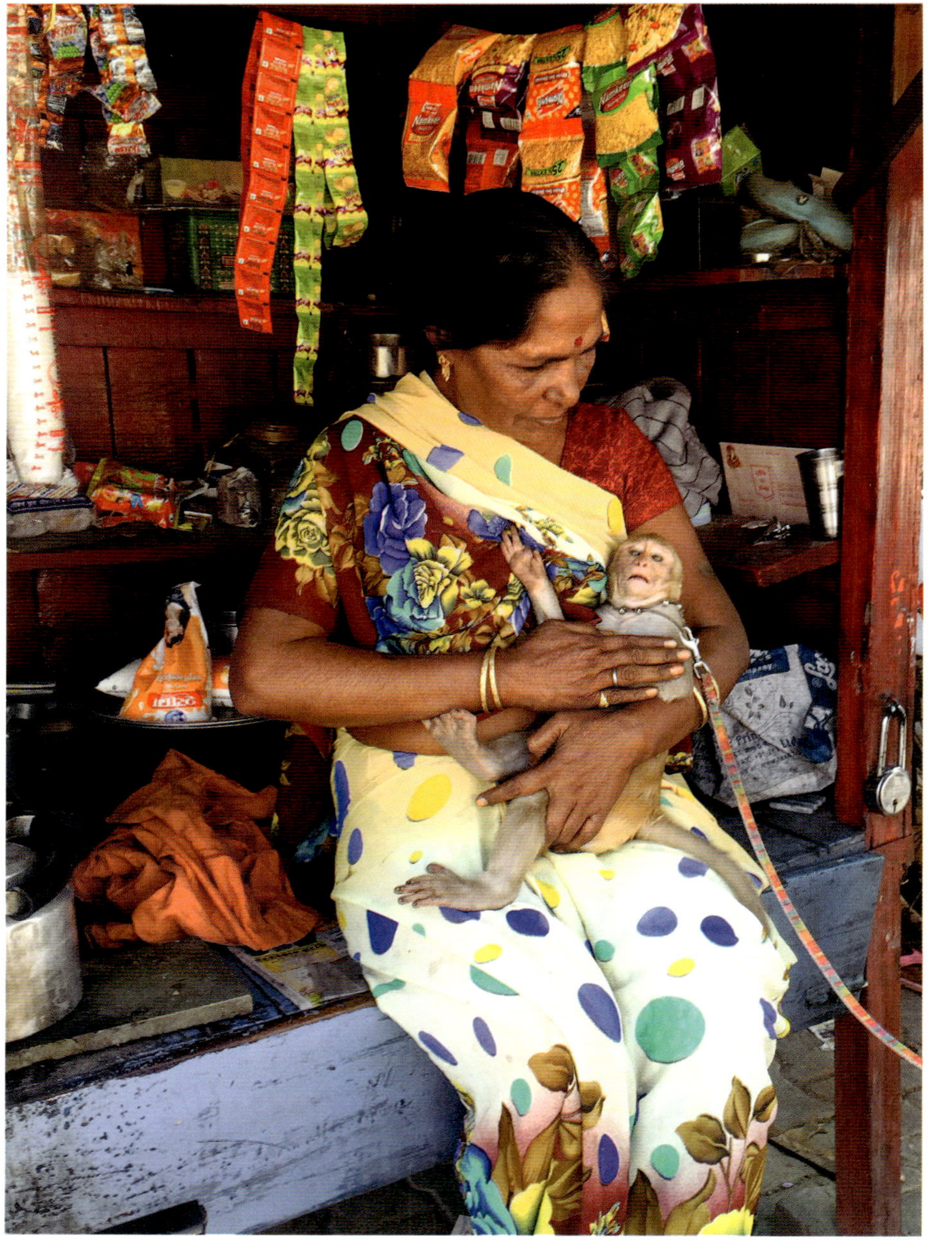

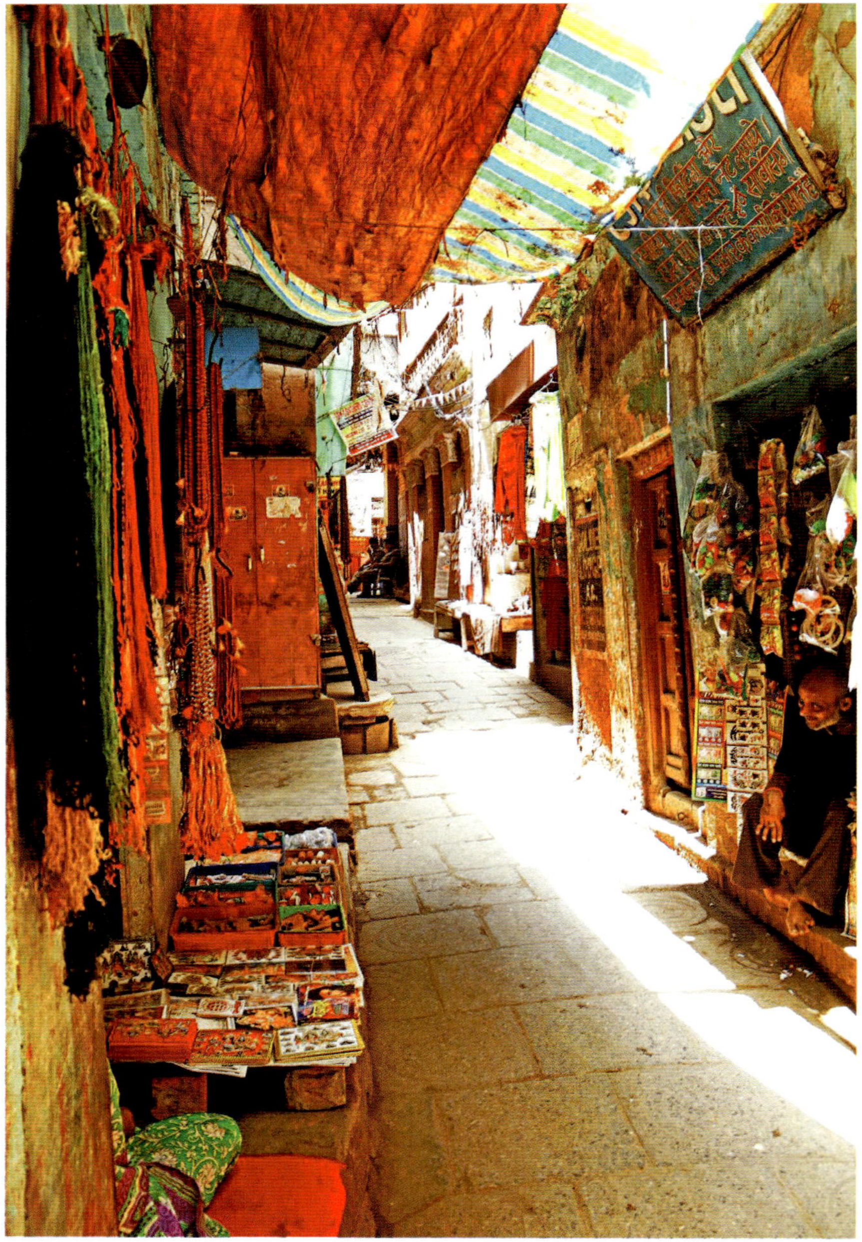

With its innumerable small shops, all kinds of spices, flavourful street food, intricate artifacts, and the silks and the brocades, Benaras is kaleidoscope of our rich cultural heritage.

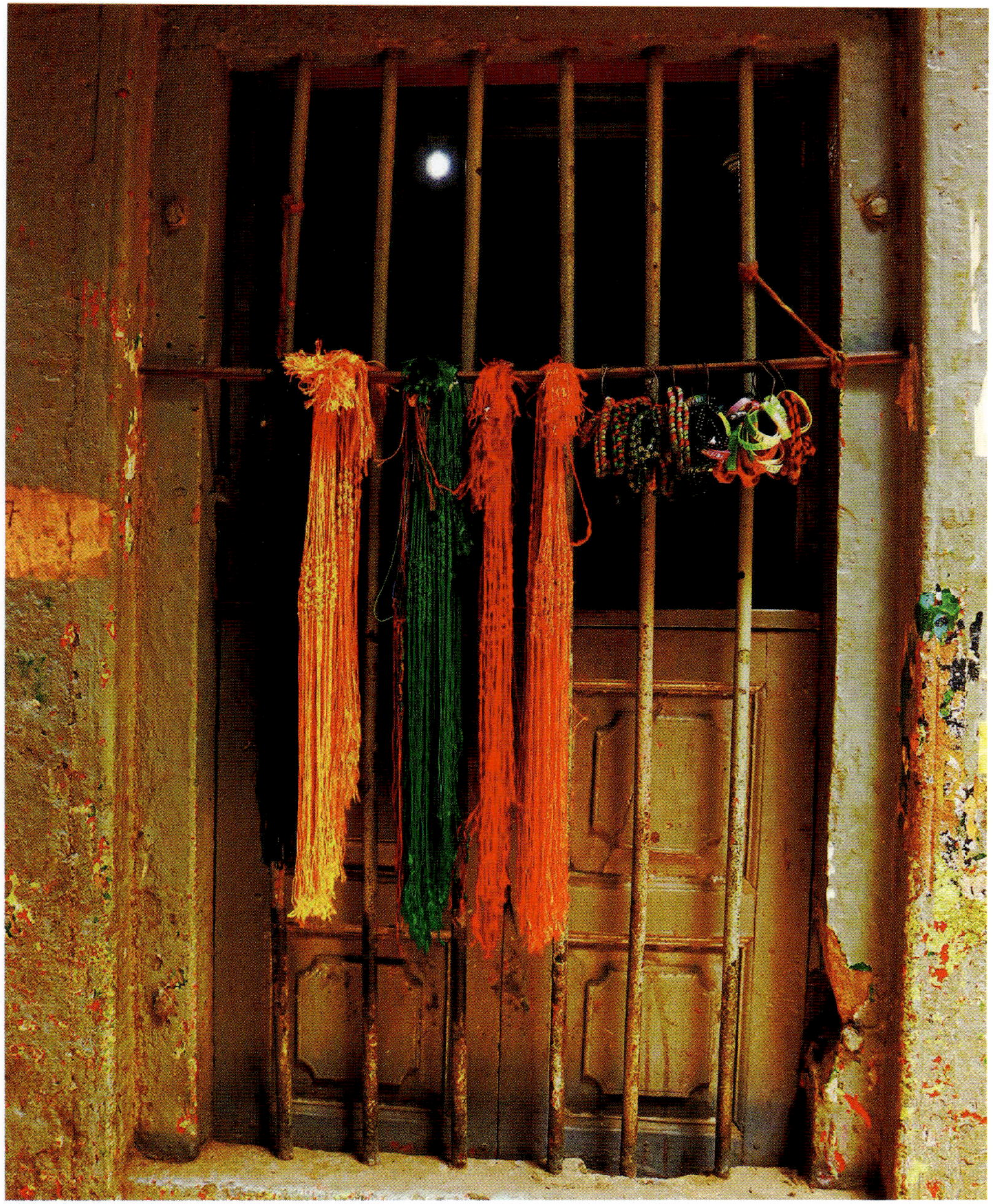

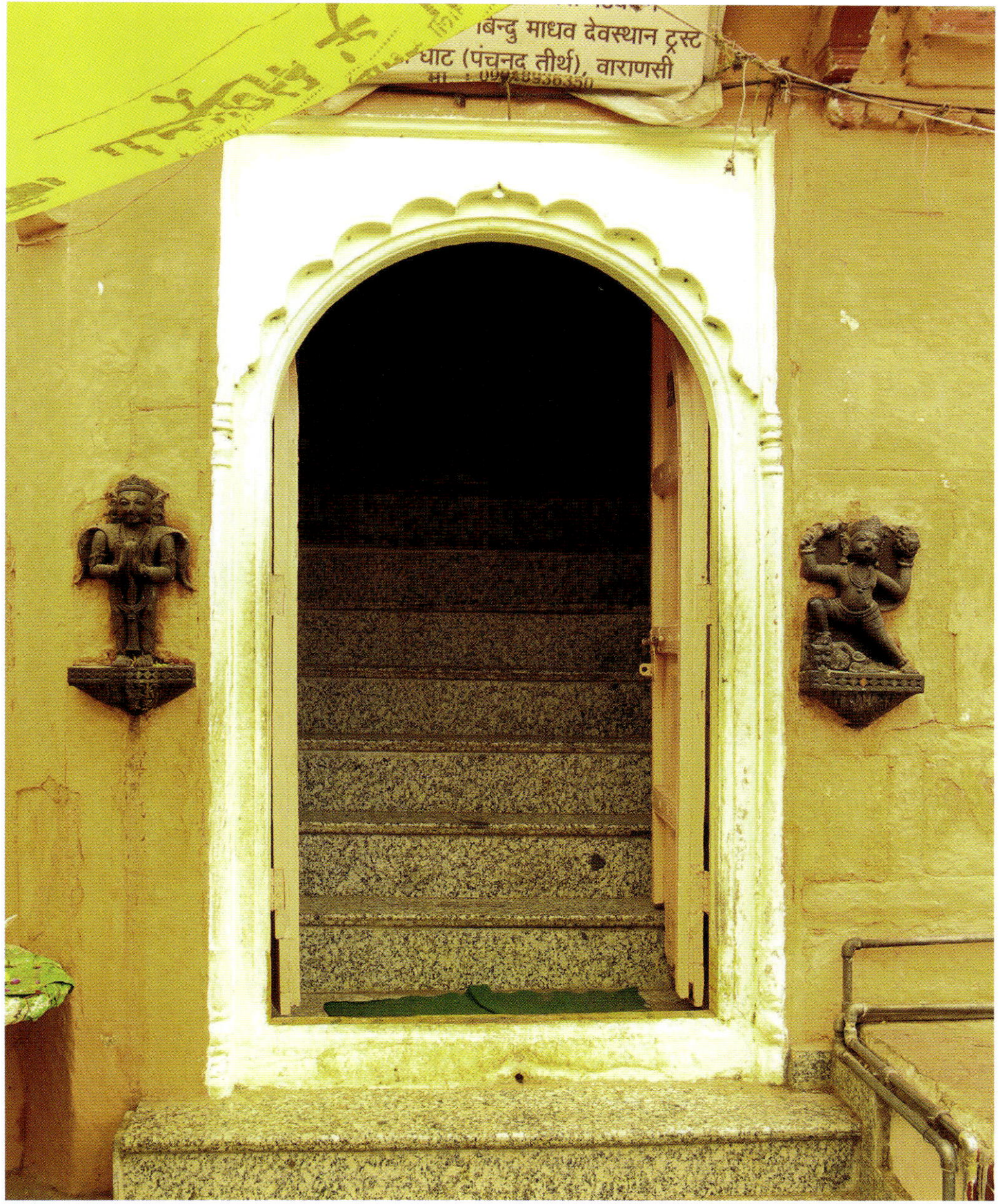
माधव देवस्थान ट्रस्ट
घाट (पंचनद तीर्थ), वाराणसी

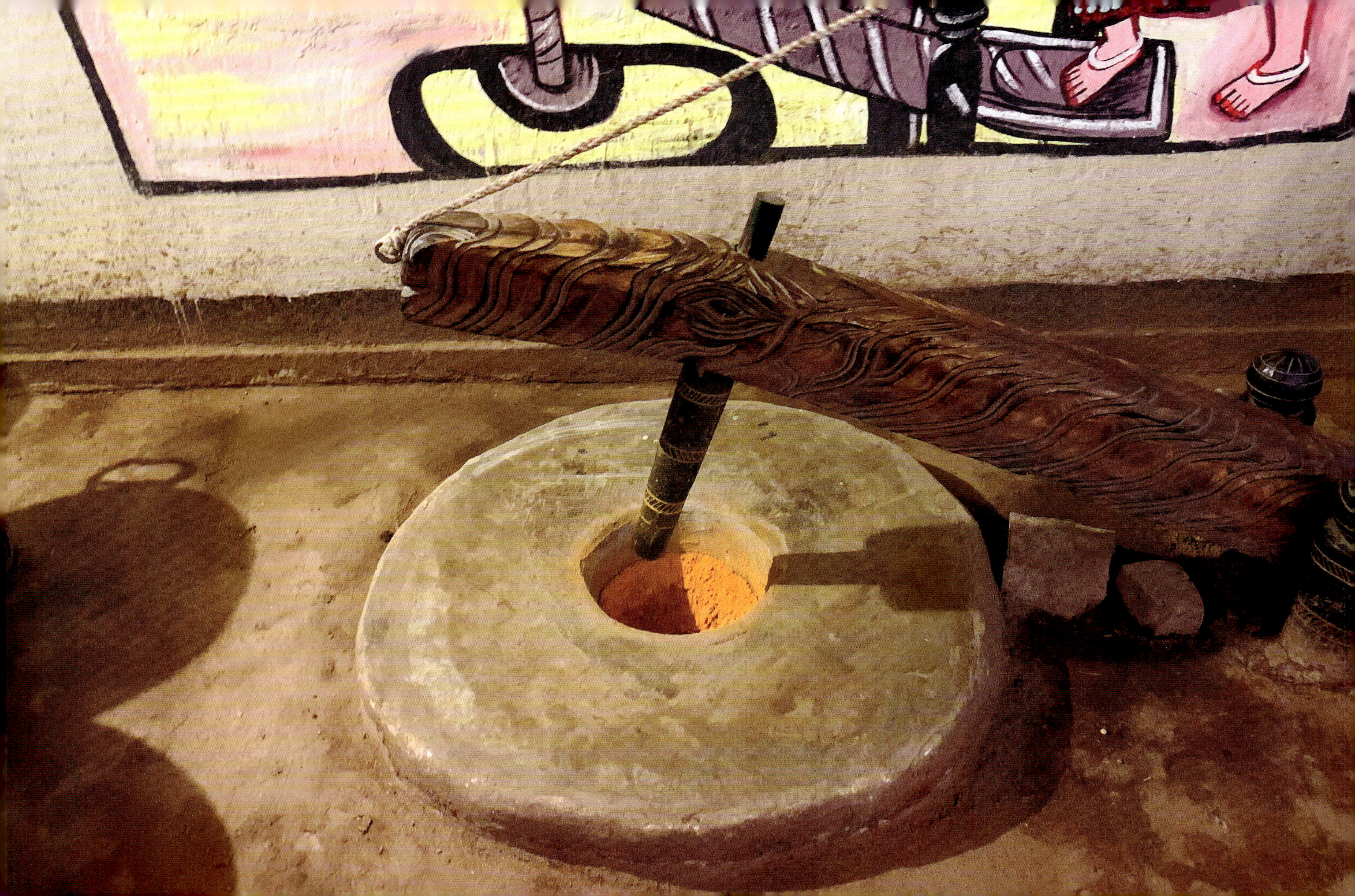

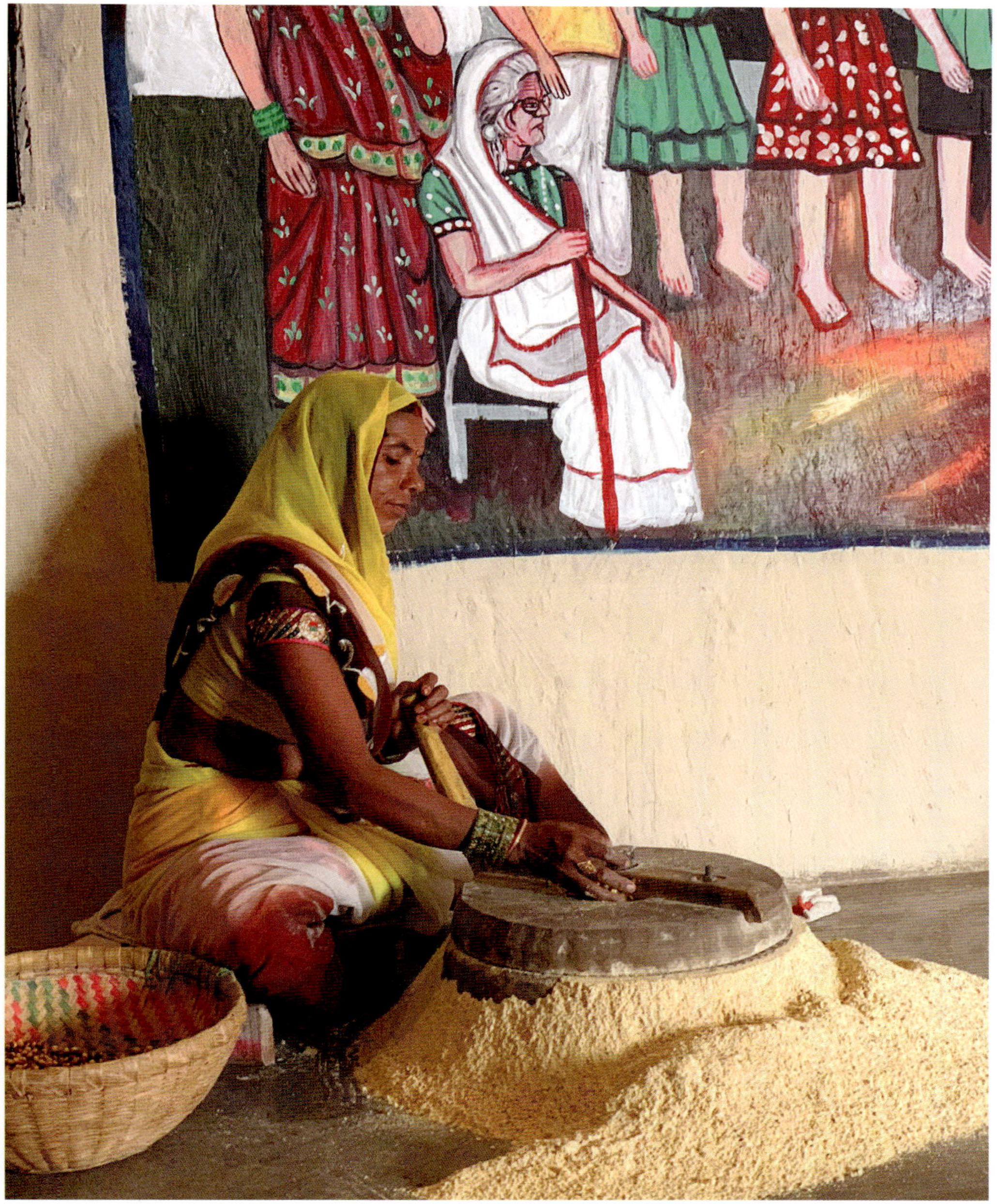

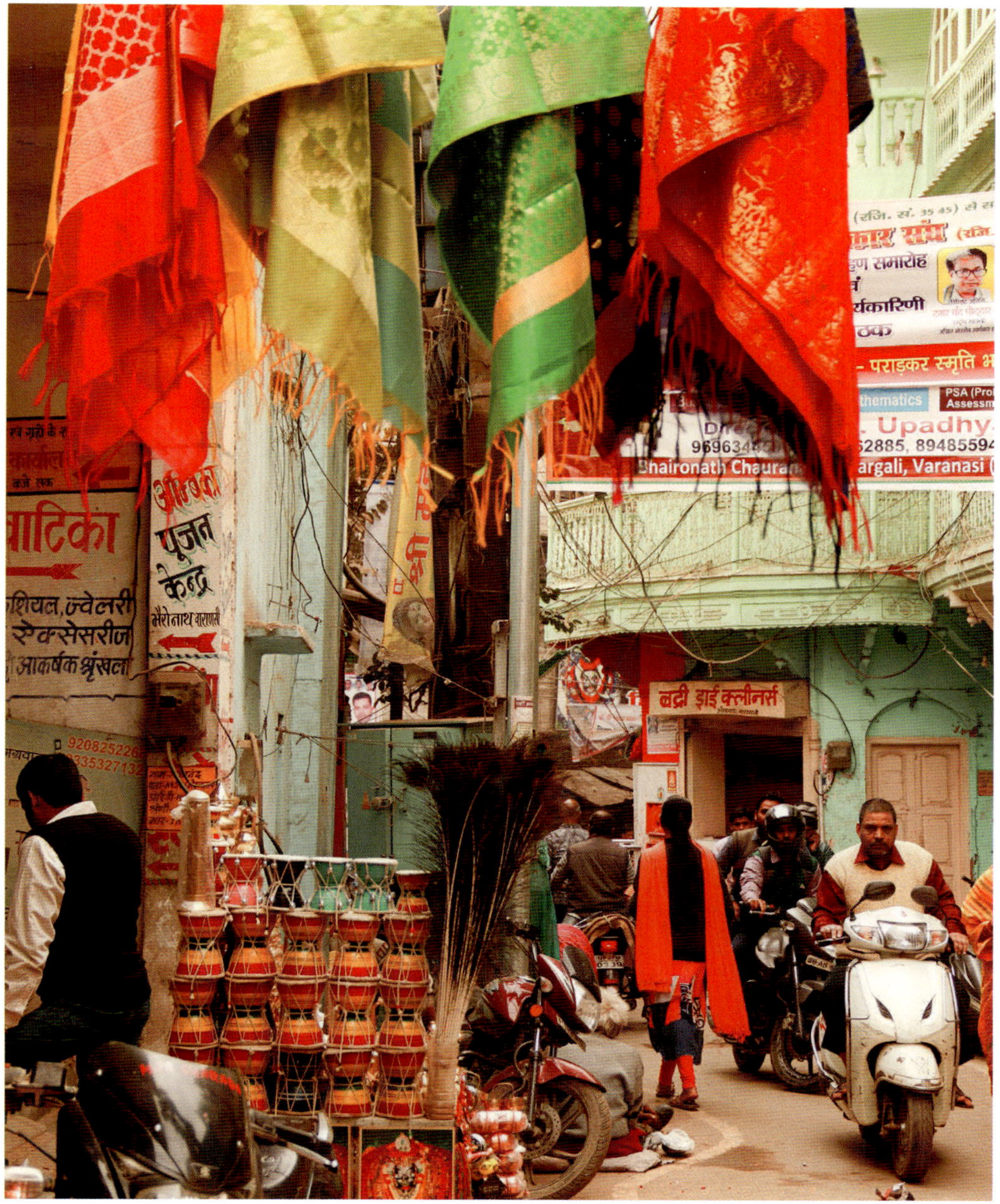
पूजन
केन्द्र
बद्री ड्राई क्लीनर्स
Varanasi

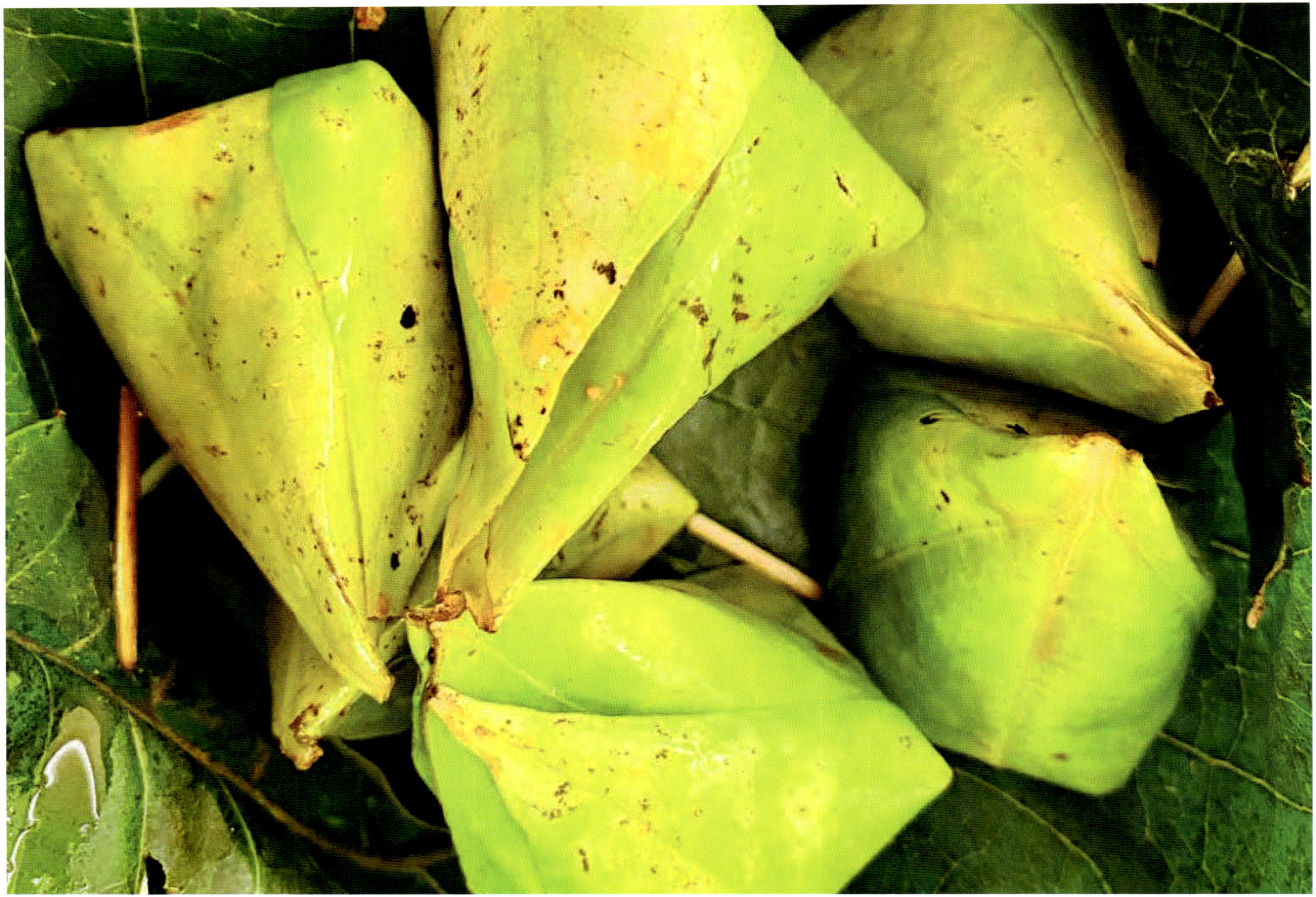

Benarasi pan and Bilva patra: One, a human delight, and the other, ambrosia, find a very special place in the ecosystem of the city. The Bilva is the favourite offering of Shiva.

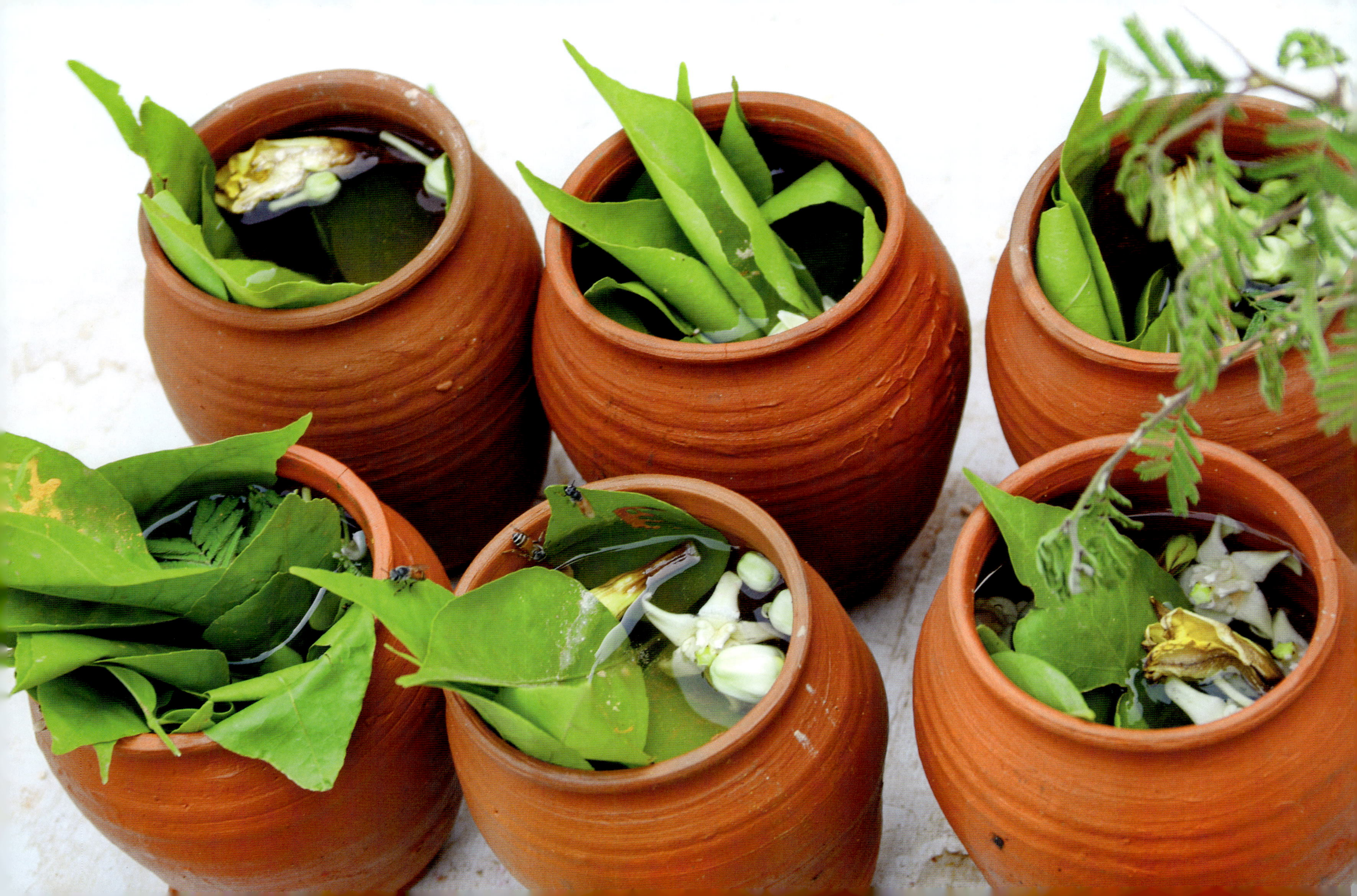

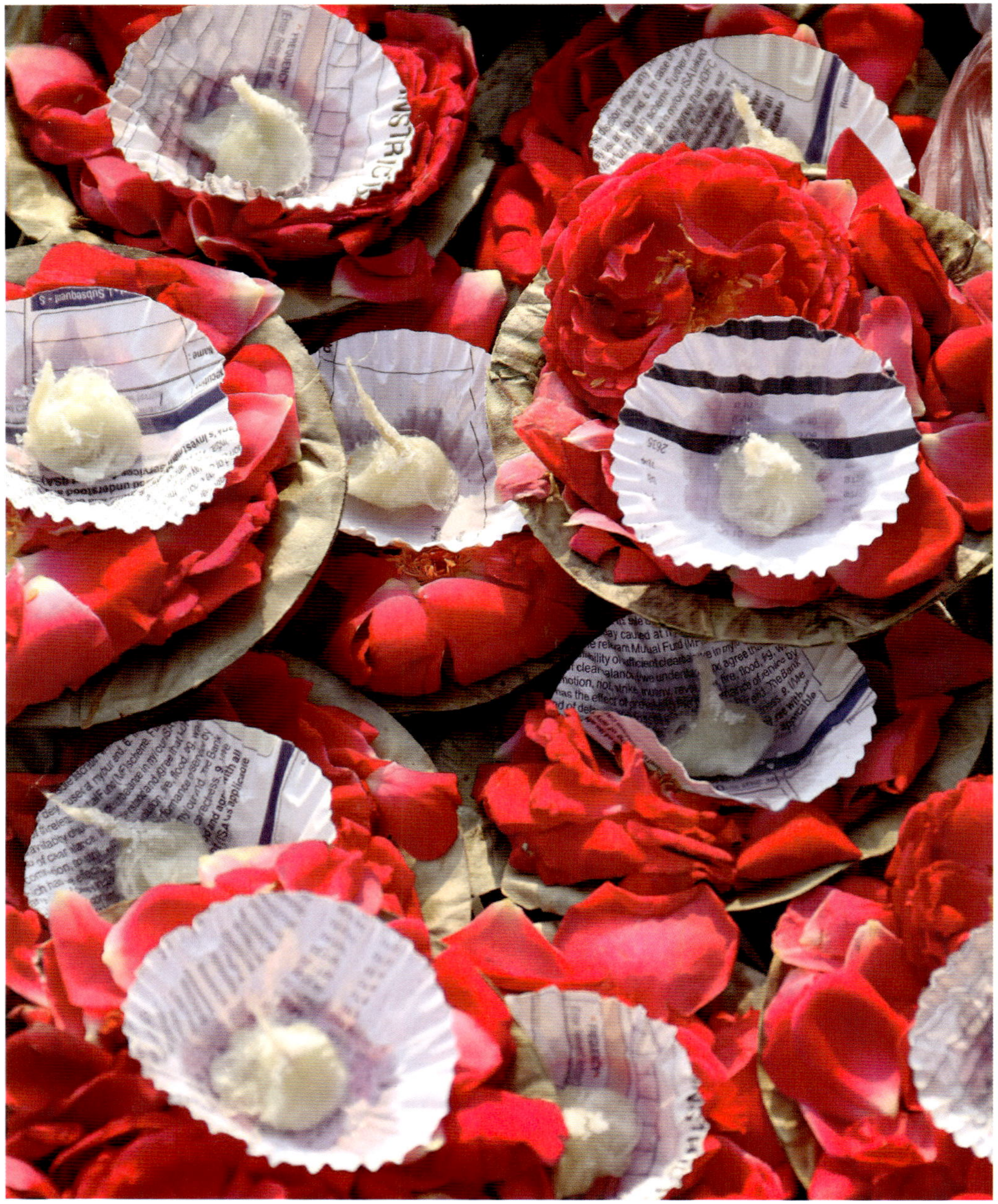

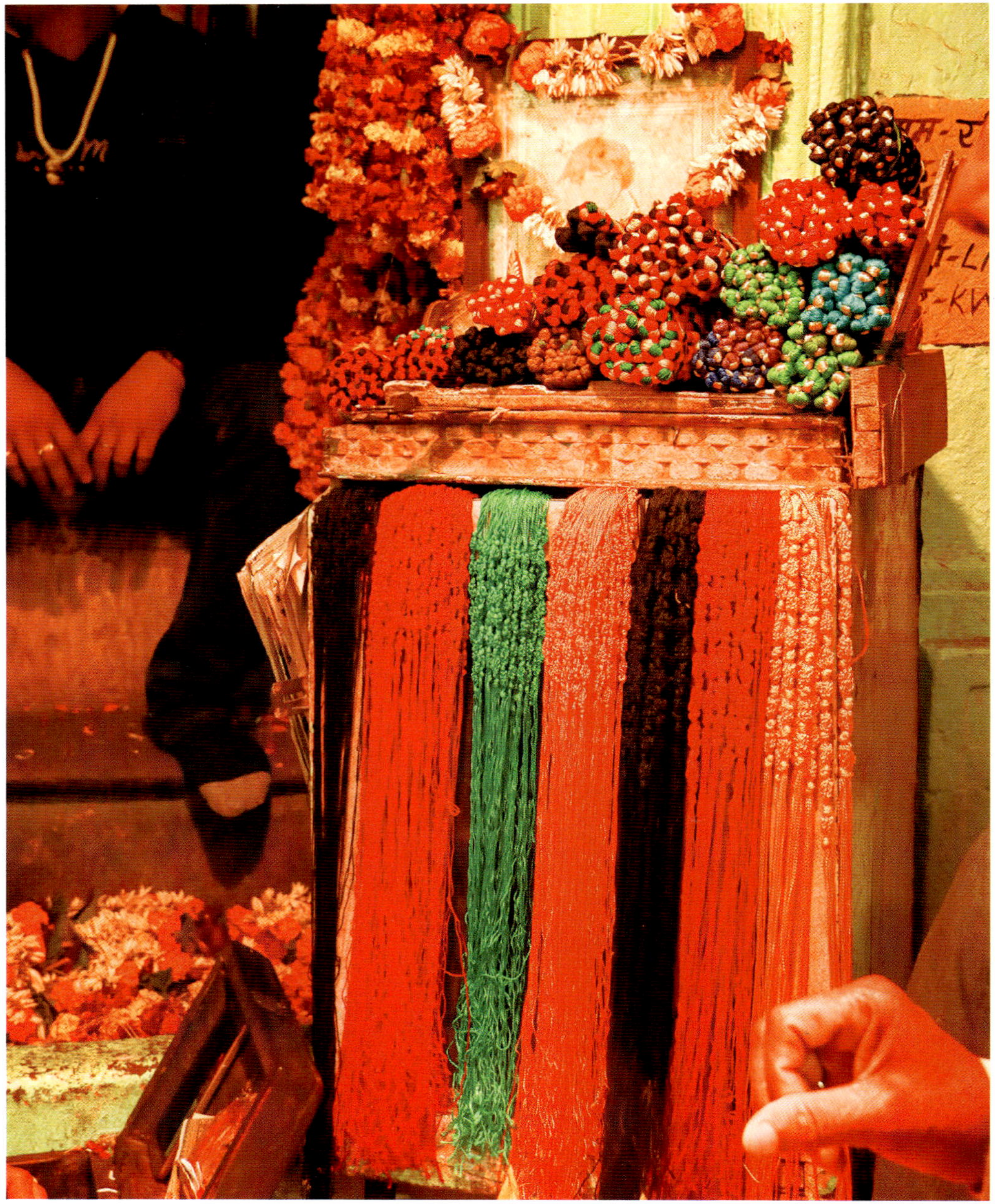

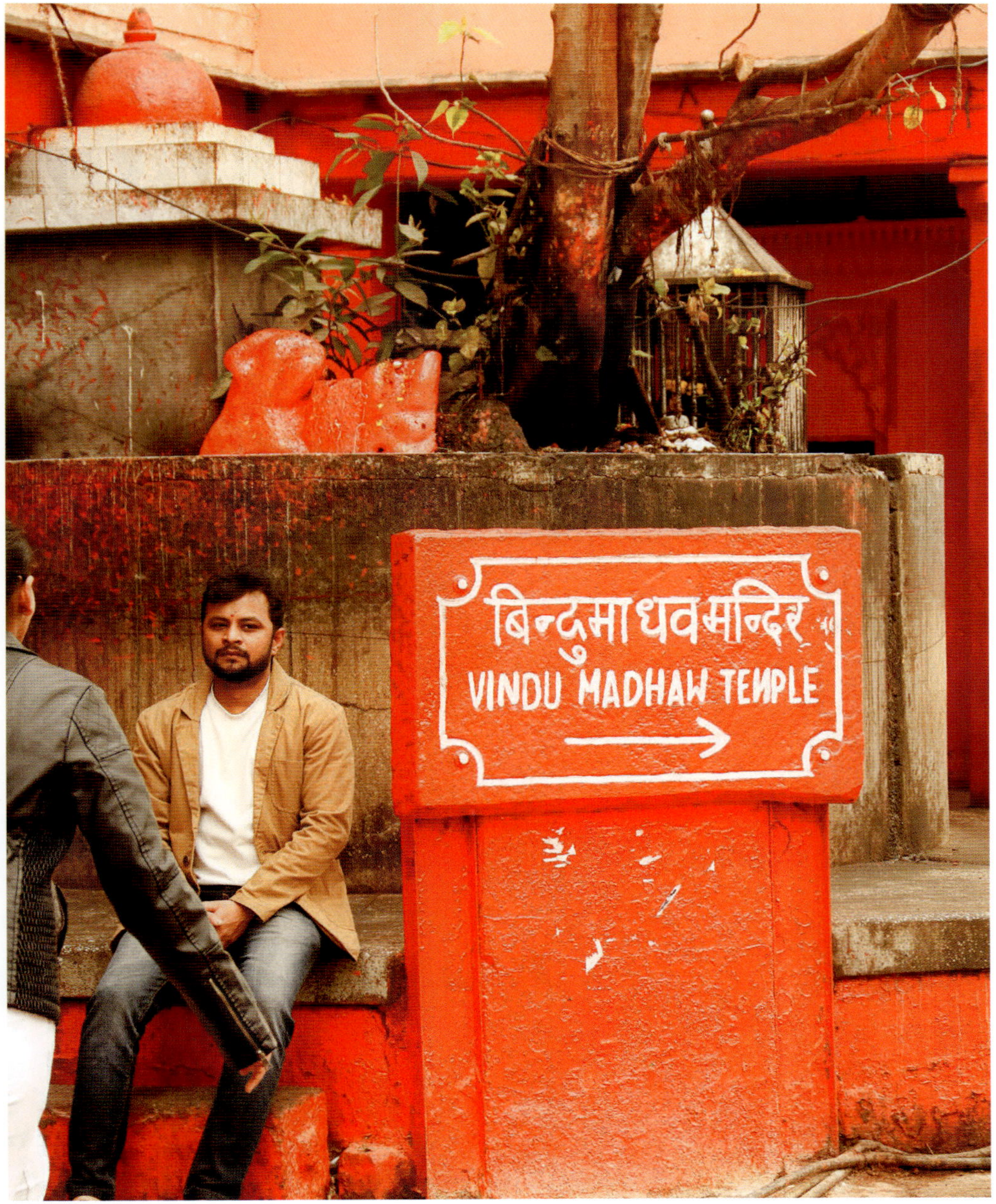
बिन्दुमाधवमन्दिर
VINDU MADHAW TEMPLE

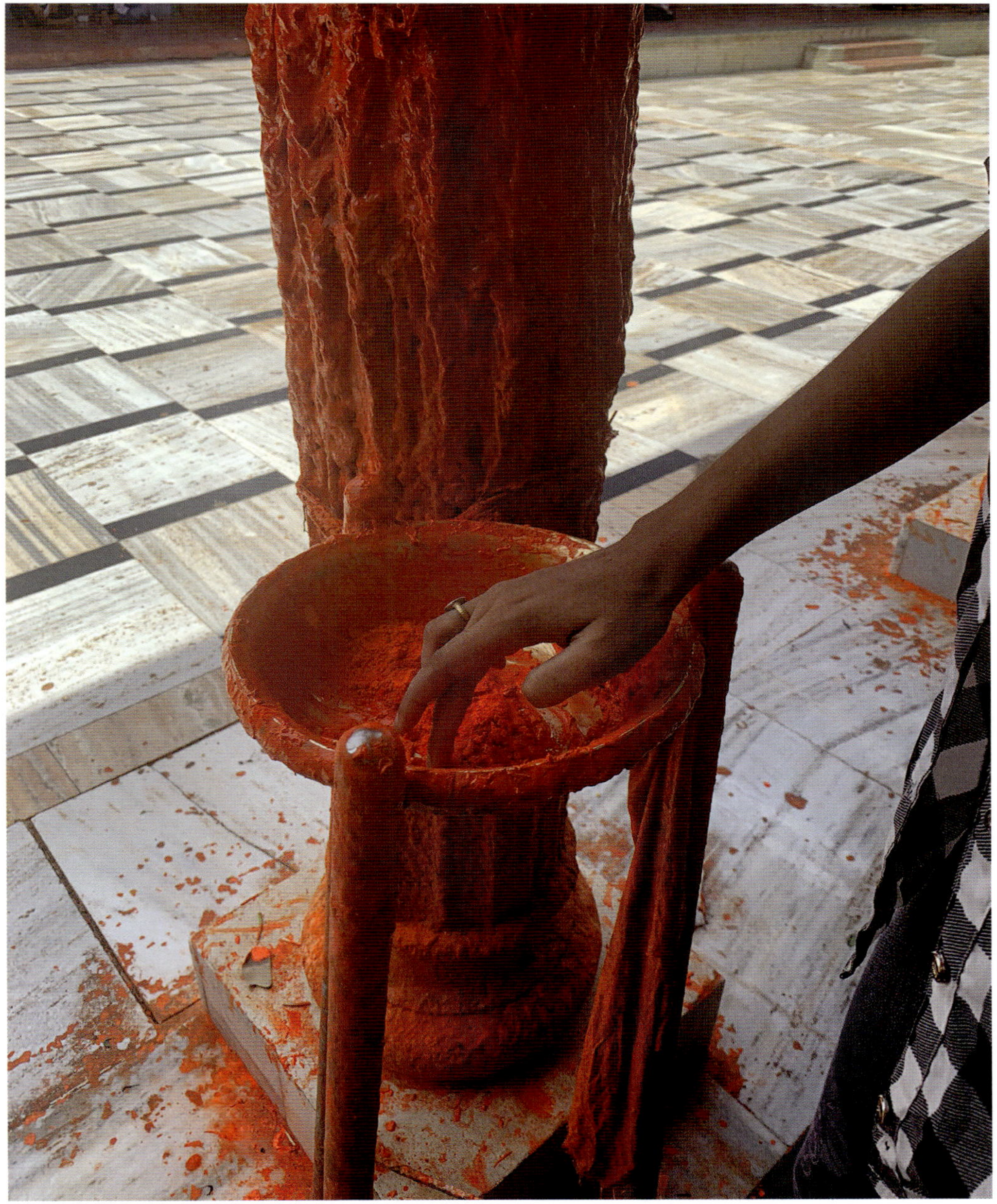

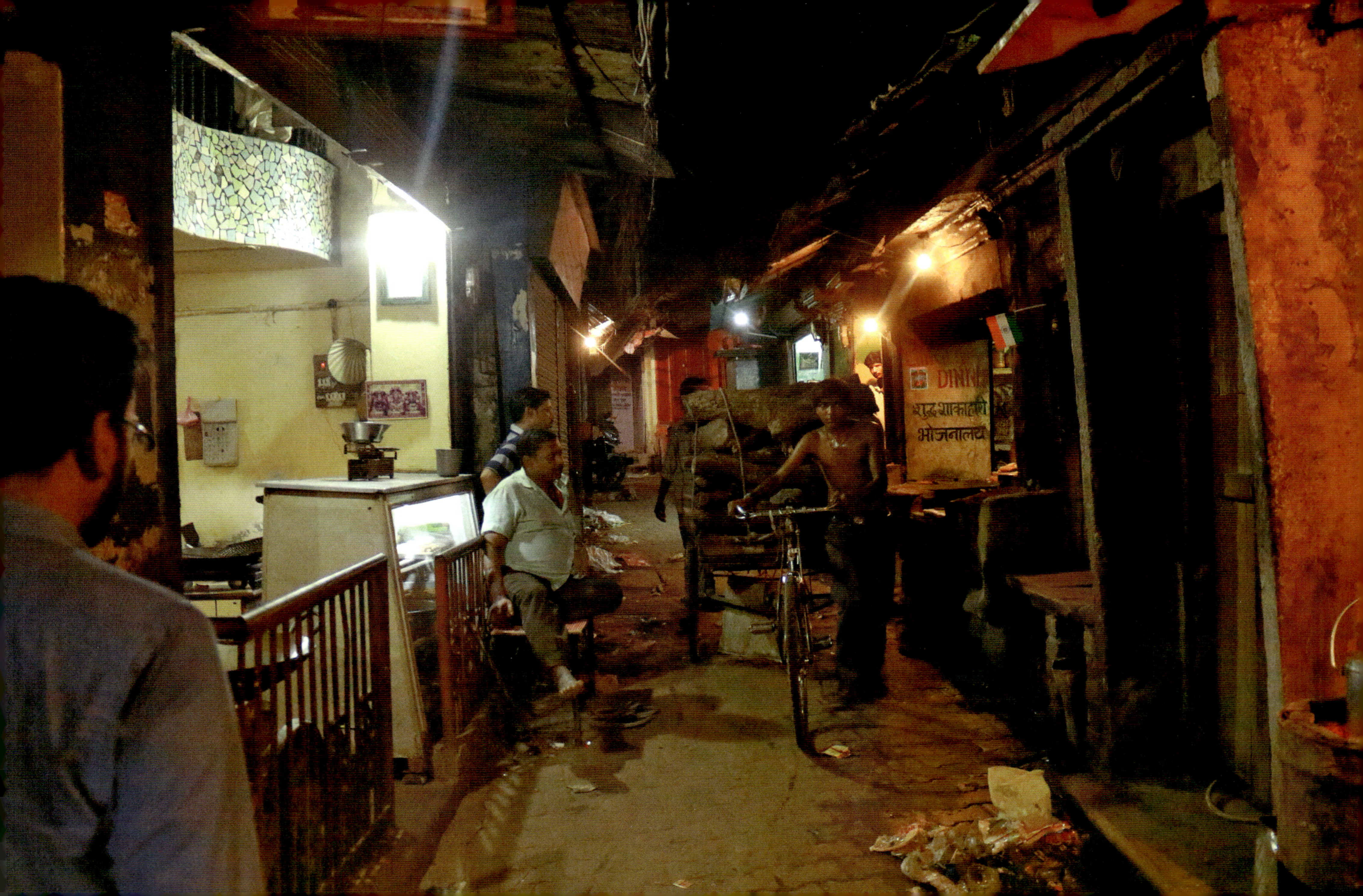
DINN
शुद्ध शाकाहारी
भोजनालय

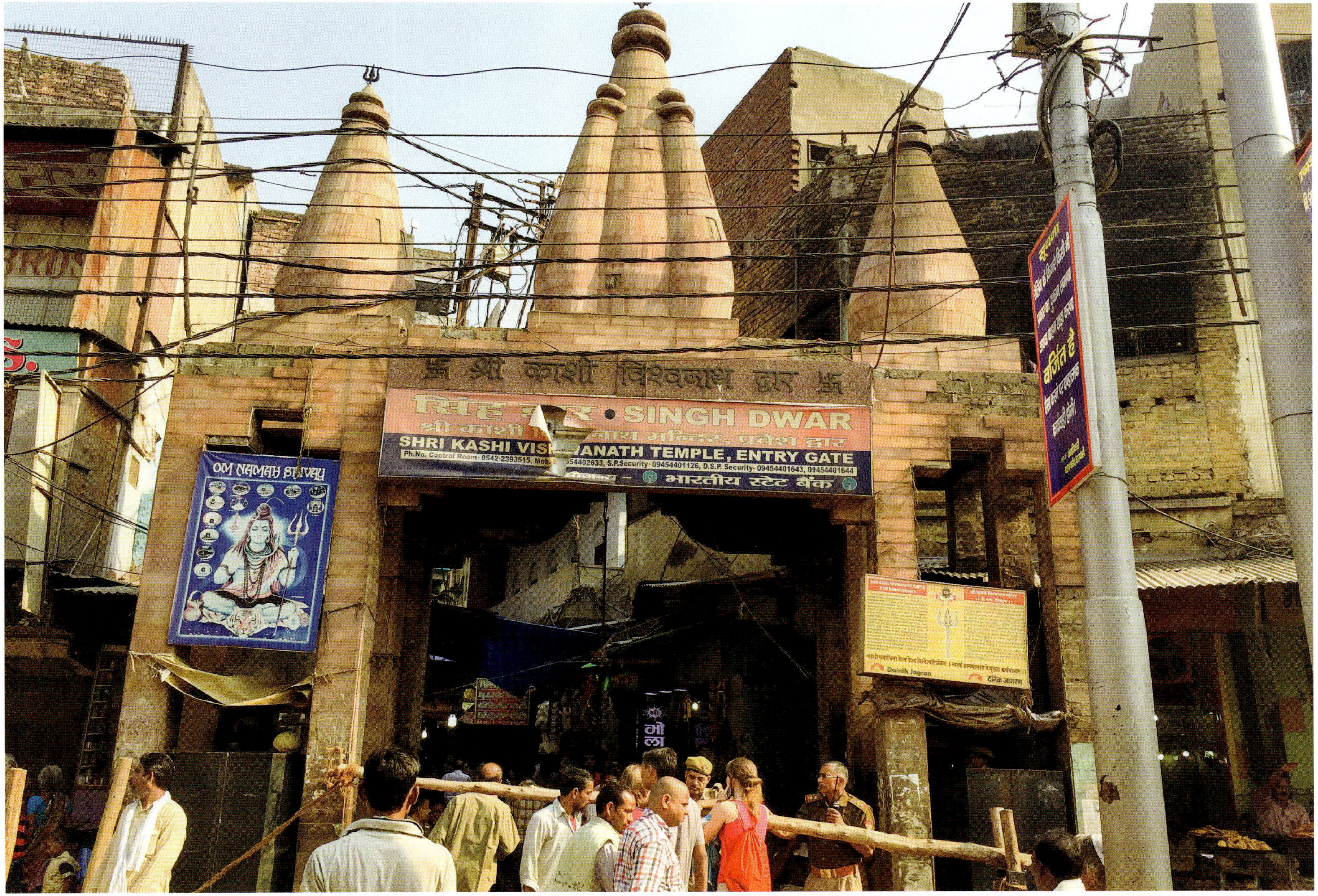


Mukti Bhawan: The stairway to heaven and freedom from the cycles of birth and death may be found here.

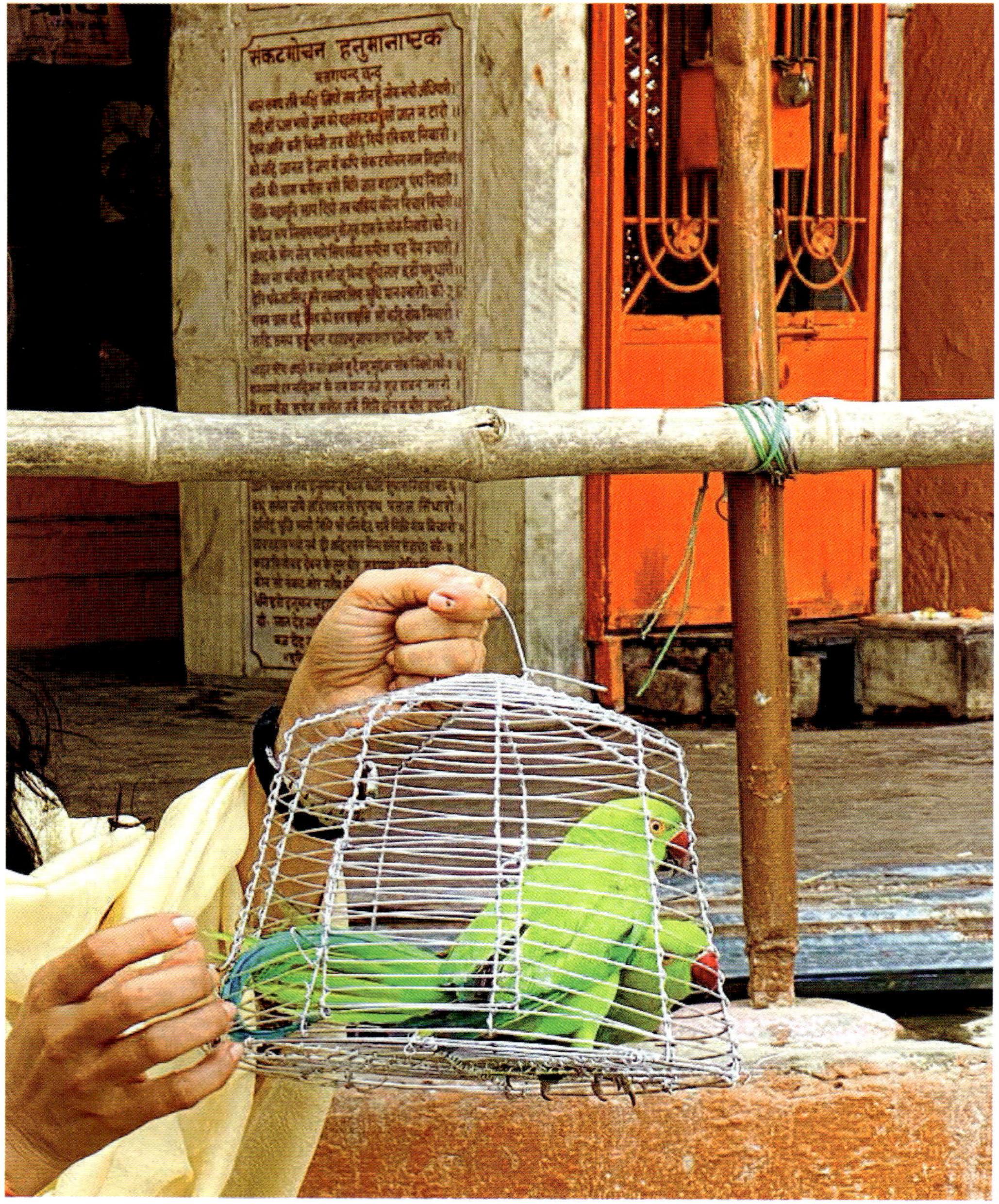
संकटमोचन हनुमानाष्टक

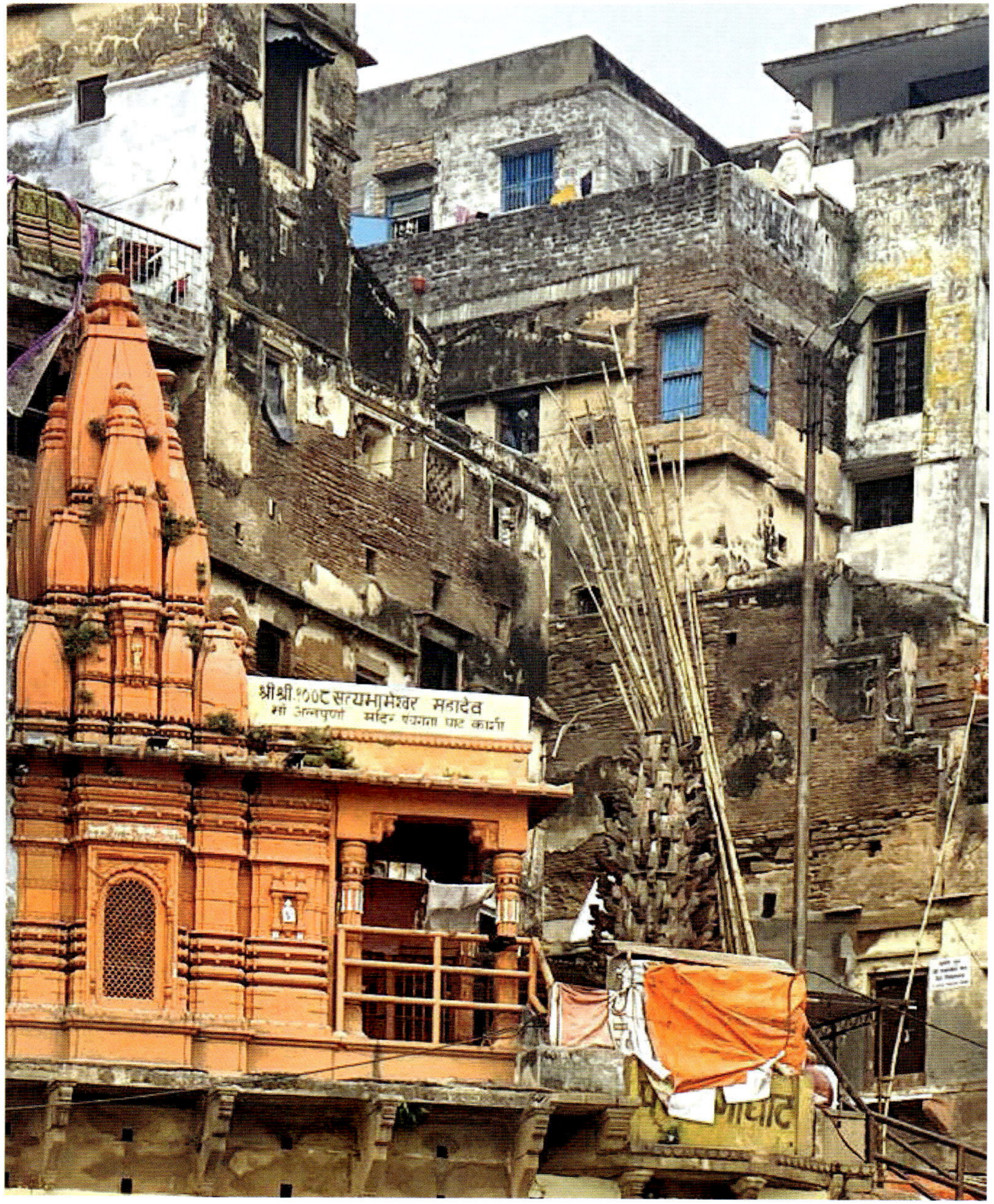
श्री श्री १००८ सत्यभामेश्वर महादेव

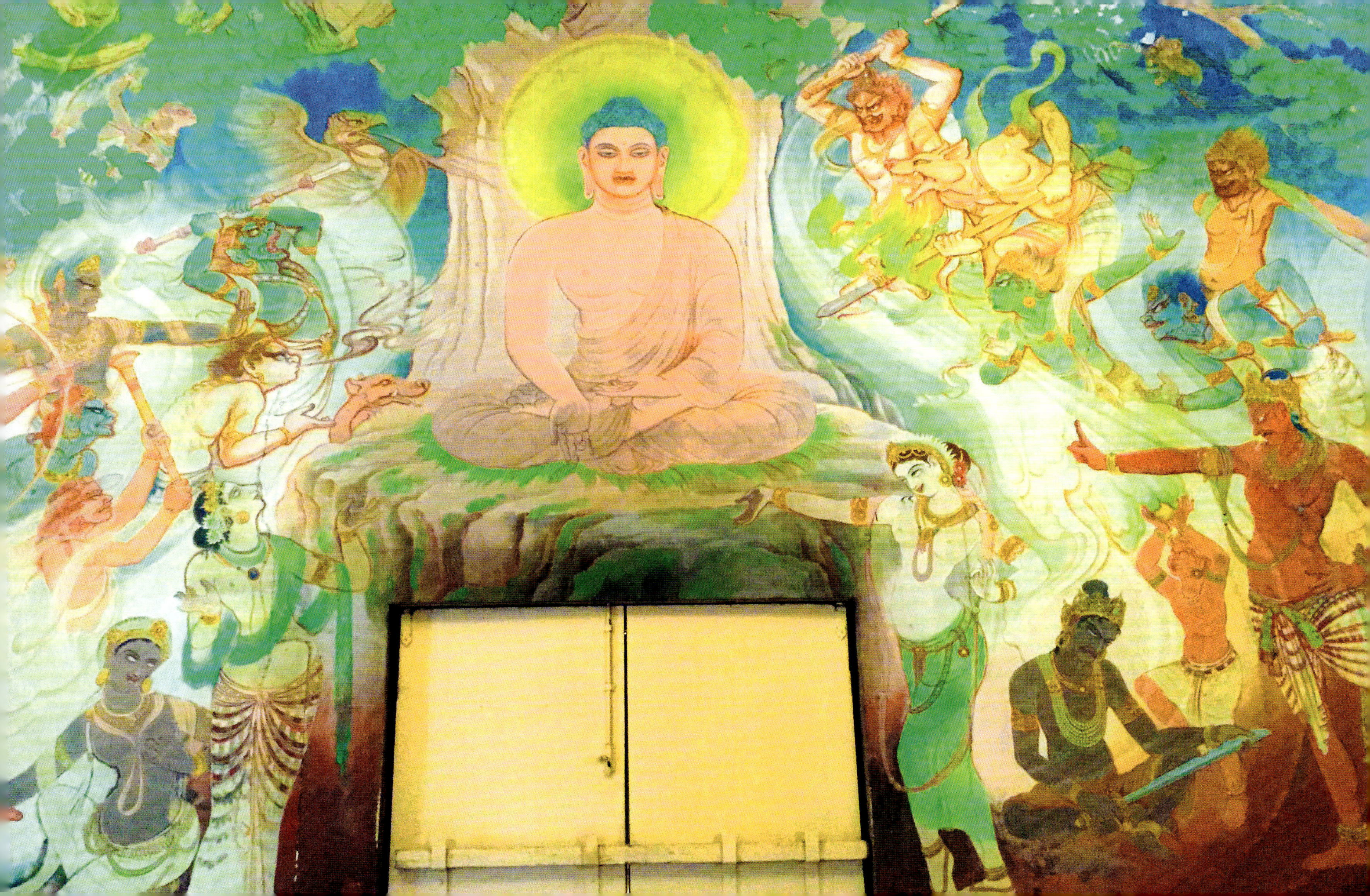

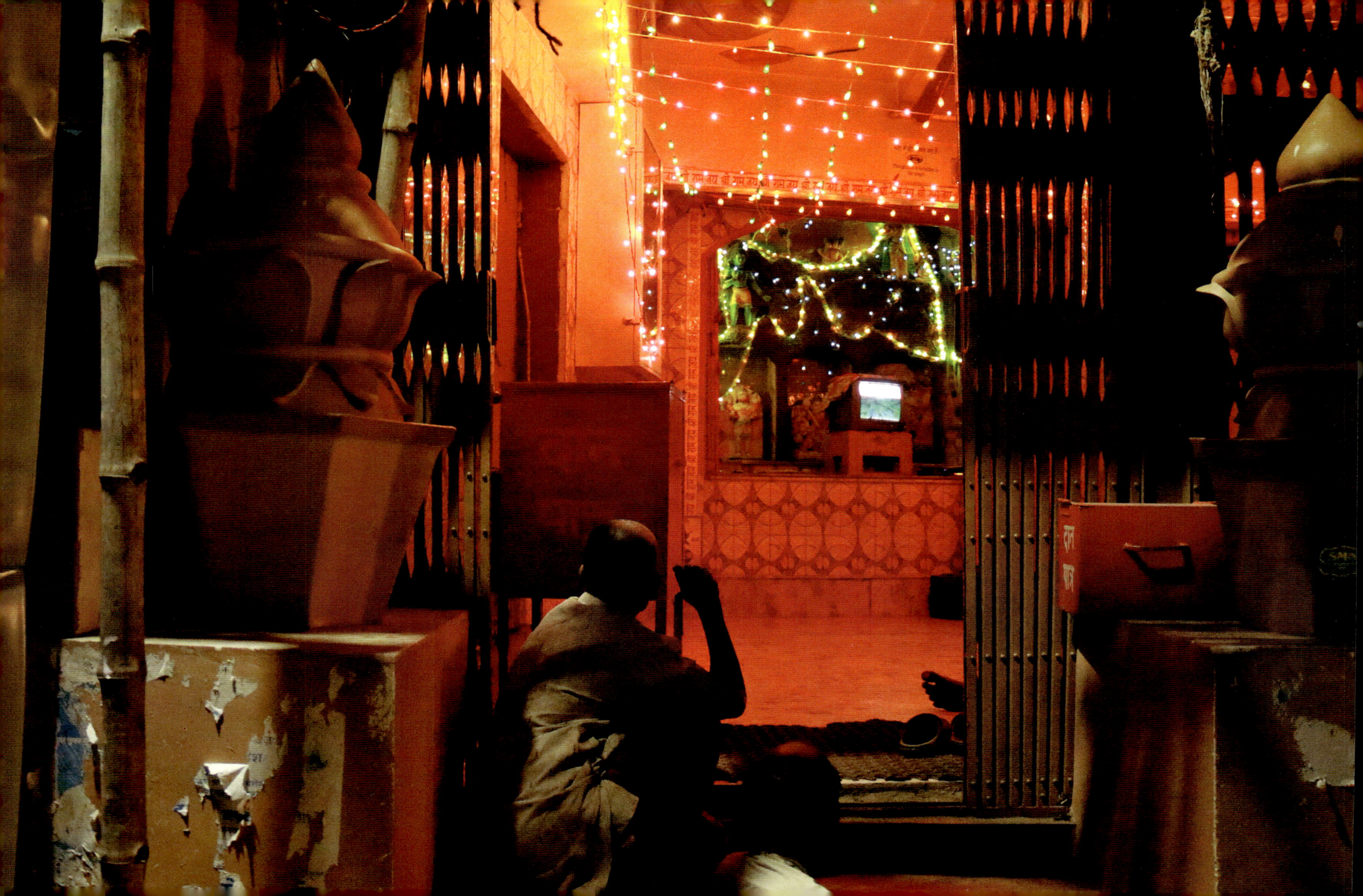

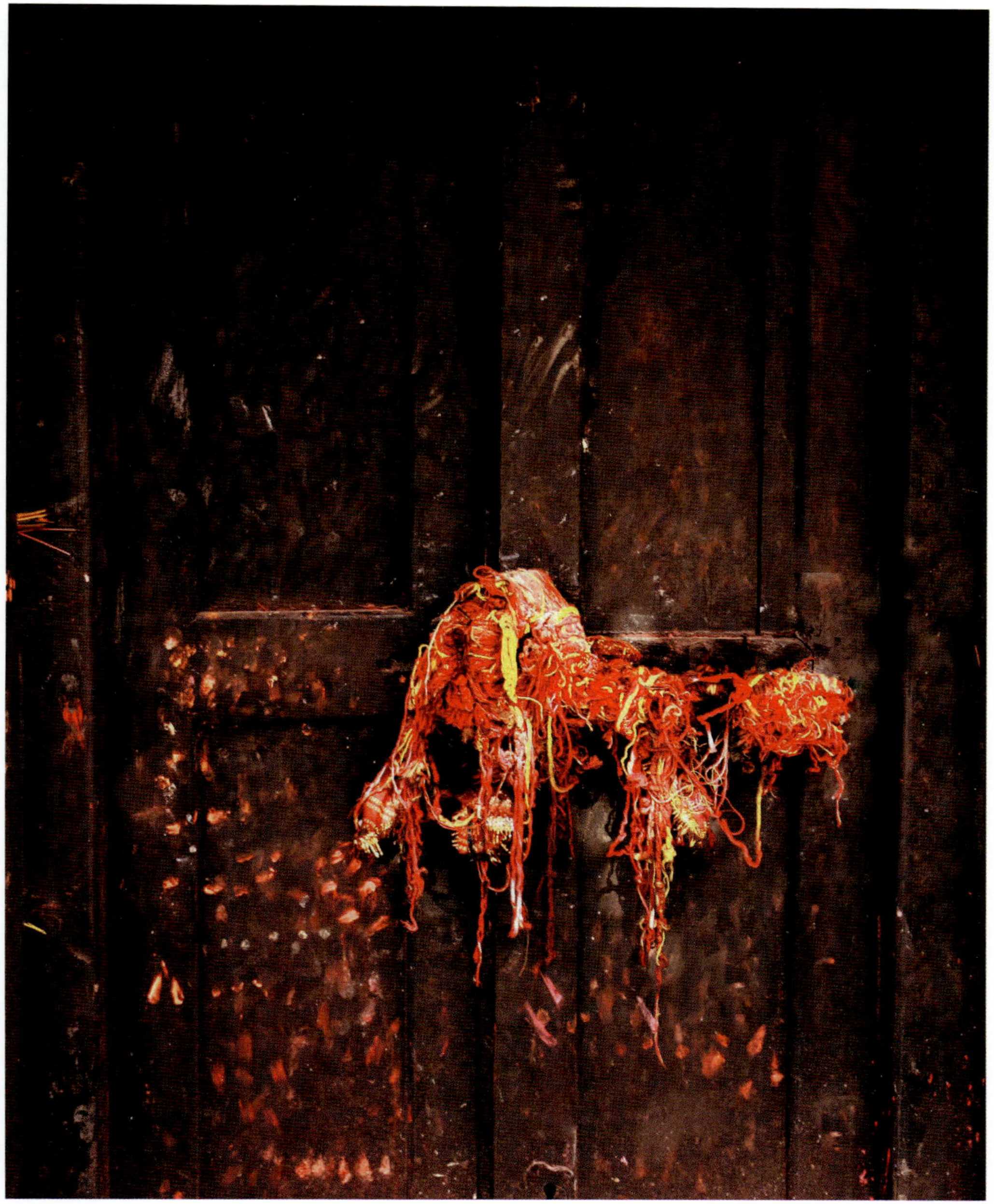

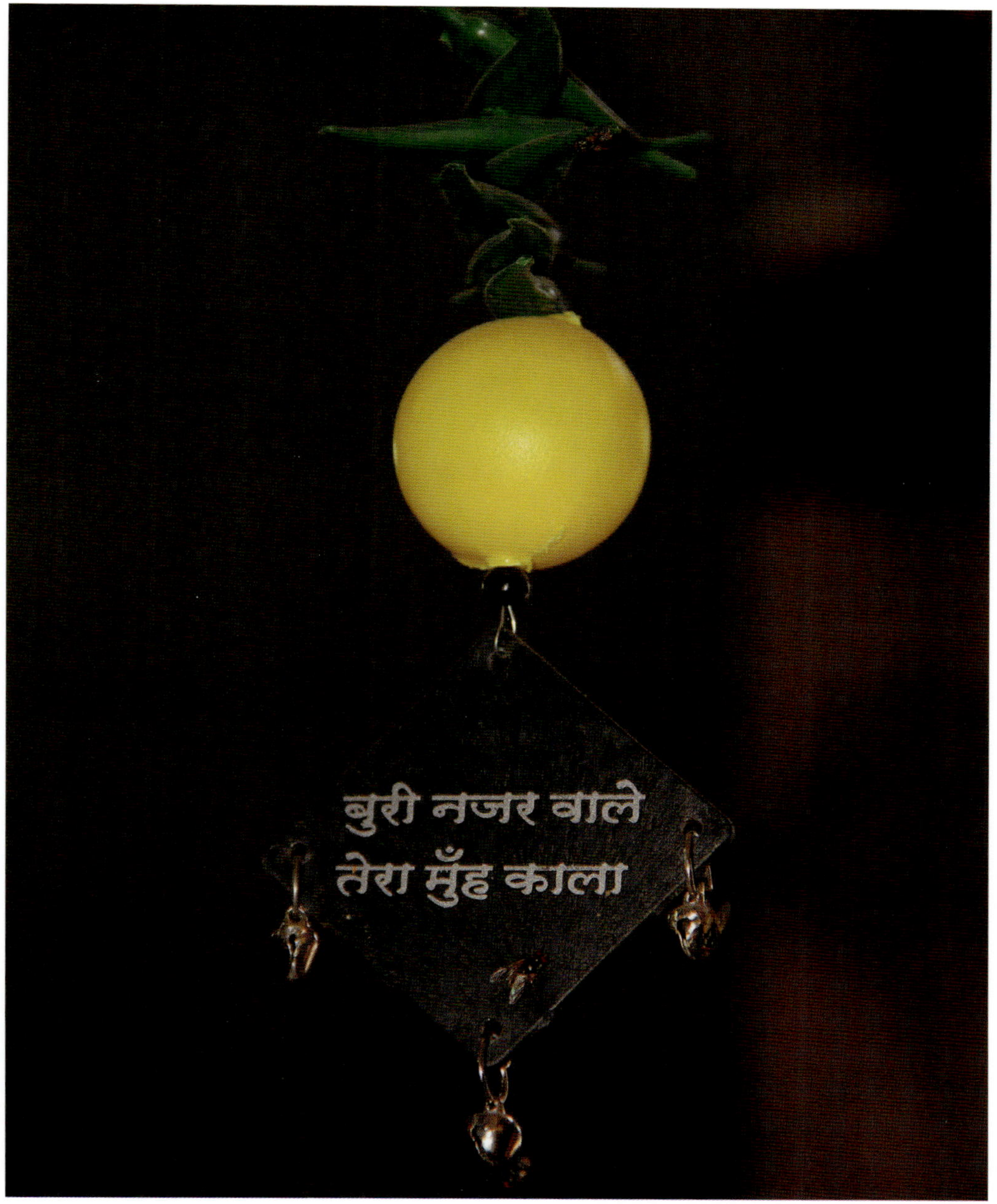
बुरी नजर वाले
तेरा मुँह काला

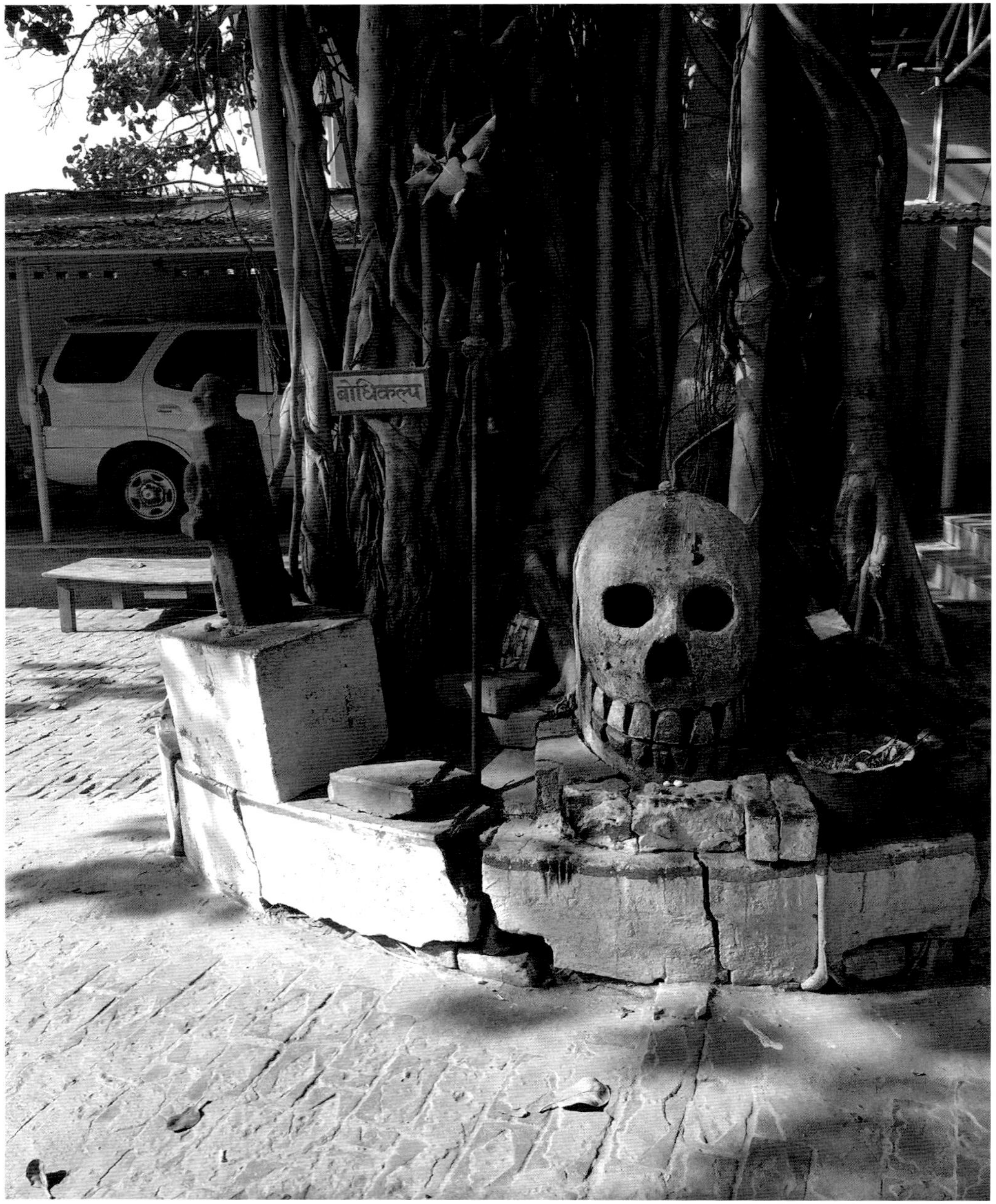
बोधिकल्प

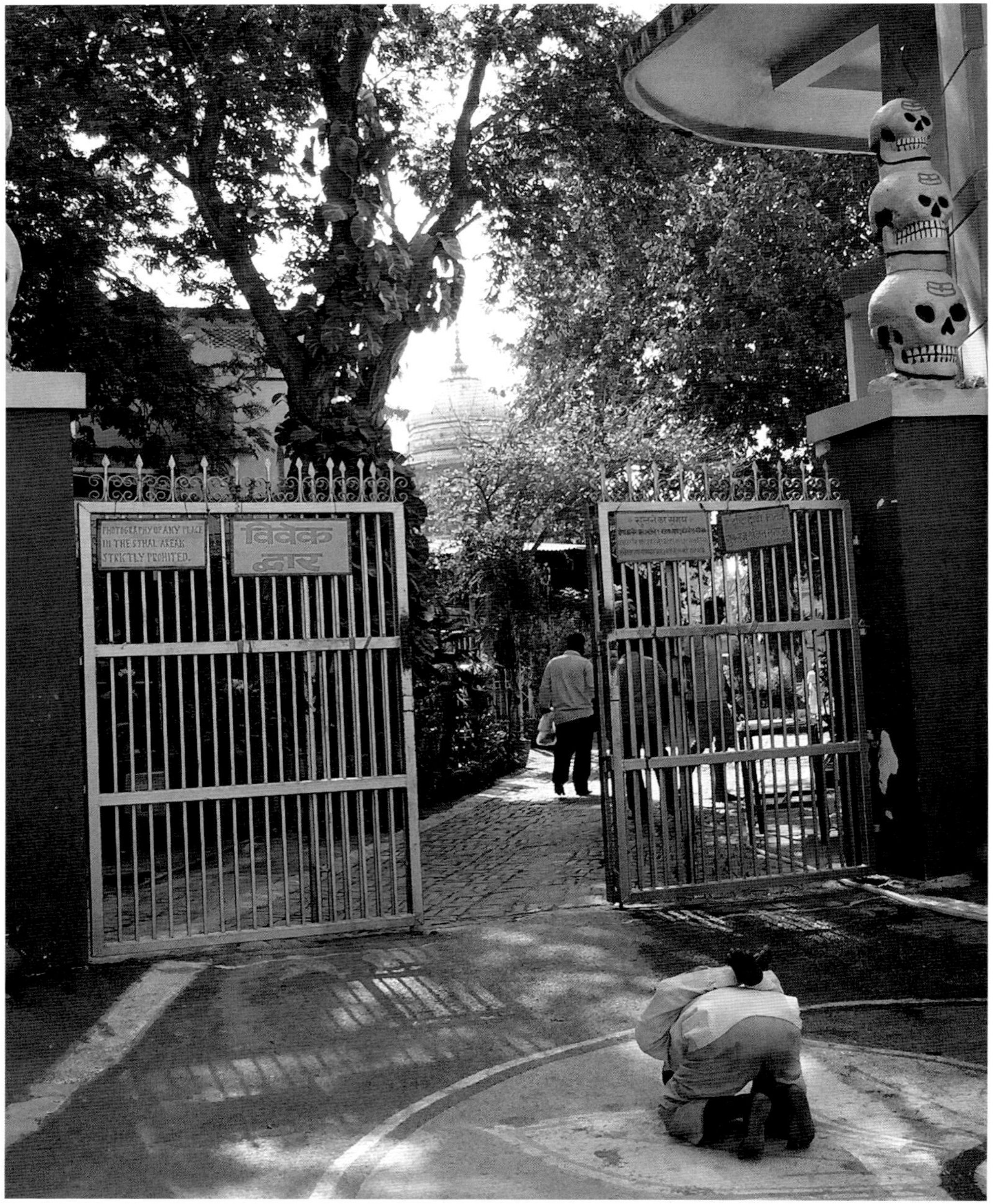
PHOTOGRAPHY OF ANY PLACE
IN THE STHAL AREAS
STRICTLY PROHITED.
विवेक
द्वार

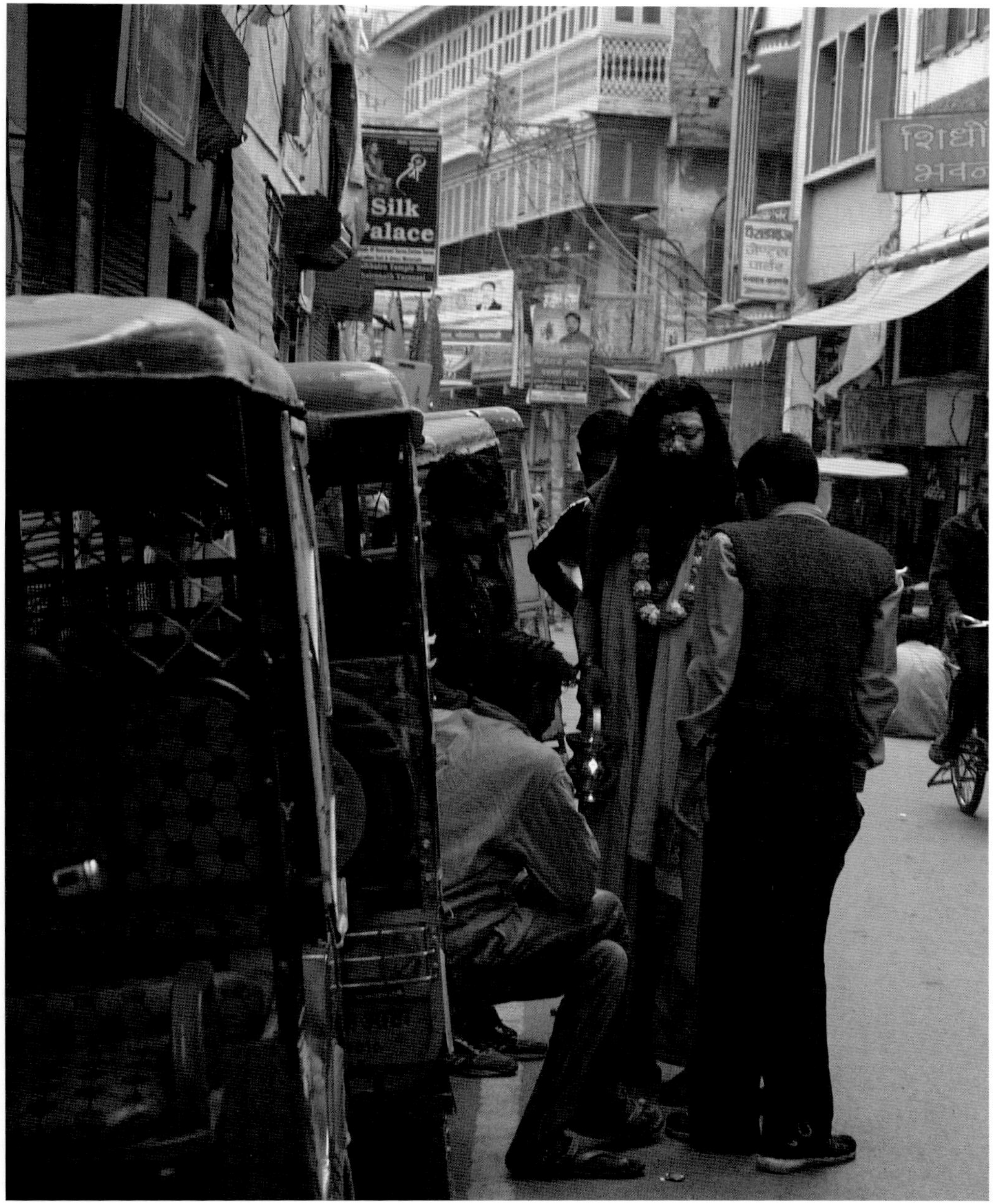
Silk
Palace

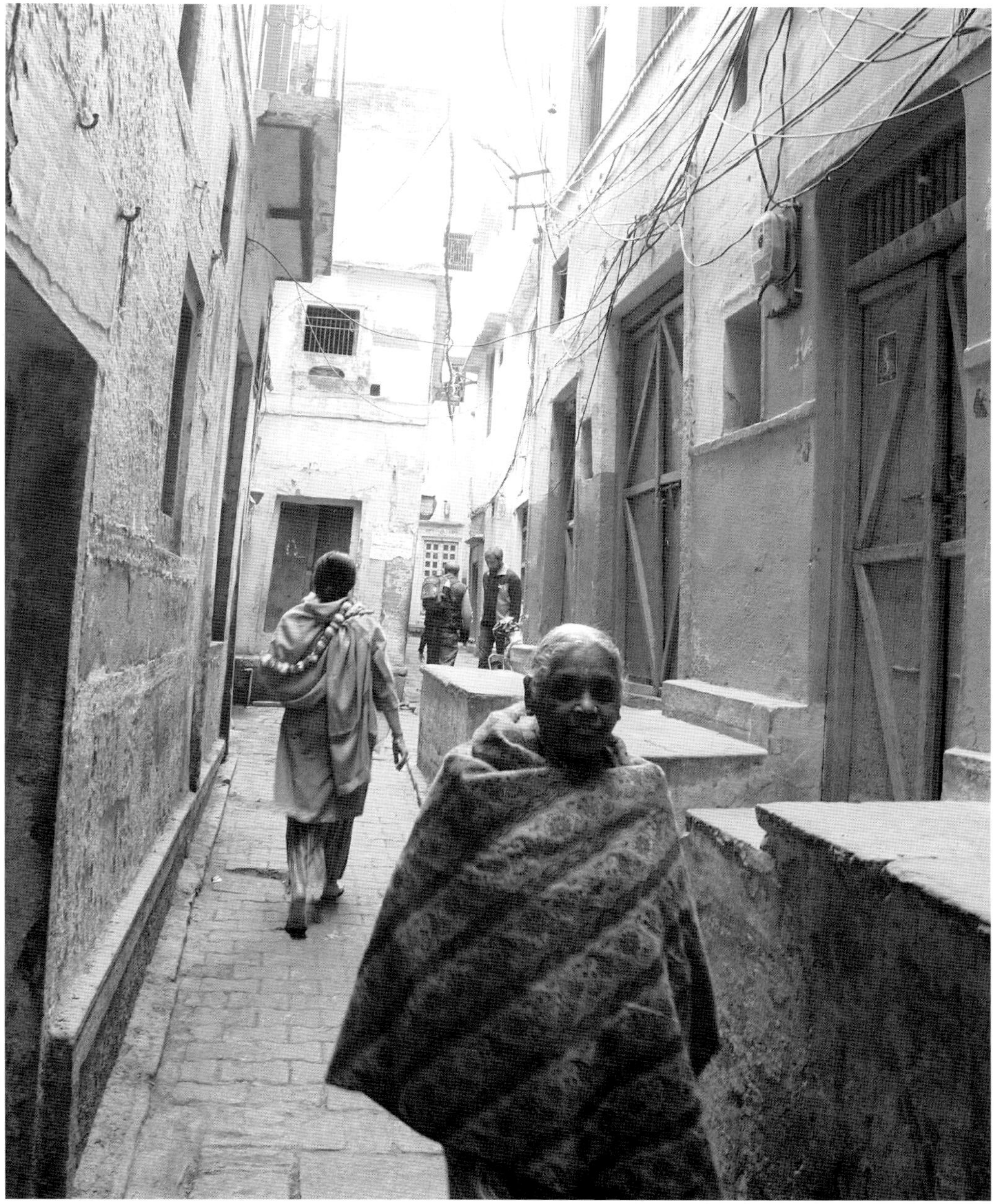

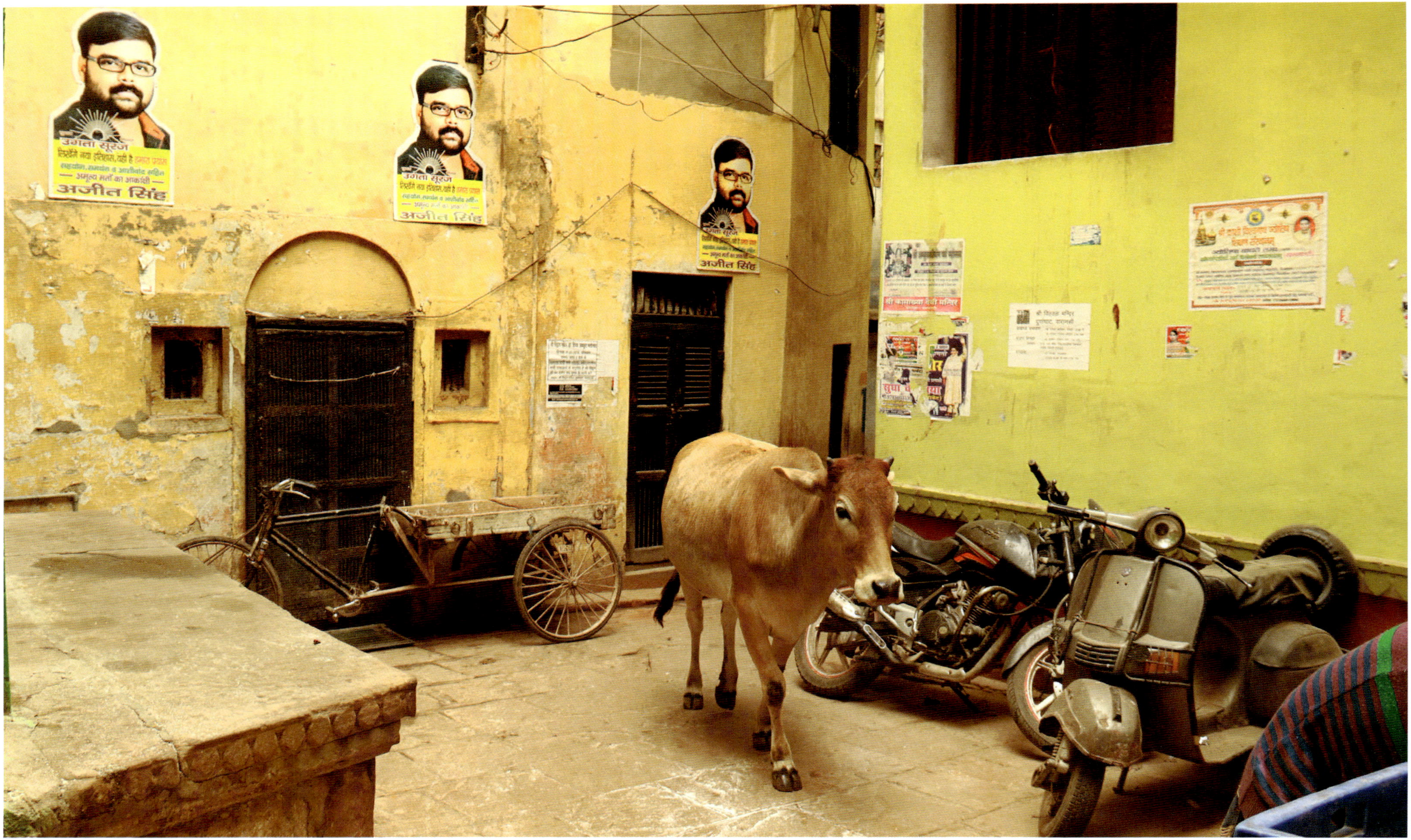
उगता सूरज
अजीत सिंह

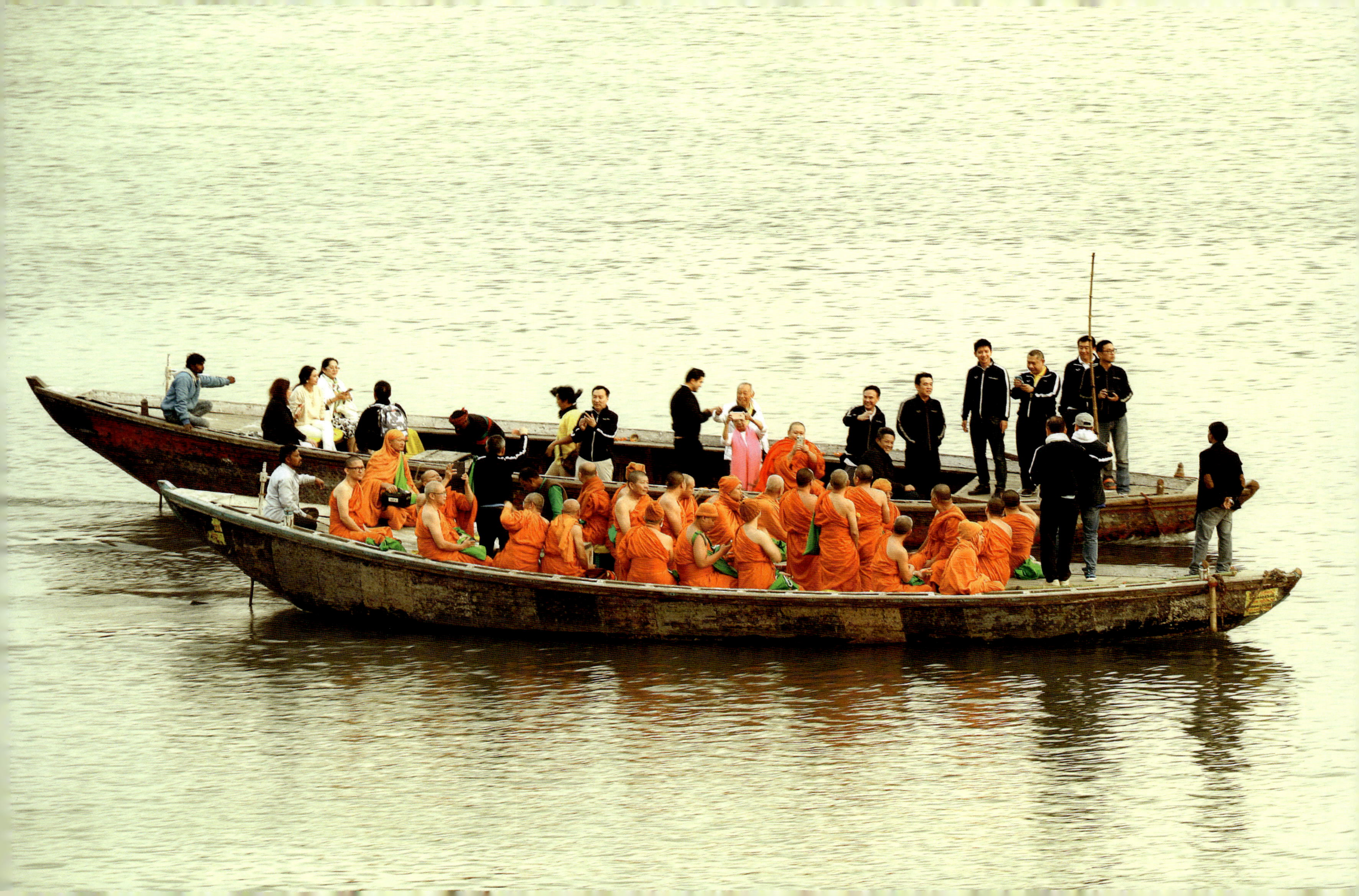

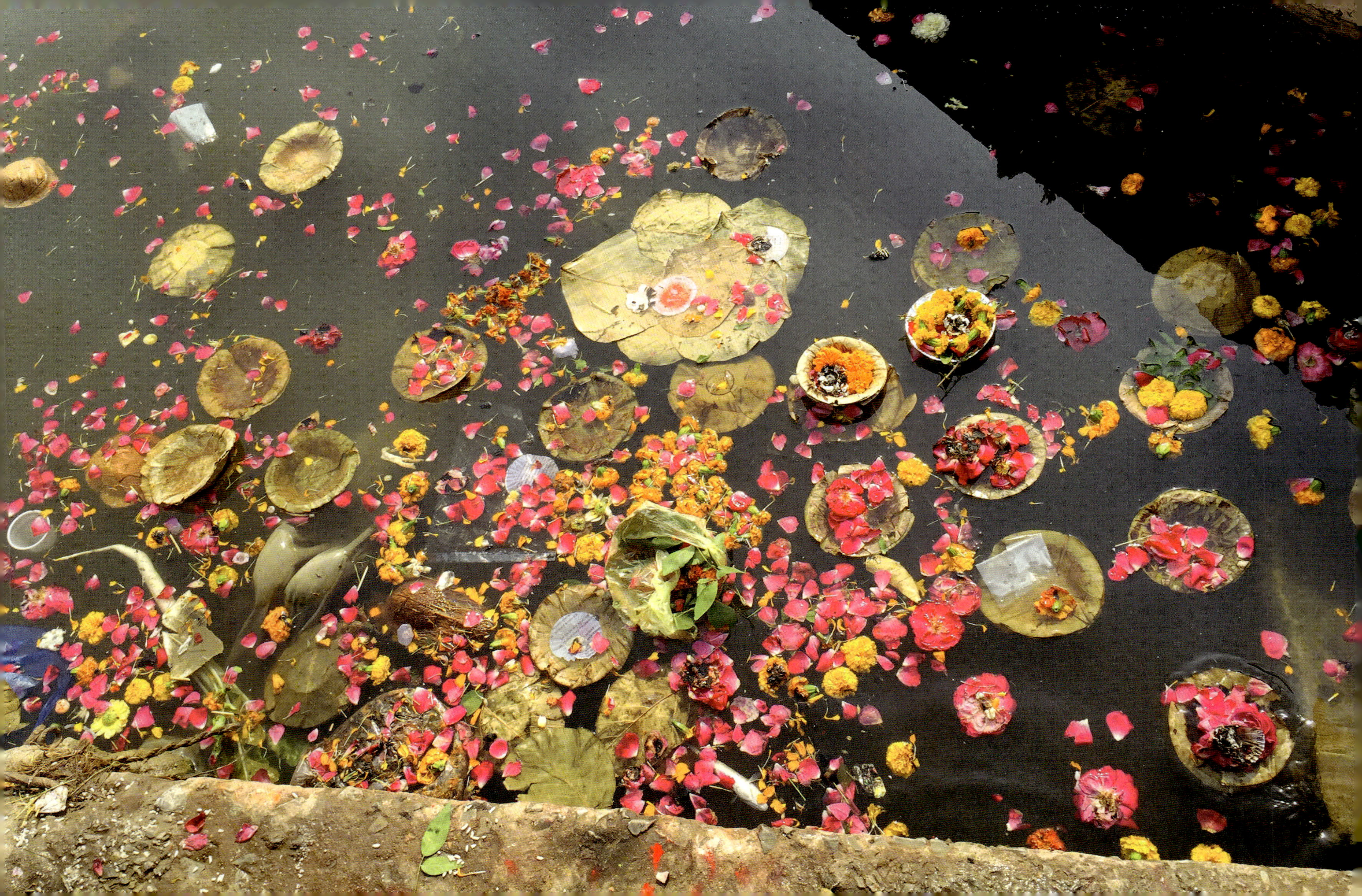

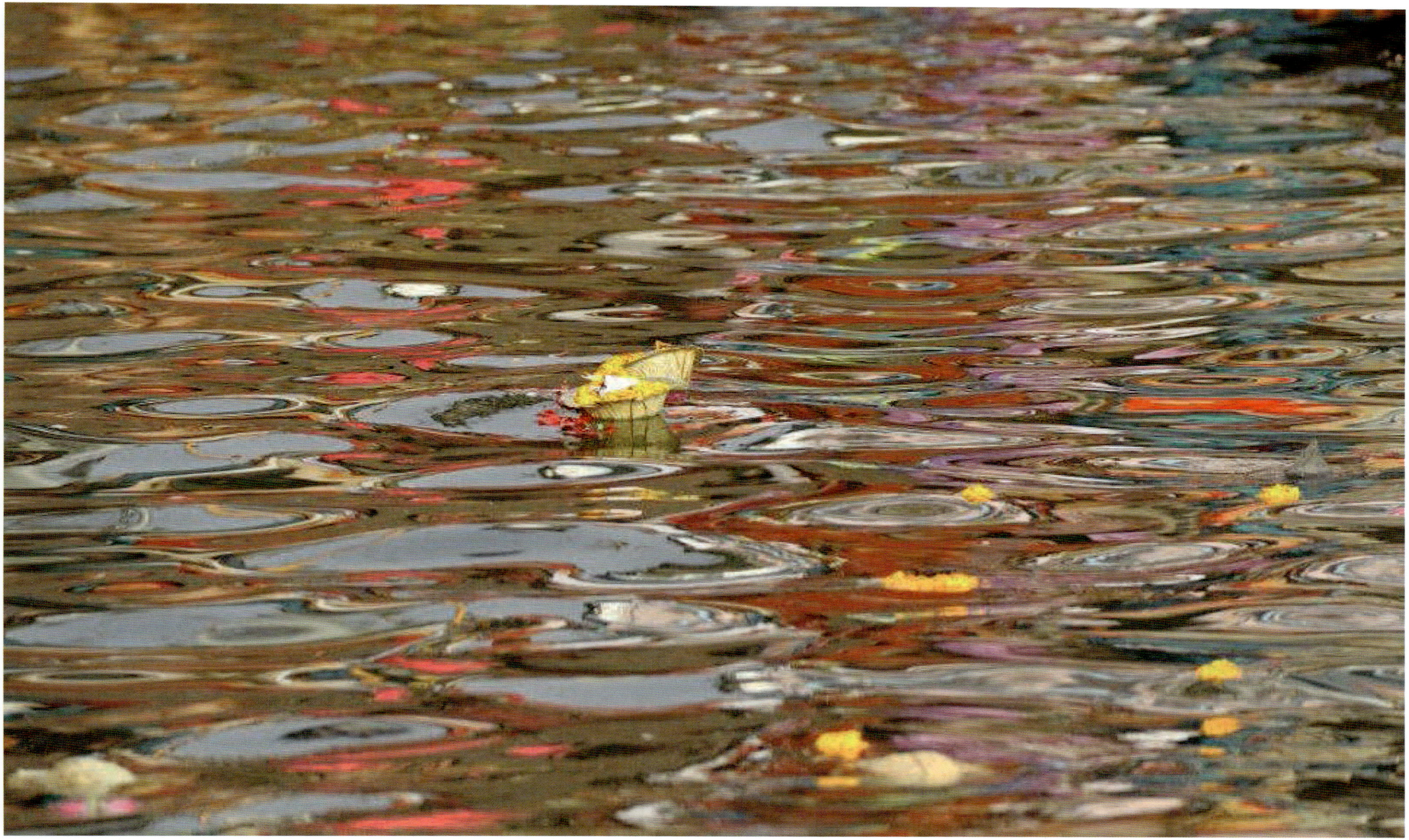

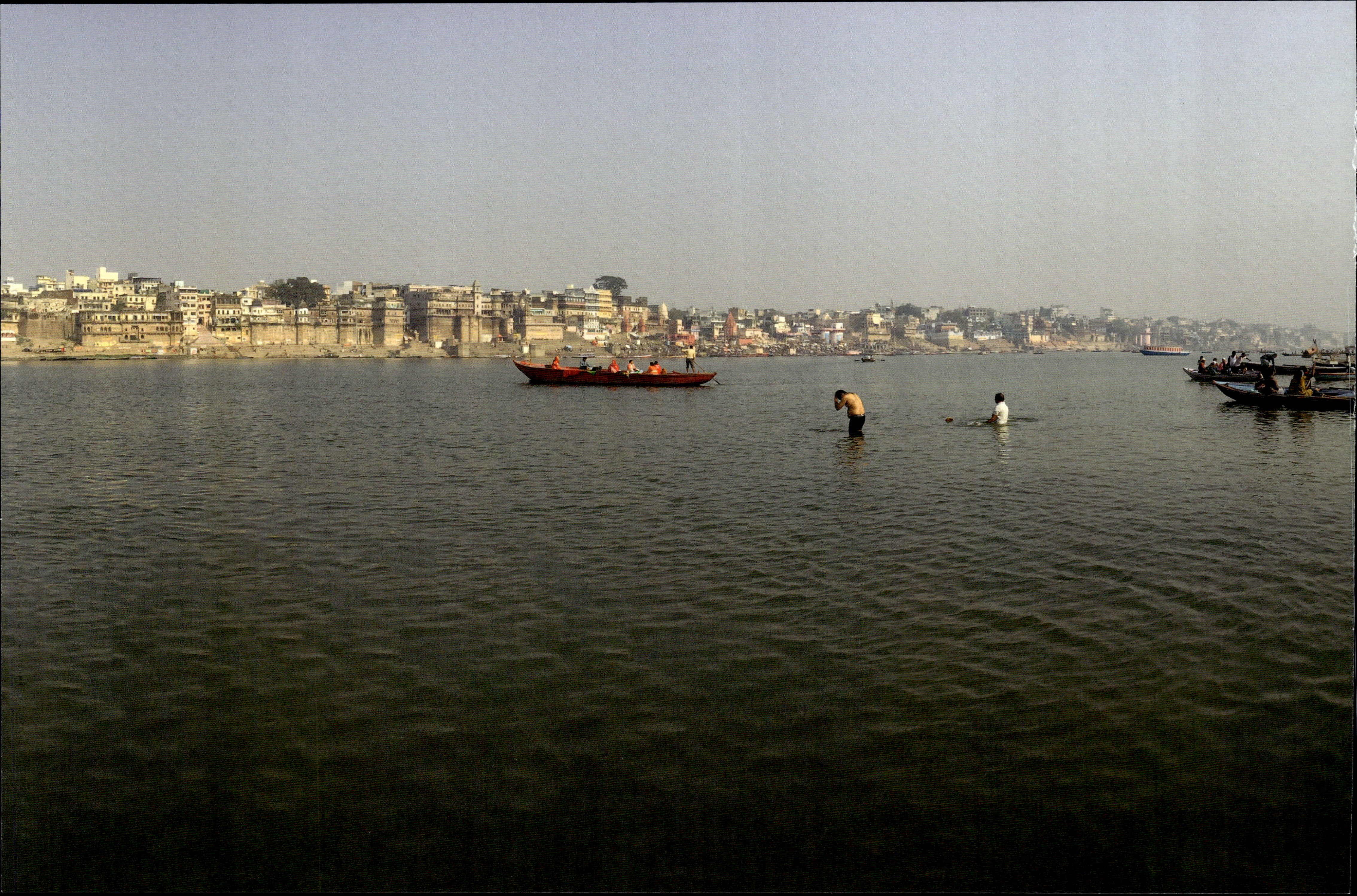

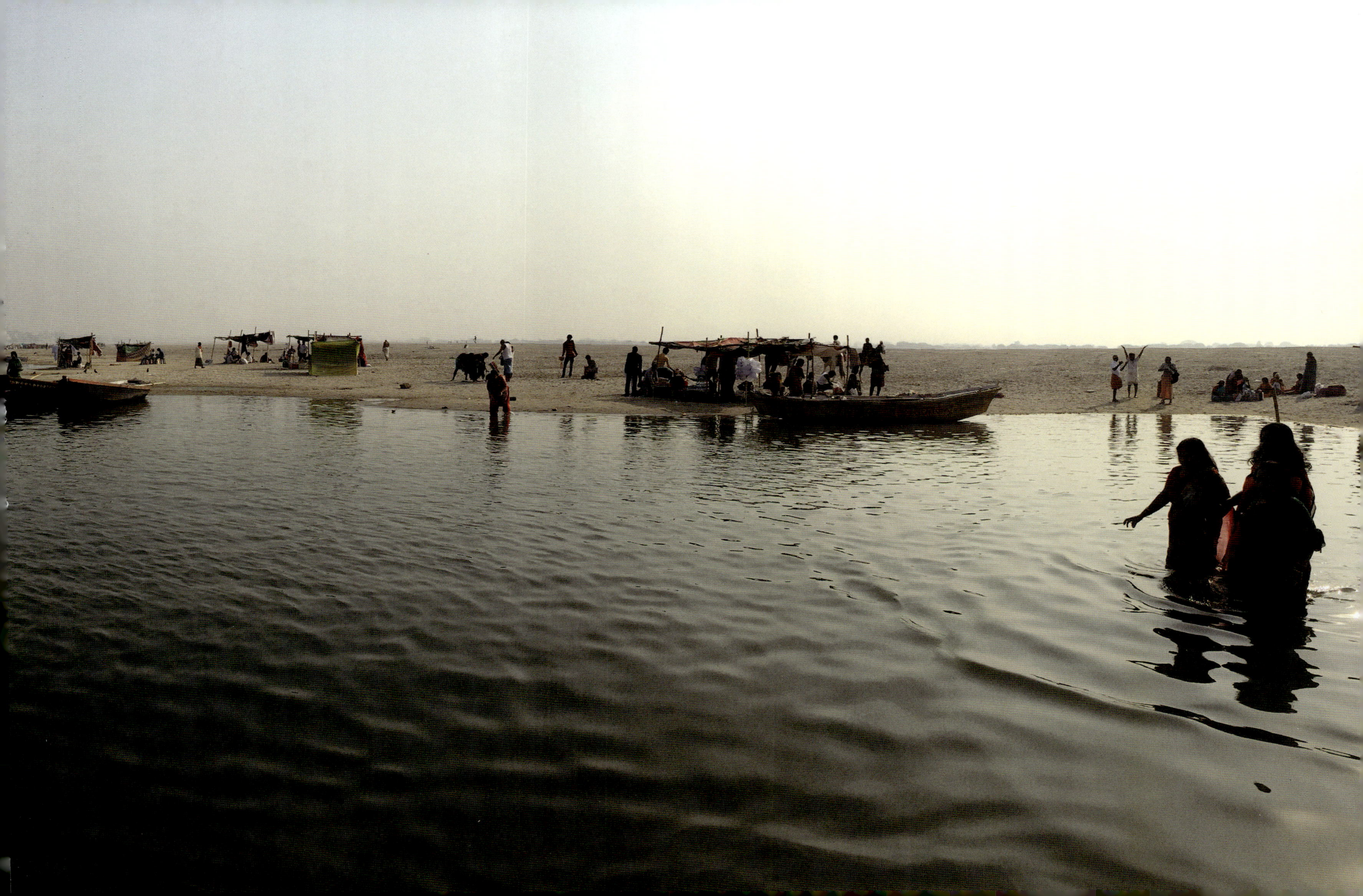

# BEWITCHING BENARAS

Sadhus sit in a deep trance, their eyes glancing inward,
Mahadev lodged in their organs.
A woman stands drenched to the bone, feverishly offering the
glittering Ganga to the skies in cupped hands, bartering with God.
Ashes fly about as death breathes from dark secret corners.

Tea vendors beckon eclectic visitors, monkeys swing from street to shoulders,
children hop and skip merrily dissolved in a cacophony of loud laughter.
Women throng tiny narrow lanes purchasing materialism.

The golden hour comes and life's lotus embraces sunlight,
flowering into the joy of beauteous splendour.
Twinkling diyas embellish the ebony dancing waters at dusk.
The Dance of Life comes a full cycle and gears for a new dawn.

No matter where you're headed, you will leave a piece of your soul behind in Benaras.
You can go away from here but you will always carry a piece of Benaras in your heart!

# ABOUT THE AUTHOR

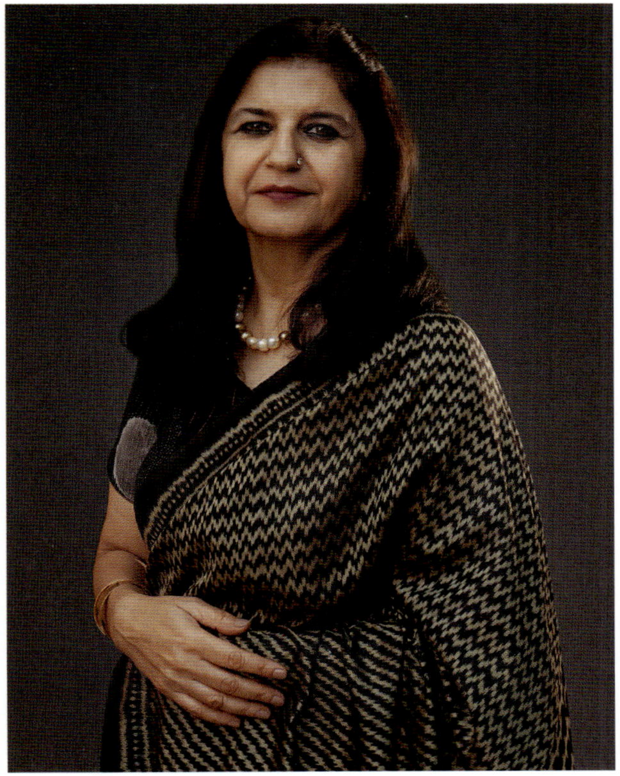

**RITU JHINGON** graduated with a BCom (Hons) degree from Shri Ram College of Commerce, University of Delhi, and holds an MBA in marketing. She has worked extensively in the areas of corporate communications and corporate social responsibility (CSR). Over the last decade, she has been focusing on social-impact projects related to women and children and has delivered numerous projects that have led many communities towards sustainable growth. Her work has been recognized globally and she has been honoured as one of the top 50 CSR professionals in the world. She has also been an active sportsperson and has received many state and national awards for her participation in aquatics.

Ritu has never been particularly religious. Her association with places of worship and temples began as a way of personal reflection. She believes that the act of photography is essentially a cry against our own mortality—with every image we capture, we hope to freeze time and immortalize ourselves. She feels that photography is the alchemy through which mundane things can be magically transformed into something incredible.

She lives in New Delhi with her doctor son, Samay.

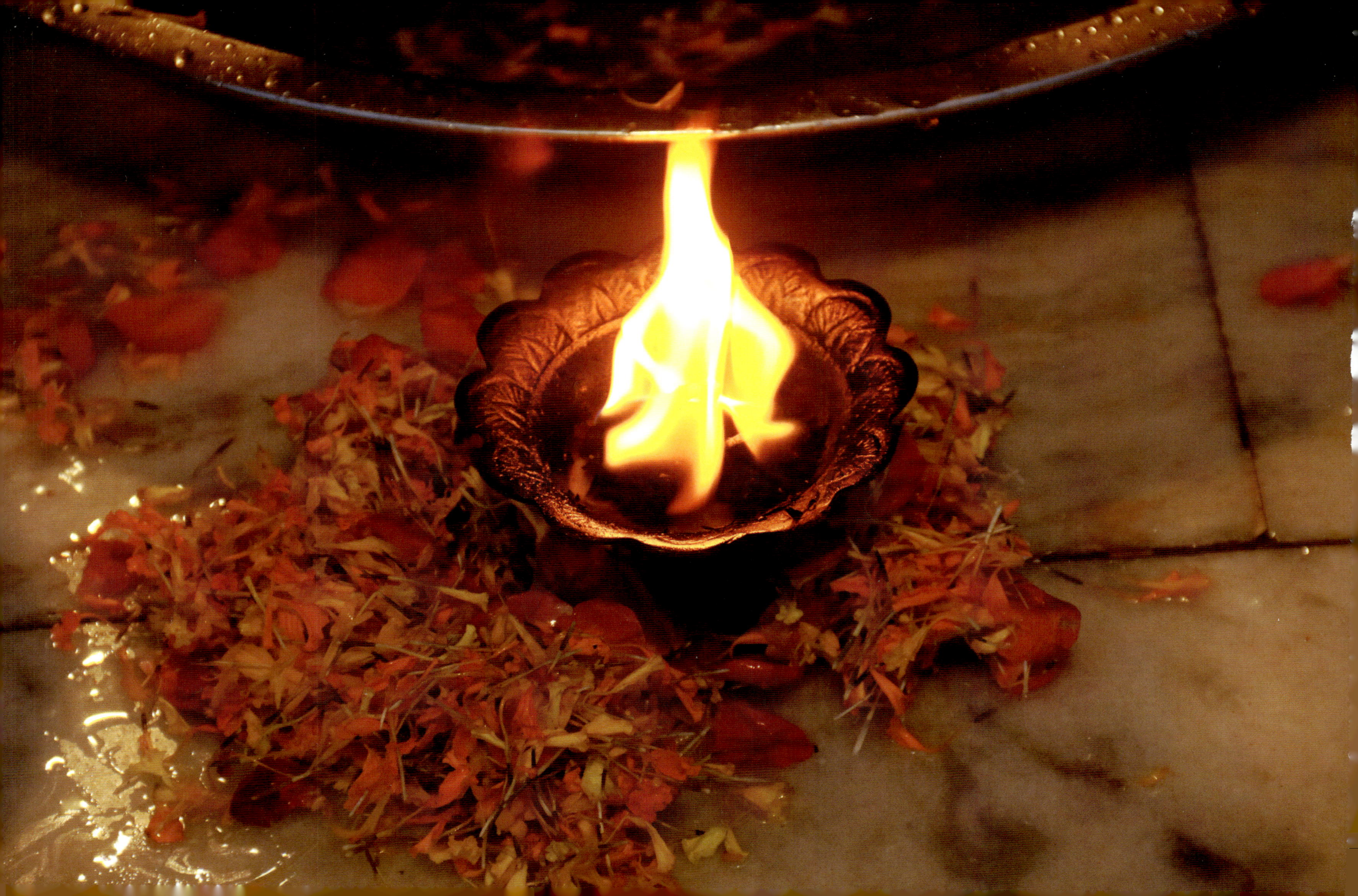